HEART OF THE PROMISED LAND
OKLAHOMA COUNTY
AN ILLUSTRATED HISTORY

HEART OF THE PROMISED LAND
OKLAHOMA COUNTY
AN ILLUSTRATED HISTORY

Bob L. Blackburn

Color Photographs by David Fitzgerald

"Partners in Progress" by Mary Ellen Meredith

Introduction by Jack T. Conn

Sponsored
by the
Oklahoma County Historical Society

Windsor Publications, Inc.
Woodland Hills, California

Supervisory editor: Barbara Marinacci
Coordinating editor: Phyllis Rifkin
Picture editor: Anna R. Igra
Copy editor: Connie Zweig
Editorial director, business biographies: Karen Story,
   assisted by Phyllis Gray and Mary Mohr
Project Coordinator: Katherine Cooper
Compositor: Barbara Neiman
Proofreaders: Doris Malkin, Jeff Leckrone

LIBRARY OF CONGRESS CATALOGING IN PUBLICATION DATA

Blackburn, Bob L., 1951-
   Heart of the promised land.

   Bibliography: p.
   Includes index.
   1. Oklahoma County (Okla.) — History.
2. Oklahoma County (Okla.) — Description and travel.
I. Meredith, Mary Ellen. II. Oklahoma County
Historical Society. III. Title.
F702.O55B55   976.6'38   81-70497
ISBN 0-89781-019-8   AACR2

Frontispiece
Dedicated to "riders of the range," this statue stands
watch over the south entrance to the Oklahoma State
Capitol. Photo by David Fitzgerald.

Table of Contents

The Cowboy Hall of Fame, renowned museum and Western heritage center, sits atop Persimmon Hill in a wooded section of Oklahoma City. Photo by David Fitzgerald.

By World War I automobiles were common sights on the streets of Oklahoma City. As early as 1916 the Oklahoma County Assessor announced that automobiles outnumbered horses in the county 1,900 to 1,353. (OHS)

Introduction

Oklahoma — the mention of this name evokes images: of powerful nations of Indians contending for what civilized man has always held most dear, home and way of life; of cowboys in their distinctive regalia moving a river of beef to northern markets; of oil men battling financial and physical odds to pour from the earth a flood of energy; of farmers fighting nature to produce wheat, corn, and cotton to feed and clothe the nation's millions; of modern business executives creating vast entrepreneurial empires. Oklahoma — in the eye of one's mind, the name of this great state produces pictures of mighty pine and gnarled mesquite, of vast prairies and granite mountains, of treeless plains and treelined rivers, of purple mesas and waving oceans of grass. In short, Oklahoma is a land rich in geography, rich in resources, rich in people, and rich in past, present, and future.

Oklahoma County is at the center of Oklahoma — geographically, politically, economically, and culturally — and in this one subdivision of the state can be seen in microcosm every facet of the events that shaped us. Here, prior to the dawn of recorded history, Indians of the plains met woodland tribes to barter buffalo hides for pottery; here French *coureurs du bois* paused to display the goods of Europe which they hoped to exchange for furs; here both soldier and civilian came to explore in the name of the United States. The cattle trails, celebrated in song, book, and film, coursed northward from south Texas to the railhead at Abilene by way of Oklahoma County. David Payne brought his Boomers here in the 1880s in vain attempts to settle the land. And here in 1889 on a single afternoon in April, 10,000 settlers — townsman and farmer racing shoulder to shoulder — would establish homes, plant dreams, and harvest a rich future.

Oklahoma County had no great natural advantages over the other six counties created that same April afternoon — no great rivers serving as outlets of commerce, no mines yielding ores that would attract major industries, no great military depots to be serviced, no forests to be exploited, no fisheries. Oklahoma City and County grew and prospered because of the spirit of its people, the enterprise of its businessmen, and the vision of its political leaders. With sinew and spirit, with character and courage, they built skyscrapers and factories along with farms and ranches. They made Oklahoma County the hub of the state, a center of marketing and distribution, a producer of food and fiber as well as services and manufactured goods, and in 1910 their efforts were recognized when the people of the state voted to move the capital to Oklahoma City.

Residents of the county have undergone the same triumphs and tragedies as the rest of the state and nation. Their sons and daughters have fought and died in two world wars and two undeclared conflicts; in the midst of a great depression, they watched their topsoil blow away as part of the dust bowl; they celebrated during periods of boom, and they suffered when the inevitable bust occurred. Here were performed deeds of valor as well as villainy. Here were both meanness of spirit and quiet heroism. In short, in Oklahoma County can be seen the gamut of human emotion — from love to hate, from friendship to enmity, from laughter to tears, from triumph to despair. But always it was the innate good sense and humanity of its people which overcame.

Today, as yesterday, the greatest asset possessed by Oklahoma County is its people. As did those who went before us, we must dream great dreams, pray to the Almighty for guidance, and then labor hard to achieve a better future for those who come after us. Oklahoma is yet a young land, one where pioneering — in business and commerce, in agriculture and the arts, in education and entertainment — can still produce rich rewards. The pages which follow will help the reader understand the hardships met and overcome by our pioneer forefathers, the challenges they did not shrink from, the goals they set and accomplished. As we approach the Diamond Jubilee of Oklahoma's statehood, we should recall these aspects of our heritage — and strive to imitate their greatness.

Jack T. Conn

1

Land Belongs to No Man

Oklahoma. The name conjures visions of warlike Indians on horseback, gun-toting cowboys just in from the range, forests of oil wells pumping black gold from the earth, and resilient farmers conquering drought, dust, and depression. It is all this—and more.

Oklahoma has been described as a Southern state, a Western state, a Midwestern state, even a border state, depending on the writer's perspective. The reason for this uncertainty lies partly in the varied geography, climate, vegetation, and population of the state, for within its borders are pine forests and grassland prairie, elevations of 5,000 feet and 300 feet, freezing winters and scorching summers, flat plains and steep mountains.

The people of the state are just as diverse, combining the nation's largest Indian population with descendants of Northern "Yankees," Southern planters, European immigrants, and Afro-Americans. From its people to its landforms, Oklahoma is truly a land of contrast and variety.

In the geographical center of this fascinating state is Oklahoma County. Straddling the old Indian Meridian, which was the dividing line between Oklahoma Territory and Indian Ter-

Facing page
Osage Indians were fierce warriors and hunters who ventured far in search of buffalo. In this painting by C. Wimar, two hunters are chasing a cow and calf through terrain typical to Oklahoma County. (OHS)

10

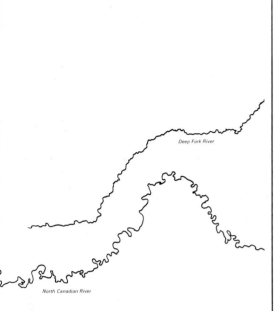

North Canadian River

Deep Fork River

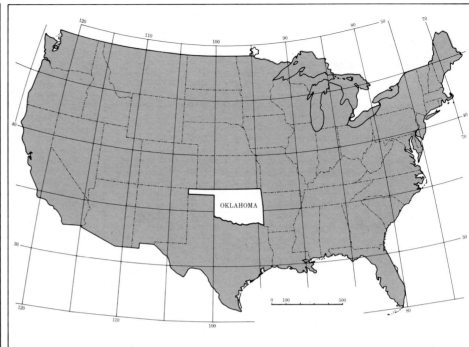

OKLAHOMA

Above
The two rivers draining Oklahoma County, the North Canadian and Deep Fork, served as highways for Indians and explorers and provided water for later settlers.

Above right
Oklahoma is a transition state, separating the Old South from the Midwest and the timbered Mississippi Valley from the high plains. The variety of environmental and cultural elements found within its borders makes Oklahoma one of the most unique states in the union. From Historical Atlas of Oklahoma, *University of Oklahoma Press, 1976.*

ritory, the rectangular-shaped county encompasses 750 square miles of dense timberland, open prairie, and rolling hills. Within these boundaries are average elevations ranging from 850 feet above sea level in the east to 1,250 in the west.

This eastward slope has determined the flow of the two major rivers draining the county: the North Canadian and the Deep Fork. The North Canadian, formed by the junction of Wolf Creek and Beaver River in the northwestern corner of the state, crosses the county from west to southeast, eventually flowing into the Canadian River before leaving the state. Prior to white settlement in the region, the North Canadian River was exceedingly crooked with numerous rapids. Like most rivers originating on the plains, the river had a good flow of water in the spring and early summer, dropping to only a trickle in the fall and winter.

The Deep Fork, which forms near the north-central section of the county and empties into the North Canadian, also flows from west to east. An early traveler—who saw the Deep Fork before it was changed by damming and irrigation—described the river as ''a rapid stream, and of a purity seldom to be found in the rivers of the prairie. It evidently had its sources in high land, well supplied with springs.'' Like the North Canadian, the Deep Fork was at high flow during the spring and early summer.

The diverse terrain of Oklahoma County is matched by a mercurial climate influenced by the merging of tropical Gulf and Polar Continental air masses. Although the average temperature in the county is 60 degrees, overnight temperature drops of 40 and 50 degrees are not uncommon when these two air masses collide. As a local saying goes, ''If you don't like the weather, wait a few minutes and it will change.''

For decades farmers of Oklahoma County have either prospered or perished as a result of climatic vagaries, for the unpredictable move-

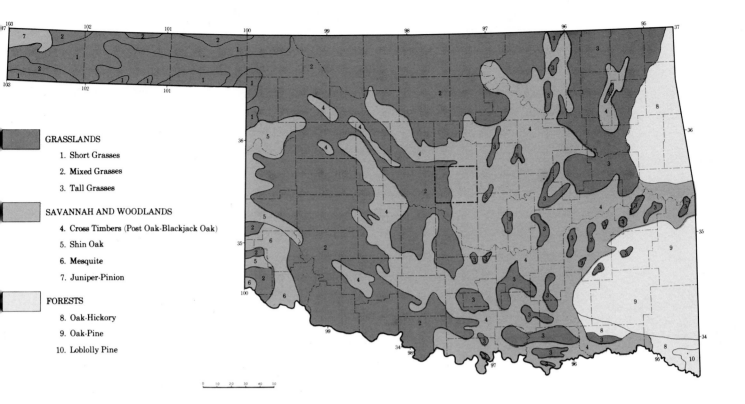

GRASSLANDS
1. Short Grasses
2. Mixed Grasses
3. Tall Grasses

SAVANNAH AND WOODLANDS
4. Cross Timbers (Post Oak-Blackjack Oak)
5. Shin Oak
6. Mesquite
7. Juniper-Pinion

FORESTS
8. Oak-Hickory
9. Oak-Pine
10. Loblolly Pine

ments of air masses produce varying amounts of precipitation. The average annual rainfall in the county is 30 to 34 inches, but extremes of 20 and 45 inches have been recorded. More important than the amount of rainfall is its distribution throughout the year. Although more than 65 percent of the precipitation falls in the spring and summer, two- and three-month periods without rain during the summer are not un- common occurrences. Conversely, large amounts of rainfall in short bursts are also part of everyday life in Oklahoma County. Anyone who has experienced a spring thunderstorm in central Oklahoma knows the awesome but fascinating power of nature.

Climatic and topographical factors have combined to divide the county into two physical subregions: the crosstimbers and the western red prairie. The crosstimbers, which roughly covers the eastern half of the county, is characterized by a thick belt of trees with interspersed fields of open grasslands. Consisting primarily of blackjack oak, hicko- ry, post oak, and shinnery, the crosstimbers before white settlement fascinated early travelers.

As Thomas James, an early explorer, noted, the crosstimbers "ap- pears to be an immense natural hedge dividing the woodlands of set- tled portions of the United States from the open prairies which have been the home and hunting ground of the red man." Frustrated ex- plorers who had to cross the tangled vegetation described it in less com- plimentary terms. After days of struggling through the stunted forest belt, Washington Irving called it a "close dungeon of innumerous boughs." Little did he foresee what riches the crosstimbers region held for future settlers.

Oklahoma County is located in the heart of the state. As seen in this map, much of the county originally was tim- bered, while the western one-third was covered with mixed grasses. From Historical Atlas of Oklahoma, *Univer- sity of Oklahoma Press, 1976.*

As depicted in this romanticized engraving, the terrain of Oklahoma County was home to a wide variety of animal life, from snakes and coyotes to buffalo and antelope. From Century Magazine.

The other half of the county is part of the western red prairie subregion. Consisting originally of rolling grasslands with narrow belts of trees along creeks and gullies, this half of the county has since become one vast farmland. The reddish soil creates some of the most productive farmland in the state, yielding bountiful crops of winter wheat year after year. As these prairies sweep toward the west, the land becomes more level and less rolling, eventually giving way to the high plains on the western edge of the state. Thus the transition line from timbered forest to rolling prairie bisects Oklahoma County.

The animal life of the county is just as varied. When the first Americans traveled through the region they found antelope, elk, deer, raccoon, opossum, coyote, wolf, skunk, prairie dog, badger, mink, squirrel, otter, beaver, rabbit, and bear. One group of mountain men killed 20 bears along the North Canadian on one hunting venture. That same band of hunters commented on the number of beaver in the region, expressing a desire to trap the creeks and rivers on a future visit. Early travelers to the region also discovered a wide variety of birds, especially wild turkeys, quail, prairie chickens, ducks, geese, and the now extinct passenger pigeons.

The animal that drew most attention from both Indians and whites was the American bison, or buffalo. Ranging in vast herds as far north as Canada and as far south as Texas, the shaggy-haired bison frequented the grassy prairies of central Oklahoma. On his visit to the county in 1823, Washington Irving encountered several herds of buffalo. After a spirited chase of one of these beasts, Irving described the animal in glowing terms: "His short black horns curve out of a huge frontlet of shaggy hair; his eyes glow like coals; his mouth is open,

This ornate ceramic bowl illustrates the high art forms and religious symbolism achieved by the Spiro civilization. It was excavated from the Spiro Mound in 1930. (OHS)

his tongue parched and drawn up in a half crescent; his tail is erect and tufted and whisking about in the air; he is a perfect picture of mingled rage and terror."

Thousands of acres of bluestem and goldentop grasses, two of the many plant forms found in central Oklahoma, attracted bison to the county. More than 100 different types of trees are also native to the region, including oak, maple, sweet gum, hickory, ash, walnut, pecan, dogwood, sycamore, cottonwood, elm, willow, cedar, hackberry, and wild plum. Although more common to the eastern half of the county, dense stands of hardwood trees were found in the western reaches of the county, most notably the stand of timber known as Council Grove, located approximately six miles west of Oklahoma City.

The hills, prairies, rivers, animals, and plant life of Oklahoma County have long provided a comfortable environment for human habitation. The first men and women known to have wandered through the region appeared more than 11,000 years ago, part of mass migrations from the west. These Stone-Age nomads were big-game hunters who followed woolly mammoths and other prehistoric creatures. For the next 9,000 years the cave dwellers advanced slowly, learning agricultural skills, the use of the bow and arrow, and the ability to make pottery. Undoubtedly, many Stone-Age men hunted along the creeks and rivers of Oklahoma County.

From 2000 B.C. to A.D. 500, prehistoric man in the region advanced more rapidly, extending farming ventures to the planting of corn,

George Catlin drew and painted the Toyash Wichita village in Devil's Canyon while accompanying a peace expedition in 1834. Although the Wichita lived part of each year in such camps, they roamed the plains and woods of Oklahoma every fall in search of buffalo. (OHS)

beans, squash, pumpkins, and sunflowers. They also built dwellings on mounds near their cultivated fields. With these advances appeared a Native-American culture known as the Spiro era, marking the golden age of Oklahoma prehistory. Spiro people refined agricultural practices, developed art forms, conducted far-reaching trade, and learned the use of metals. Although their settlements were concentrated in eastern Oklahoma, hunting and trading bands undoubtedly traveled into and through Oklahoma County.

Like the Romans, the Spiro people could not depend on sophisticated social systems and advanced art forms to protect themselves from more aggressive invaders. Sometime after A.D. 1200 less civilized nomads from the western plains invaded and vandalized the Spiro settlements. These successors to the Spiro civilization were the tribes inhabiting Oklahoma when the first Europeans arrived.

When Francisco Vasquez de Coronado marched north from New Spain in 1540, five tribes resided in or hunted through Oklahoma. The most numerous were the Caddo, Wichita, and Pawnee, while the Osage and Apache roamed the state's borders. Although each tribe at various times dominated certain regions of the future state, the boundaries of dominance were fluid, often changing yearly. Moreover, because each of the tribes depended largely on buffalo for subsistence, hunting grounds became the preserve of the tribe able to defend it.

When Coronado ventured through the Oklahoma Panhandle in 1541, the most numerous tribe inhabiting the future state was the Wichita. A warlike and roving people, the Wichita lived along the Arkansas, Canadian, and Red River valleys. Spanish and French explorers who

encountered these Native Americans described them as sedentary people who lived from March to October in grass huts, near which they
cultivated fields of tobacco, corn, and beans. During the winter months
the Wichita ventured onto adjacent prairies to hunt for buffalo, which
they used for food, clothing, and tools.

The Wichita also were shrewd traders, gaining a favored position between French and Spanish settlements to the east and south and the
Plains tribes to the west. As their role in this trade grew, the Wichita
moved their villages progressively closer to the plains on the edge of
the crosstimbers. By the 1740s Wichita tribesmen had established trading centers near the western edge of the tree belt. The largest and most
active post was San Bernardo, one of the so-called Twin Villages located on the Red River. From this stronghold, Wichita traders frequently traversed the future boundaries of Oklahoma County.

The Wichita shared much of their domain with the Pawnee and the
Caddo, two tribes which belonged to the same linguistic group. When
first encountered by Europeans, the Pawnee controlled a large region
of central and southern Kansas, from which they frequently entered
Oklahoma. Described as a large and powerful tribe by early Spanish explorers, the Pawnee earned a formidable reputation because of their
hunting and raiding ventures as far south and west as New Mexico.

The Caddo in 1541 controlled territory along the Red River in the
southeastern part of what would become Oklahoma. Like their allies,
the Caddo were farmers who lived in villages, but they also hunted
buffalo on the plains west of the crosstimbers. Hunting and raiding excursions took Caddo warriors to a broad belt of land bordering the Red
River as far west as the present Texas Panhandle. Their presence in
western and central Oklahoma is confirmed by tribal tradition, which
tells of a great battle in the crosstimbers between the Caddo and Choctaw, a battle lost by the Caddo. Such a battle indicates the extensive
hunting and warring range of tribes such as the Caddo.

The Apache lived to the west of these tribes, and at the time of Coronado's expedition, roamed the high plains of the Texas Panhandle and
western Oklahoma. Following the migrating buffalo across an ocean of

This group of Osages visited France in 1827 and 1828. Although they had reigned supreme in the eastern sections of future Oklahoma for more than 20 years, by the 1820s a combination of federal pressure and encroaching eastern tribes was forcing the Osages north. (OHS)

grass, the nomadic Apache developed a mobile life-style revolving around the shaggy beast of the plains. Hunters ate the meat, formed the bones into tools and weapons, and used the hides for clothing and shelter. Coronado encountered the Apache on the plains and described their eating habits, their few possessions, and their tipis.

Typical of Indian history both before and after white men appeared in the New World, tribal spheres of influence changed constantly. From 1541 to the 1700s, the Wichita, Pawnee, Caddo, and Apache experienced mounting territorial conflict with other tribes, most notably the Osage and the Comanche. The Comanche, a tribe of the Shoshonean linguistic group, emerged from their early mountain haunts in the central Rockies after they acquired horses and began to move southward in search of better land. By 1700 Comanche bands ranged from the Platte River in Kansas to the Red River in southern Oklahoma. A victory over the Apache in 1723 established their dominance on the plains of western Oklahoma. Although Comanche warriors shunned white settlements and trading posts in the crosstimber region, small hunting and raiding bands often entered and crossed Oklahoma County in search of game and booty.

The Osage were the most warlike of all the tribes pressing into Oklahoma before 1800. From their ancestral homes in south-central Missouri and northern Arkansas, Osage hunting and raiding parties persistently chipped away at the domain of the Caddoan tribes in

Oklahoma. By the mid-1700s Osage pressure had forced the less warlike Wichita to move south to the Red River Valley. For the next 100 years the Osage fought numerous wars to increase their control over northeastern Oklahoma. Until the relocation of the Five Civilized Tribes, the Osage were the dominant Indians of the region.

Tribal dislocation and migration long had been an integral part of Native-American development, but the appearance of Europeans accelerated the pace of such changes. The first Europeans to fly their flag over what would become Oklahoma were Spaniards. After Coronado's march across the Panhandle in 1541, daring adventurers such as Friar Juan de Padilla, Andres Do Campo, and Juan de Oñate entered Oklahoma in search of treasure and converts, establishing Spanish claim to the region. However, Spanish control of their New World empire was tenuous at best in the northern provinces. As late as 1700 Oklahoma remained merely a little-used highway for further exploration and trade.

Spanish dominion in the region was challenged by the French in 1682, when Réné Robert Cavelier, Sieur de la Salle came down the Mississippi River to claim the drainage basin for France. The first Frenchman to enter Oklahoma was probably Louis Juchereau de St. Denis, who ascended the Red River in 1714. In 1719 Bernard de la Harpe and Claude du Tisne both arrived in search of trade with the Indians. Including the expeditions of Pierre and Paul Mallet and Fabry de la Buyere, the French established a valid claim to the region for their king.

French merchants established profitable connections with tribes such as the Wichita. By the mid-1700s several fortified commercial centers were operating in the crosstimbers region. From Daily Oklahoman, *1955.*

After La Harpe's visit to the region in 1719, French *coureurs du bois* (runners of the forest) established close trade relationships with the Wichita living in villages along the Canadian and Arkansas rivers. With guns, ammunition, knives, axes, beads, and cloth, the Frenchmen traded for countless bales of beaver skins and buffalo robes, which they floated downriver to New Orleans. French traders even extended their influence to the Comanche and Apache on the plains, using their Wichita allies as middlemen. In less than 50 years, using merchants instead of soldiers and trade goods instead of guns, the French brought Oklahoma and Oklahoma County into their empire.

The first American to record his visit to the future Oklahoma County was Thomas James, a merchant who wanted to establish commercial ties with the Plains Indians. From Missouri Valley Historical Review. *Courtesy, Missouri Historical Society.*

French control of the region lasted until 1763 when defeat in the French and Indian War forced France to cede the Louisiana Territory to Spain. Little changed for the Indians of the region, for Spaniards lived too far south to exert effective control on trade. In 1800 France regained title to the region, only to sell it to the expanding American nation in 1803. This famous land transaction became known as the Louisiana Purchase.

To determine what the new territory would mean for the United States, President Thomas Jefferson initiated the first American exploration of the trans-Mississippi West. During the next 50 years, more than 13 American exploration parties traversed what would become Oklahoma. Five of these expeditions entered the woods and prairies of Oklahoma County.

The first American to record his visit to the county was Thomas James. Born in Maryland in 1782, James was a true son of the frontier. His parents heeded the lure of the West in 1803, settling first in Kentucky, then in Illinois. In 1807 they arrived in southern Missouri. When he turned 27, James signed on for a trading expedition up the Missouri River. Two years later, in 1822, James organized and led another expedition to the West, hoping to trade guns and blankets to the Comanche for buffalo robes and beaver pelts.

On this expedition, James led his 12 men up the Arkansas to the South Canadian, which he ascended to the mouth of the North Canadian. After abandoning his keel boats for pirogues (hollowed-out logs of shallow draft), James made his way west to the crosstimbers and entered Oklahoma County. Ten years later he described the land in central Oklahoma as "a very fertile and beautiful country, which will in a few years teem with a dense population. The prairies are interspersed with valuable woodland, and will make as fine a farming country as any in the Union."

The next American to record his visit to the county was Washington Irving, America's well-known author who made "a tour of the prairies" in 1832. During his seven-day stay in what would become Oklahoma County, Irving participated in several exciting buffalo hunts, witnessed the "ringing" of a band of wild horses, experienced the "dreary belt" of the crosstimbers, encountered a band of Osage warriors, hunted bear and turkey, and observed the "grand prairie." Irving later publicized his visit in *A Tour on the Prairies*, published in 1835.

In this painting Richard (Dick) West describes the suffering and dislocation experienced by the Five Civilized Tribes in the "Trail of Tears." Forced from their ancestral lands in the Southeast, the tribes moved west to Indian Territory. (OHS)

After Irving's adventurous exploits, most expeditions to and through the central section of the future state were military ventures attempting to pacify the Plains tribes. Peace with the Comanche, Kiowa, and Wichita was essential to federal Indian policy from 1820 to 1860, for a protected region in eastern Oklahoma was needed as a vast Indian reserve where tribes from east of the Mississippi River could be relocated. The largest tribes to suffer such relocation were the Cherokee, Choctaw, Chickasaw, Creek, and Seminole, known collectively as the Five Civilized Tribes.

After a devastating series of removal treaties, wars, and the infamous "Trail of Tears," the Five Civilized Tribes occupied most of what would become eastern Oklahoma, a region commonly referred to as Indian Territory. The Cherokees claimed the northeast quarter of the territory; the Choctaws and Chickasaws shared all the land between the South Canadian and Red rivers; and the Creeks and Seminoles inhabited the wedge of land between the two enclaves, including the region that would become Oklahoma County.

By 1860 these tribes had developed prosperous and politically advanced Indian nations. With schools, plantations, factories, and towns, the Five Civilized Tribes were advancing steadily when the War Between the States erupted. Soon, the heart of the promised land would become a prize for the winner of a 30-year struggle for dominance in Indian Territory.

Facing page
Washington Irving, the noted author from New York, spent one week in Oklahoma County in 1832. In his journal he described several exciting buffalo hunts such as the one depicted in this engraving. (OHS)

Although Indian tribes on the plains had no conception of land ownership, they nonetheless jealously guarded their hunting ranges. From Harper's Monthly.

2

Fight for the Promised Land

With the warm evening sun to his back, 55-year-old Jesse Chisholm guided his team and wagon along the south bank of the North Canadian River. The mixed-blood Cherokee had just completed a successful trading venture among the Caddo and Wichita and was returning to his trading post at Council Grove. It was a trip he had made countless times since 1858, the year he had established his home in the future Oklahoma County.

The three-year trading experience had been fruitful. Chisholm had earned the trust of the Plains tribes, served as guide and interpreter for several United States Army peace missions, and rescued more than 10 captive children from nomadic bands of Comanche, all while operating a successful business along the banks of the North Canadian.

Chisholm was more than a scout and a businessman. He was a frontiersman, an individual who reveled in the expanse of the untamed wilderness. Central Indian Territory in 1861 offered him that isolation. The Seminole and Creek Indians, who legally owned the land, were far to the east and south beyond the range of depredating Plains tribes. To the west and north were the nomadic Comanche, Kiowa, Caddo, and Wichita, who left little

Frederic Remington

Above
Jefferson Davis, President of the Confederate States of America, sent delegates to the Five Civilized Tribes soon after the Civil War began, embroiling Indian Territory in a conflict which lasted for more than four years. From Pollard, Southern History of the Civil War, 1866.

Right
Jesse Chisholm, mixed-blood Cherokee trader and trapper, operated a trading post in Oklahoma County from 1858 to 1861. He earned the trust of the Plains tribes and acted as interpreter for several United States Army peace missions. (OHS)

mark on the land as they followed migrating buffalo herds across the plains. To mountain men like Chisholm, Council Grove and the surrounding country on the eve of Civil War was a rich land comfortably removed from the rest of the world.

The isolation was soon to end, however, for politicians 1,500 miles to the east were fomenting a conflict that would begin a long period of change for Indian Territory. That conflict was the Civil War. When news about the war reached Council Grove, Chisholm and his Indian neighbors hoped their homeland would be spared from the growing tempest. Their hopes were quickly destroyed.

Confederate leaders, who viewed the Indian lands as a source of food, horses, lead, and manpower, sent delegations to the tribes soon after the outbreak of hostilities; by the summer of 1861 all of the Five Civilized Tribes had signed treaties of allegiance with the South. Despite the official treaties, many Cherokee, Creek, and Seminole full-

blood warriors remained loyal to the Union. Even a few mixed-bloods, such as Jesse Chisholm, opposed the break with the United States.

Opothleyaholo, a Creek chief who disregarded the alliance with the Confederacy, gathered more than 7,000 Creek and Seminole Indians into a neutral camp northeast of present-day Oklahoma County on the Deep Fork River, declaring he would not participate in "the white man's war." Apprehensive about this large, potentially hostile force, Confederate leaders directed Colonel Douglas Cooper to disperse the warriors. The result was the first engagement of the Civil War in Indian Territory, the Battle of Round Mountain.

Although Confederate leaders lured more than 5,000 Indians into uniform, federal forces reclaimed control of the northern half of Indian Territory as early as September 1863. Superior gunpowder, availability of artillery, and greater manpower were the deciding factors in a series of bitter conflicts.

Above
Stand Watie, prominent in Cherokee affairs for two decades, was one of the last Confederate generals to surrender. He continued to attack Northern posts and supply trains until the Indian nations capitulated in 1865. (OHS)

After 1863, when a virtual stalemate developed, the most successful Confederate military leader in Indian Territory proved to be Stand Watie, a mixed-blood Cherokee who harassed Northern posts, attacked supply trains, and terrorized Northern sympathizers. Despite his efforts the Confederacy fell, and the Indian nations capitulated during the summer of 1865.

Beyond the destruction of lives and property, the most significant outcome of the Civil War in Indian Territory was the Reconstruction Treaties of 1866. These treaties, which punished the Five Civilized Tribes for their alliance with the South, granted rights-of-way through Indian Territory to railroad companies. By 1888 the land would be ribboned with rail lines, serving as an effective wedge for opening Indian lands to white settlement.

The harshest provisions, however, forced the Indian nations to cede approximately half of their domain to the United States. Supposedly, the federal government would settle other tribes on those lands. It was the central section of this ceded territory which eventually would become the Unassigned Lands, the first part of Indian Territory to be opened to white settlers.

Most of the ceded land was divided between nomadic Plains Indians and tribes that formerly had been placed on reservations in Kansas and Nebraska. After a series of agreements in 1866 and 1867, the Cheyenne, Arapaho, Comanche, Kiowa, and Apache tentatively agreed to reservations in the western half of Indian Territory, beyond the 98th meridian.

West of the Cherokee, Creek, Seminole, and Chickasaw reservations and east of the Unassigned Lands, the federal government settled smaller tribes. By 1870 the only parts of Indian Territory not assigned

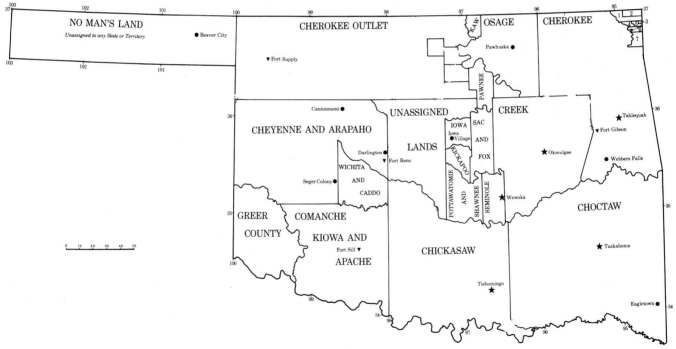

Above
The Reconstruction Treaties of 1866 left the Five Civilized Tribes with only the eastern half of Indian Territory. These treaties also allowed for the construction of railroads through Indian Territory. From Historical Atlas of Oklahoma, *University of Oklahoma Press, 1976.*

Top
An artist's sketch depicts the Council at Medicine Lodge, where the Cheyenne, Arapaho, Comanche, Kiowa, and Apache Plains tribes accepted assignments to reservations in Indian Territory in 1866 and 1867. Courtesy, Western History Collections, University of Oklahoma.

FIGHT FOR THE PROMISED LAND   29

Above
Chris Madsen, who in 1890 became a deputy United States marshal, served with troops in the West during the Indian campaigns. These troops forced wayward bands of Indians back onto their assigned reservations. (OHS)

Above right
Darlington Agency, as it appeared in 1875, served as the administrative center of the Cheyenne and Arapaho Reservation. (OHS)

to tribes were No Man's Land (the Oklahoma Panhandle) and the Unassigned Lands, which included the future Oklahoma County.

Assignment to reservations did not mean peace on the plains, for many tribes sporadically rebelled against their captors. In the spring of 1868, when Indian agents did not deliver promised gifts and rations, a number of Kiowa, Comanche, Cheyenne, and Arapaho warriors fled their reservations to resume traditional ways of hunting and raiding. Not until winter campaigns were mounted against their mobile camps did the warring nomads return to their reservations.

In 1870 similar unrest resulted in new depredations and hunting ventures, which would persist for the next four years. Led by fearless fighters such as Satanta, Satank, and Big Tree, the warriors often raided east of their reservations into present-day Oklahoma County. The boldest raid was mounted by a Cheyenne war party against a supply train bound for the Wichita agency, less than 30 miles southwest of Oklahoma County. The warriors attacked the train at Buffalo Springs, stole the trade goods, and killed four whites.

In response to these outbursts, the federal government mounted a counter-offensive to pacify the tribes of central and western Indian Territory. Between August and December, 1874, cavalrymen under the command of General Nelson A. Miles and Colonel Ranald S. Mackenzie combed the plains for Indians off the reservations. By asserting a constant pressure on the nomads, who already were weakened by scarcity of the once plentiful buffalo, troops forced the wayward bands onto their assigned reservations. The last band to surrender were the Quahada Comanches, led by mixed-blood Quanah Parker.

With the warriors under observation, troopers arrested and incarcerated key leaders, confiscated weapons, and commandeered war ponies. Without guns, horses, or effective leadership, the Plains tribes of Indian Territory were reduced to permanent life on reservations.

HEART OF THE PROMISED LAND: AN ILLUSTRATED HISTORY OF OKLAHOMA COUNTY

From 1866 to 1874 troopers and federal lawmen fought Plains Indians who sporadically entered the future Oklahoma County. At the same time, these agents of law and order faced another, more elusive enemy—the Western outlaw.

To combat the growing surge of outlawry after the Civil War, by 1866 all of the Five Civilized Tribes employed their own lawmen. The only law enforcement agency with the interjurisdictional authority to combat outlaws in Indian Territory, however, was the federal court at Fort Smith. In 1875 this court entered a new era with the arrival of Isaac "Hanging Judge" Parker, who brought "law and order" to the frontier court. He appointed an army of 200 deputy marshals, and for the next 20 years he ruled the region with an iron fist.

One of the most common crimes committed by both outlaws and raiding Indians in the crosstimbers region was cattle rustling. Robert Lake, who operated the Circle Bar Ranch along the North Canadian River in the future Oklahoma County, suffered these depredations countless times before 1889. Although he was in the Unassigned Lands illegally, Lake had a ranchhouse on the future site of Oklahoma City, a cattle pen on a small tributary to the west, and a pond where Belle Isle amusement park later would be located. Another rancher running cattle in the future Oklahoma County was William McClure, whose 7C Ranch headquarters were located farther east on the North Canadian in the lands of the Potawatomi.

Rustlers also struck herds moving north on cattle trails. Two major trails skirted the boundaries of Oklahoma County: the West Shawnee Trail and the famous Chisholm Trail. Established in 1867, after more easterly trails aroused opposition among settlers, the West Shawnee Trail diverged from the old Texas Road at Boggy Depot, veered northwest to the South Canadian, and then crossed the North Canadian near present-day Shawnee. The preferred route, however, was the Chisholm Trail.

Rancher William McClure ran cattle in the future Oklahoma County after 1867. Twenty years later he drove cattle to Oklahoma Station for loading onto railroad cars. Courtesy, Veta McClure.

Western artist Frederic Remington sketched cattle on the long treks from southern Texas. Cattle rustlers often preyed upon cattle driven along the various northward trails. From Harper's Weekly.

This famous route was named for Jesse Chisholm, the mixed-blood Cherokee trader and rancher, who in 1858 had established a trading post at Council Grove. Crossing into Indian Territory at Red River Station, the cattle trail followed a course roughly paralleling the 98th meridian, intersecting the North Canadian River less than 10 miles west of Oklahoma County. In herds averaging 1,500 head, more than 3 million longhorns were pushed to market over the Chisholm Trail from 1866 to 1889.

A minor route, which entered Oklahoma County, but did not receive as much attention or traffic was the Arbuckle Trail. Not to be confused with the Arbuckle Road in the eastern part of Indian Territory, the Arbuckle Trail crossed the Red River just north of Gainesville, Texas, passed through the future counties of Love, Carter, Garvin, and McLain, and crossed the South Canadian River just north of present-day Lexington.

The trail continued in this northerly direction, passing to the east of present-day Moore until it intersected the North Canadian River near the site of the first Oklahoma State Fair Grounds. It then passed through present-day Nichols Hills before veering to the northwest, where it joined the Chisholm Trail.

After 1867 Texas cowboys drove their herds north over such routes because trail drives were the cheapest and most efficient means of transporting their hooved produce to market. By 1890, however, trail drives had become an event of the past, victims of a more efficient means of transportation—the railroad.

In 1871 the Missouri, Kansas, and Texas Railroad (the KATY) became the first line to enter Indian Territory, extending track from the northeast corner of the Cherokee Nation to the Red River near present-day Durant. The first track into Oklahoma County would be laid 16 years later.

On July 4, 1884, Congress granted authority for two rail lines to cross Indian Territory. One of these, the Southern Kansas Railway Company, an affiliate of the Santa Fe, quickly dispatched survey teams to determine the shortest and most easily traversed route, which proved to be directly through the heart of the Unassigned Lands. Company and governmental officials approved the route in 1886 and construction began in August. With crews laying an average of one and one-half miles of track per day, the ribbon of metal slowly moved south through the Cherokee Outlet. In February 1887 the first rails were laid in the area to be known as Oklahoma County.

When surveyors first plotted the route through the Unassigned Lands, they designated several locations for water wells and coal stations. Two points were chosen in the future Oklahoma County. One was at the highest elevation between the Cimarron and the North Canadian, where surveyors found a good spring. At first the water and coaling station was designated Summit, but a month later the name was changed to Edmond. The other watering point, on the north bank of the North Canadian River, was named Oklahoma Station. At both sites Santa Fe workers constructed water towers and began digging water-bearing wells. At Edmond Station they also erected a coal bin, making this the only source of coal in the Unassigned Lands. During the summer of 1887 one passenger and one freight train passed along the isolated tracks each day.

Surveyors working on the Santa Fe Railroad route through the Unassigned Lands designated numerous sites for watering stations, including two in the future Oklahoma County—Edmond and Oklahoma Station. Courtesy, Western History Collections, University of Oklahoma.

FIGHT FOR THE PROMISED LAND

Above
Constructed in 1888, the log home of Agent Ben Miller was located east of the tracks at Oklahoma Station. (OHS)

Right
The post office at Oklahoma Station became a central gathering place for railroad employees and cowboys from surrounding ranches. (OHS)

The Santa Fe stations attracted the first permanently settled white men to the future county. Depot agents, construction crews, and hotel employees were only a few of those early city residents. The agent at Oklahoma Station, A.W. Dunham, also served as the stage agent for a line that ran from Oklahoma Station to Fort Reno. Pulled by a team of four horses or mules, the stage ride took approximately four hours each way and cost $3 for a one-way ticket or $5 for a round-trip fare.

In 1887 the Santa Fe tracks in the Unassigned Lands traversed an undeveloped and unsettled enclave which did not produce revenue for the railroad. To generate business, railroad officials and stockholders

saw a land opening as the only alternative. Their most effective allies in the struggle to destroy this economic vacuum were the Boomers, an army of persistent farmers and businessmen who had been demanding the opening of the Unassigned Lands.

The Boomer movement began in 1879 when Elias C. Boudinot, a railroad attorney and mixed-blood Cherokee, announced through the press that there was a 14-million-acre tract of land in the central part of Indian Territory that was part of the public domain. The attorney described these lands as "the richest in the world." A series of articles on the Oklahoma lands followed, stirring a new land hunger among thousands of depression- and drought-plagued farmers.

As a result of the publicity, hopeful settlers organized three Oklahoma colonies, all intent on forcing the federal government to open the lands to settlement. The most famous and best organized of the three was established and led by David L. Payne, the "Prince of the Boomers."

Born in Indiana, Payne moved to Kansas in 1858, served in the Union army, and eventually won election to the state legislature. Obsessed with the Unassigned Lands, Payne in 1879 rushed to southern Kansas to organize an army of homeseekers. Once there, the tireless leader moved from town to town, camp to camp, encouraging his followers to persist in their crusade. His typically rousing speeches included catchy phrases such as the Biblical quote, "... and the Lord commanded unto Moses, 'Go forth and possess the Promised Land.'" To Payne and his followers, central Oklahoma would be the land of milk and honey.

Payne's most effective weapon in his war for land proved to be Boomer raids. From 1879 to 1884 Payne and his cohorts "invaded" the Unassigned Lands numerous times, eluding the federal troops who were ordered to keep all whites out of the district. Of the six Boomer raids that led into the future Oklahoma County, the most famous occurred in the spring of 1880 when Payne's army marched to the North Canadian and established an illegal town.

Choosing a spot beside the river in what is now Oklahoma City, the settlers erected a stockade, constructed homes, and broke the prairie sod for planting. This thrust into the heart of the promised land ended when blue-shirted troops from Fort Reno marched in and escorted the homeseekers to the Kansas border.

Above
Elias C. Boudinot, mixed-blood Cherokee lawyer, ignited a tempest in 1879 when he announced that land in central Indian Territory was public domain. This stirred a hunger for land among depression- and drought-plagued farmers. (OHS)

Above left
These Boomers, camped near Winfield, Kansas, were some of the hundreds of land-hungry men and women who invaded the Unassigned Lands. In 1889 these lands were opened to settlers legally. (OHS)

Living in mobile camps and cooking under the open sky, many Boomers suffered countless hardships in their quest for land. This last Boomer camp was set up in 1889. (OHS)

Although defeated in isolated battles such as the conflict on the North Canadian, Payne was winning the war through publicity and controversy. The Boomer raids generated interest in the unopened lands, while Payne and his men carried the fight into the printed media.

Payne also intentionally sought arrest several times, forcing the issue into the courts where he pled the cause of the ''poor man, the laborer.'' This tactic proved effective, eliciting a decision from a judge in Wichita that the Unassigned Lands were indeed public domain and that Payne was not guilty of violating any United States law.

Another weapon in the land-seekers' arsenal was the *Oklahoma War Chief,* a newspaper edited by Samuel Crocker, one of Payne's top assistants. With this outlet for propaganda, the Boomers controlled an efficient means for presenting their cause to the public.

Payne died in 1884, five years before his mission was accomplished, but the war for land was continued by several of his lieutenants, most notably Samuel Crocker, William L. Couch, and W.H. Osburn. While these able men rallied the Boomers in raid after raid, the mood of Congress changed. Years of favorable publicity combined with the efforts of railroad lobbyists to sway congressional attitudes concerning the Unassigned Lands.

In 1888 delegates were sent to the Seminole and Creek nations with instructions to pay the tribes for their residual rights to the unoccupied land. On March 3, 1889, Congress at last approved the Springer Amendment, which provided for the opening of the Unassigned Lands to white settlement. President Harrison then proclaimed the date of the first land run—April 22, 1889.

The Buffalo Soldiers: Black Fighters on the Frontier

Indians called the uniformed black men buffalo soldiers, Boomers called them yellow legs, and the army called them the Ninth and Tenth Cavalry Regiments. All agreed they were capable fighters and disciplined soldiers hardened by years of frontier life and Indian wars.

The Ninth and Tenth Cavalry units, organized soon after the Civil War, consisted of black soldiers and white officers recruited for frontier service. Initially, some leaders questioned the fighting ability of black regiments, but the critics were proven wrong during the late 1860s and early 1870s when the black soldiers bravely fought Kiowas, Comanches, Cheyennes, and Arapahoes on the southern plains, and Apaches in the desert Southwest.

In 1881, after years in the field fighting Indians, the Ninth Cavalry returned to the southern plains, where troops were assigned to various posts from Fort Riley in Kansas to Forts Supply, Reno, and Sill in Indian Territory. Although the Indian conflicts had ended, the black soldiers did not rest. Instead, they were thrust into a four-year fight for the "Promised Land," a battle that pitted the United States Army against a ragtag army of Boomers led by David L. Payne.

The first of these conflicts between the Boomers and the buffalo soldiers began on a hot summer day in July 1882, when Payne and a small band of his followers secretively made their way to the future Oklahoma County. There they pitched their tents and began plowing the land in the rich North Canadian river valley. Within days, a scouting party of black soldiers under the command of Lieutenant C.W. Taylor discovered their presence and ordered them to leave. When Payne and his people refused to move, the soldiers bound and carried the non-resistant raiders to their wagons. The black soldiers then transported the captives to Fort Reno, on to Texas, and then to Fort Smith, Arkansas.

Failure only fired the spirits of Payne and his disciples. In February 1883 buffalo soldiers again encountered the Boomers at Camp Alice, a makeshift town on the North Canadian. And in a replay of their earlier meeting, the alleged trespassers were expelled. Six months later another confrontation occurred at the point

David L. Payne, the "Prince of the Boomers." (OHS)

where the Payne Trail crossed the Cimarron River. Then, in July 1884, in an attempt to deter future raids, army officials moved six companies of the Ninth Cavalry to a temporary camp on the Chikaskia River, in the direct route of the Boomers. Predictably the tactic only forced the Boomers to change their route of entry and point of encampment.

In August 1884 the Boomers established the town of Rock Falls in the Cherokee Outlet, but again, black soldiers arrived, destroyed improvements, and escorted the settlers to Kansas. This trip was extended by a month-long trek through Indian Territory, a punishing journey, which Payne labeled an act of illegal confinement and intimidation. But the buffalo soldiers were simply doing their duty and admittedly doing it well.

The role of black soldiers in the Boomer wars ended in January 1885 when the two regiments were transferred to the northern plains where they eventually would become involved in the crisis leading to the battle of Wounded Knee. During their short stay in the Unassigned Lands, the buffalo soldiers had ably served their country in an unpopular war with homeseekers. Ironically, it was largely the publicity generated by these conflicts that eventually would lead to the opening of the Unassigned Lands.

3

The Greatest Horse Race

As the sun rose over the horizon on central Indian Territory, more than 50,000 hopeful men, women, and children anxiously waited for the great race to begin. It was April 22, 1889, the day of the land run.

As noon approached, many 89ers boarded trains that would carry them into the frontier enclave at a slow but steady speed. Others double-checked teams and wagons or exercised their horses, ready to sprint for desired town lots or quarter-sections. Whether on horseback, in wagons, or aboard trains, they all shared a common dream—to stake claim to a portion of the promised land.

True to the best American tradition, the 50,000 or more people waiting for the land run represented all walks of life. Standing shoulder-to-shoulder were blacks and whites, Northerners and Southerners, businessmen and cowboys, city folk and farmers. They came from all sections of the country, attracted by the lure of the land.

Most of the contestants were from neighboring states. More than 16 percent were from Kansas, 12 percent from Missouri, and 9 percent from Texas. The rest were largely from drought-

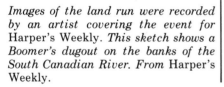

This long wagon train crossed the Cherokee Outlet a few days before the land run. On April 22 they assembled along the northern border of the Unassigned Lands for the opening signal. Courtesy, Western History Collections, University of Oklahoma.

Images of the land run were recorded by an artist covering the event for Harper's Weekly. *This sketch shows a Boomer's dugout on the banks of the South Canadian River. From* Harper's Weekly.

plagued Midwestern states such as Iowa, Ohio, Indiana, and Illinois. These native-white settlers would be joined in the Oklahoma Country by more than 500 blacks, making the land run a true melting pot of the American nation.

Robe Carl White, a young man from Iola, Kansas, was typical of these adventurers. Like many men on the western frontier, White was from a family that had moved west with the advancing line of settlement. His family had migrated from the Northeast to Illinois, then to Missouri, then to Kansas. When news of the impending land run spread like wildfire across Kansas, the slumbering pioneer spirit in young White was rekindled. Leaving his country teaching job in early April, the young Kansan joined three friends and rode horseback to Arkansas City, Kansas, to prepare for the invasion.

Choosing the northern border of the Unassigned Lands as their starting point, White and his friends entered the Cherokee Outlet, which separated Kansas from the region to be opened. The other three start-

HEART OF THE PROMISED LAND: AN ILLUSTRATED HISTORY OF OKLAHOMA COUNTY

ing lines were in the Kickapoo Reservation on the east, beyond the South Canadian River on the south, and in the Cheyenne-Arapaho lands on the west.

The rules governing the land run from these borders were simple. Any man or single woman 21 years of age or older could claim 160 acres; the first to drive a stake into a quarter-section would be the owner. When more than one person entered a 320-acre site with the intention of establishing a town, they could divide the land into town lots, which then could be claimed as individual parcels of land. The only restriction was that all legal claimants had to start from outside the Unassigned Lands at 12:00 noon on April 22. Those who violated this law, appropriately called ''Sooners,'' later would cause endless legal problems.

In its haste to open the district, Congress failed to provide a plan for government in the Unassigned Lands after the run. The only federal officials in the region would be a few soldiers and a handful of deputy

An artist covering the land run visited Main Street in Purcell, Indian Territory, where many Boomers gathered for final preparations (above). He also sketched the Boomers as they approached the southern boundary of the area to be opened (below). Courtesy, Western History Collections, University of Oklahoma.

THE GREATEST HORSE RACE

One of the most convenient and reliable means of entering the Unassigned Lands was by rail. These passengers board one of several special trains originating from Arkansas City, Kansas, on the day of the land run. Courtesy, Western History Collections, University of Oklahoma.

United States marshals from Kansas and Muskogee. There would be no territorial government, no provisions for town governments, and no plans for platting townsites. In short, the heart of the promised land would be without law.

Despite these potential problems, the 50,000 or more home-seekers were eager for the adventure. As noon approached, the restless participants fought for the best starting positions, knowing that a few seconds could mean the difference between claiming good bottomland and settling for scrub-oak wasteland.

At the appointed time, cavalry buglers and flagmen positioned themselves on the highest elevations possible. As the seconds ticked away, they raised their bugles, flags, and guns. In near unison they gave the signal and the race began. A wall of overloaded wagons, high-spirited horses, and slow but steady trains all moved forward together.

Most of the 12,000 land-seekers who entered what would become Oklahoma County scattered across the countryside on 160-acre homesteads. The majority were men who had left their families and possessions at home, for speed was essential. One man who used speed effectively was William McClure, who had operated the 7C Ranch in the Kickapoo and Potawatomi lands since 1867. McClure knew the land of Oklahoma County, for he had run cattle on the unoccupied range for years. On the day of the run, he posted hired hands at intervals along the best route to his desired claims near Oklahoma Station. When the opening gun sounded at 12:00, he bolted on horseback across the sand hills at a run. Six miles into the district he met his first hired hand, mounted a fresh horse, and pushed on at a steady speed. After meeting his next employee at Lightning Creek, he again changed horses. With this advantage, he arrived at Oklahoma Station a full 30 minutes ahead of the crowd, with time enough to claim 160 acres a short distance to the northwest of the townsite of Oklahoma City and two town lots at what became First and Harvey.

Robert Lake was another man who used experience to his benefit. For three weeks prior to the run, this rancher exercised himself and his horse to build endurance. At noon on April 22, equipped with camp gear, bacon, and biscuits, he positioned himself along the eastern line of the run. When the signal sounded, he turned his mount toward the south, while the other horsemen raced in a direct westerly line. From his years in the region, Lake knew that the best fords and trails could be found to the south. By choosing the best route and by conserving his horse's energy, this crafty rancher arrived at his desired quarter-section minutes before other 89ers.

Although most successful 89ers arrived with only a horse, a bedroll, and a gun, they soon were joined by family members driving wagons loaded with the provisions necessary for survival. One family from Missouri brought to their father's claim, one mile north of Arcadia, a team of oxen, six horses, 40 cattle, a half dozen chickens, and a rooster. They also had a covered wagon filled with a bushel of dried beans, 150 pounds of dried fruit, two butchered hogs, a butchered calf, and enough lard to last a year. Such provisions would be needed during the coming year.

William T. Rogers, an 89er who claimed 160 acres three miles north of Edmond, recalled the first few weeks after the run: "We lived in a shelter made from the canvas we had used on the wagons. As we had no stove we had to cook over an open fire. We had long legged kettles and skillets that we placed in the hot coals. I sold two of the oxen to help pay expenses until we harvested a crop. We lived mostly on beans and turnips." For farmers such as Rogers, the quest for prosperity would be a long, uphill battle.

Boomers pause along the border of the Unassigned Lands to purchase a last cup of coffee for 10 cents. Courtesy, Western History Collections, University of Oklahoma.

Oklahoma Station is pictured here as it appeared two hours before the land run began. At noon a group of men with the Seminole Townsite Company stepped off the railroad right-of-way and began platting the town. (OHS)

Although those who lived in towns did not suffer from isolation, drought, and late crops, the first-day residents of Oklahoma City and Edmond faced other problems that would have to be overcome. One of the most perplexing was how to determine the legal boundaries and ownership of town lots, a result of several controversial and conflicting townsite surveys.

The first and most aggressive townsite organization in the county was the Seminole Townsite and Development Company, which, in league with Santa Fe officials, had positioned agents at the two railroad stations prior to the run. A few minutes after noon on April 22 those agents left the railroad right-of-way and began surveying streets and blocks in both Oklahoma City and Edmond.

Conflicts developed only hours later. At 1:15 officials of the Oklahoma Town Company arrived in Oklahoma City by wagon from the South Canadian River. Led by Doctor Delos Walker, this company began surveying town lots south of Grand Avenue (now Sheridan), which was the southern extent of the Seminole townsite. Thus, two separate 320-acre townsites were established near Oklahoma Station. One was Oklahoma City proper, extending north of Grand Avenue and west of the Santa Fe tracks. The other was South Oklahoma City, extending south of Grand. A year later the two would be combined into one city.

In Edmond similar town development conflicts surfaced when colonists from Springfield, Missouri, and Chicago, Illinois, arrived during mid-afternoon. Within two days these groups had prepared a plat and

HEART OF THE PROMISED LAND: AN ILLUSTRATED HISTORY OF OKLAHOMA COUNT

declared it the official survey of Edmond, but it was in direct conflict with the Seminole Townsite survey. The quarrel was intense, for both factions intended to auction or sell town lots. A compromise was finally reached that combined the two plats. The overlapping townsite surveys still can be seen in the angling of streets in downtown Edmond.

While these legal conflicts unfolded, first-day settlers crowded into the two townsites. In Oklahoma City, where an estimated 4,000 to 6,000 people arrived on April 22, the scramble for the best lots resulted in mass confusion. One young man who entered Oklahoma City on the third train from Arkansas City looked for a friend who had staked a claim on Main Street. As the boy later wrote, "I kept looking for Main Street, but couldn't see a street or anything that looked like a street. All I could see was a lot of tents arranged in a haphazard way, much like someone had thrown a handful of white dice out on the open prairie."

The settlement pattern of Oklahoma City was indeed haphazard, for the federal government had taken no part in the town plat. The only reference points for determining claims were a few street markers placed hurriedly near the railroad. For lots, each claimant had to judge how much land he could defend. Surveyors associated with either the two townsite companies or compromise committees later moved through the mass of tents with surveying tools.

The Oklahoma Town Company, for example, sent out one party of surveyors with a rope that had a knot tied 30 feet from the end. They

One of the first objectives of any Boomer after he claimed his land was to establish ownership by possession. This was done by unloading furniture or by erecting a tent. In this photograph, taken on the first day in Oklahoma City, one settler even erected a frame building. Courtesy, Western History Collections, University of Oklahoma.

THE GREATEST HORSE RACE   45

Two months after the opening, Edmond was still only a scattering of tents and frame buildings on the open prairie. Courtesy, Central State Museum, Central State University, Edmond.

walked along the streets with the rope, measuring 30' x 150' lots for men who claimed ownership. In return, claimants paid the surveyors one dollar for a title issued by the townsite company.

In Edmond the first surveyors marked off several 25' x 140' lots minutes after the run began—and more than an hour before the first legal claimants arrived. Because of the smaller area and fewer contestants involved, the mass confusion typical of Oklahoma City did not spread to Edmond. At 3:30 on April 22, only about 40 persons had claimed town lots. Two days later the population still was less than 400.

Threatening settlers in both towns were lot-jumpers, men who forcefully took lots from weaker claimants. Robe Carl White, the young 89er from Kansas, was one such victim. Only 19 years old and too young to claim a lot, White nevertheless had staked claim to a lot on Main Street in Oklahoma City. That evening he noticed two men walking slowly down the street heavily armed and carrying pup tents. When directly in front of White's unimproved lot, the two men unloaded their tents and told the young Kansan to move on. After a short confrontation, White "compromised" by giving them the lot.

Not all lot-jumpers chose their victims so carefully; some resorted to violence. The only effective agent of law and order in Oklahoma City capable of suppressing such lawlessness during the first few days was a United States infantry unit commanded by Captain Daniel F. Stiles. Stiles, whose instructions were to preserve order and to prevent

As seen from the north only weeks after the land opening, Oklahoma City looked like a "handful of white dice out on the open prairie." (OHS)

violence at Oklahoma Station, had arrived by train on April 19, 1889.

Camped east of the Santa Fe tracks on the military reservation (near present-day 2nd Street and Stiles), the captain and his men carefully confined their actions to keeping the peace and did not attempt to adjudicate claim disputes. As Stiles often told frustrated lot-claimants, "I am not here to decide which of you owns that lot, but to keep peace between you until it is decided."

Several times Stiles and his men prevented riots and mob violence, not by sheer numbers but by the authority they represented. Indicative of the soldiers' influence was a speech given by a politician who led a large mob of men opposing Captain Stiles: "We have gone to the point of force, and we have been met by force; and while by strength of numbers we might overpower this handful of troops, we should regard them, not according to their own strength, but according to the power they represent—the power of the government. There is but one thing for us to do—disperse and go home." The politician's respect for authority was typical of men in the frontier community.

However expedient, martial law was unacceptable to men accustomed to self-rule and local government. From the first day of settlement, political agitation was an integral part of life in young Oklahoma City, and conflicts concerning townsite companies and land ownership were a natural part of that agitation. The men of the boomtown were split into two quasi-political parties, the Seminoles and the Kickapoos. The Seminoles included the beneficiaries of the Seminole survey; the other party consisted of everyone else.

This spirited controversy prompted an impressive array of street-corner oratory, for both sides were eloquently represented. The Seminole leadership relied on the skills of Sidney Clarke and General James B. Weaver, both proven politicians.

Clarke was a tall, lean man from Kansas, who had sponsored the legislation opening the Unassigned Lands. Before the sun set on April 22, Clarke was perched on a wagon spouting support for the Seminole cause and coloring the Kickapoos as "hungry land sharks." Weaver, the Greenback Party's presidential candidate in 1880, also touted the aims of the Seminoles, making frequent references to equal rights, free speech, and a free ballot.

Facing these two politicians were equally impressive orators. Judge J.L. Brown, a small, feisty gentleman from Kansas, would jerk his head and lambast the Seminoles for "stealing lots." He dwelled on that sub-

Kentuckian John Blackburn was secretary of the Seminole Townsite Company and one of the early leaders in the history of Oklahoma City. He helped survey the townsite, aided Seminole politicians, and served as the town's first deputy mayor. (OHS)

HEART OF THE PROMISED LAND: AN ILLUSTRATED HISTORY OF OKLAHOMA COUNTY

Edmond escaped many of the problems encountered in Oklahoma City. Here, looking north on Broadway, grass in the streets gives the new town an appearance of youth. Courtesy, Central State Museum, Central State University, Edmond.

ect to such an extent that the Seminoles labeled him with the alliterative sobriquet, "Lot-Jumping Jim."

M.R. Glascow, a six-foot three-inch giant, was another Kickapoo, whose deep voice had the people spellbound in Oklahoma City that first day. In mid-afternoon, standing on the bed of a wagon, Glascow spoke of the Magna Carta, the Declaration of Independence, and the Bill of Rights, comparing the objectives of the Kickapoos to the plight of freedom-seeking citizens. Citing Patrick Henry's immortal speech, the spellbinder replaced each "King George" with "the Seminoles." Such rhetoric only added to the magic of Oklahoma City on April 22, 1889.

The first effective governmental body in Oklahoma City was the Committee of Fourteen, a group of men chosen on April 23 to establish streets, alleys, and blocks, and later to settle ownership disputes. After the committee determined where the survey should begin, a subcommittee heard arguments in ownership cases. Moving from lot to lot, they often found as many as a dozen conflicting claims. In such instances, the committee heard evidence and summarily settled the cases on the spot. When attentive crowds grew too inquisitive, assistants surrounded the members with a triangle of three cottonwood boards nailed together. The committee then made decisions from within the barrier.

The survey of the Committee of Fourteen proceeded north through South Oklahoma City until it approached Grand Avenue, the southeastern extent of the Seminole survey. By controlling the Oklahoma City townsite from the first minutes after the run, the Seminole Townsite and Development Company had forced settlers to accept its

survey. Therefore, if the Committee of Fourteen were allowed to survey North Oklahoma City again, many of the original claimants could have lost their land.

A compromise finally was reached: the two plats were laid end-on-end, with irregular lots between Grand and Main, much like a stone mason forces cement between two non-aligned stones. The jogs in north-south streets at Grand (Sheridan) were the result of this compromise. As Angelo Scott later wrote, ''These irregularities are very literally the scars of a bloodless conflict.''

During the next few days two temporary municipal governments were established, one in South Oklahoma City and one in Oklahoma City proper. Five days after the run, the men of South Oklahoma City elected a provisional government with G.W. Patrick as mayor. The leadership of this body changed often during the next few months before provisional government was suspended altogether.

On April 26, a mass meeting was convened in Oklahoma City proper, at which time temporary officials were nominated to hold elections on May 1. On election day, the men of Oklahoma City wrote their candidates' names on pieces of paper and dropped them into a large coffeepot. As in the temporary election, William L. Couch was the winning candidate for the mayor's office.

As demonstrated by this first election in Oklahoma City, Couch was probably the best-known man in the community. Born in 1850 in North Carolina, Couch and his family had migrated west to frontier Kansas

HEART OF THE PROMISED LAND: AN ILLUSTRATED HISTORY OF OKLAHOMA COUNTY

n 1866. Struggling to raise a family and earn a living, young Couch farmed, bought and sold horses, and raised livestock. In the winter of 879, after hearing David L. Payne deliver a speech about the Unassigned Lands, he joined Payne's Oklahoma Colony.

Couch later led and participated in several Boomer invasions while serving as one of Payne's most trusted lieutenants. On opening day, his dream realized, Couch staked a claim to 160 acres west of Oklahoma City, then rode into the bustling town. Well known as a leader and respected for his tenacity and hard work in opening the district, Couch quickly rose to a position of authority.

Although without federal sanction, Couch's provisional government began work immediately. One of the first ordinances made lot-jumping a crime punishable by a $100 fine. A similar enactment required lot-claimants to secure title from the Seminole Townsite and Development Company, a proposal that antagonized a number of residents. Despite these overt attempts to stabilize the Seminole claims, the provisional government generally limited itself to ordinances meant simply to maintain public order during the first few months of settlement.

To most of the men and women of Oklahoma City and Edmond, politics and city government were secondary concerns. More important to them were business affairs, the quality of life, and simply getting along. While politicians fought over city charters, town plats, and special elections, the people of the frontier communities were establishing homes and erecting buildings. Overnight, tent cities appeared, while frame buildings emerged in a matter of days.

With fertile land, adequate rainfall, and excellent railroad connections, Oklahoma County overnight became a checkerboard of farms and bustling towns. The day before, only railroad tracks and small depots had broken the symmetry of the gently rolling plains; after the run of '89, thousands of hopeful businessmen, workers, and farmers began transforming the untamed land into a vibrant county that soon would dominate the state. To these men and women, Oklahoma was indeed the promised land—and Oklahoma County its heart.

William L. Couch, a Boomer leader before the land opening, became the first elected mayor of Oklahoma City. In the early days of the town, his provisional government maintained public order. (OHS)

The famous jog at Grand (Sheridan) Avenue was the result of two townsite plats laid end-on-end. (OHS)

4

Rural Pioneers Struggle for Survival

On April 23, 1889, the 5,000 or more successful homesteaders of Oklahoma County turned toward an uncertain future and made plans to win their "bet with the government." First, they had to overcome weeks of filing, defending, and proving claims of ownership of their 160-acre homes. This accomplished, they faced a year of no crops, no source of ready cash, and no relief from the elements. If they managed to survive that first grueling year, they still had to contend with isolation, agricultural depression, and back-breaking toil.

Aside from these long-term considerations, the first need usually was housing. During the first few days the better-prepared settlers slept in covered wagons or in tents, which provided basic protection. Frontier life, however, could not continue without a place to cook, store supplies, and offer a brief release from hard work. In the eastern half of the county, as well as along creek and river beds in the prairie regions, this need was met by log cabins.

When a family decided what size cabin was needed, timber was cut in uniform sizes. Some pioneers preferred logs eight inches in diameter, while others chose 14-inch timbers. With the logs cut,

This low-lying structure is a half-dugout, half-sod house. Notice the close proximity to the small corn field, usually the first crop planted by struggling pioneers. (OHS)

hewed, and placed in a pattern, neighbors assisted with the "raising." The more experienced cabin builders worked at the corners, where they cut interlocking notches in each log. With walls in place, workers added rafters, installed planks for decking, and covered the roof with homemade shake shingles. The walls then were chinked with wedge-shaped pieces of oak and daubed with clay-mud or plaster. Pine doors and flooring, window frames, and a leather thong on the door finished the well-built log cabin.

There was little timber in the western half of the county, forcing prairie settlers to build dugouts or sod houses. Dugouts, as the name implies, were holes dug into the ground with pole roofs covered by planks and sod. Most were small, measuring anywhere from 12' x 14' to 16' x 18'. The problems associated with dugouts were numerous, including leaky roofs, dampness, spiders, scorpions, and snakes.

The sod house had many of the same drawbacks, but offered more room. Constructed of prairie sod cut into slabs several inches thick, a foot wide, and two or three feet long, sod houses were much like brick structures. The sod blocks, held together by tough bluestem and goldentop grasses, were stacked into walls, leaving spaces for doors and windows. After extending logs and planks from wall to wall, more blocks were arranged for a roof. Although most sod houses survived only a few years, they provided quick and inexpensive protection from the elements. In most cases farmers replaced both soddies and log cabins with frame houses soon after the first good harvest.

Once constructed, shelters had to be furnished. Because most 89ers were financially troubled farmers searching for a better life, furnishings usually were expedient and simple. One hard-pressed man who claimed a farm in the northeastern part of the county later described his meager possessions: "I made all the necessary furniture from poles, dry-goods boxes and stumps. My dishes were fashioned from gourds. I made several water jugs from clay."

A family near Arcadia was more typical of Oklahoma County pioneers. As the woman of the household later remembered: "There was no floor in the house, but the dirt was packed hard. I ripped up feed sacks and sewed them together to cover the floor. My dish cupboard was a dry-goods box nailed to the wall with a curtain in front. We made three stools of split logs with pegs for the legs and made a table of a large box. We made our bed from peeled poles and ropes. I brought my dishes, cooking utensils and bedding with me." For such frontier families, ingenuity and hope for better days were the only relief from such poverty.

With homes established, the pioneers' thoughts turned to water and food. Initially, water was obtained from creeks, rivers, or springs. Hauled in barrels, creek water was adequate at first, but muddy runoff, disease, and seasonally low flow made this source unstable and even dangerous. If affordable, most early pioneers dug water wells as soon as possible. Fortunate farmers found water at 20 to 40 feet, while others either hit dry holes or found only "gyp water," which was too heavily saturated with minerals for human consumption.

While water could be found in the new land, food had to be brought in during or immediately after the run. Settlers had to have sufficient provisions for at least one year, for the land run occurred too late in the spring to clear the land for a crop. In fact, a combination of tough prairie grasses with deep root systems and substandard plows caused many farmers to take more than two years to clear the land. The only

Above
After a good harvest and enough time to procure necessary materials, farmers were able to build log cabins with rock chimneys and shingled roofs. (OHS)

Left
Simple plank cabins provided an alternative for small families or single settlers. This hut was located on the Wheeler Turner claim, one mile south of Edmond. Courtesy, Central State Museum, Central State University, Edmond.

The North Canadian River supplied pioneers with building materials, fuel, and water. (OHS)

planting that first year was done in small gardens where farmers hoped to raise enough cabbage, beans, and corn for the coming season. More than one family that first winter lived on a simple diet of cornbread, turnips, sorghum molasses, and rabbit meat.

Many settlers survived temporarily by leaving their farms to work elsewhere. The federal government allowed homesteaders to vacate their claims for up to six months, during which time they could try to find jobs and earn enough money to remain on their farms the other six months. Some men joined railroad construction crews; others toiled for more prosperous farmers and ranchers who could pay hired hands. Even if such jobs paid only one dollar a day, it helped buy flour, coffee, salt, and other staples.

Despite their efforts to establish homes in the new land, many farm families in Oklahoma Territory could not overcome the obstacles confronting them that first year. In September 1890, Congress responded to the hardship by appropriating $47,000 in relief funds. A territorial board of relief used the money to buy commodities which were distributed through county agents.

Daniel Downing was a typical recipient of such relief. He was the father of four children and the owner of 160 acres of land and several head of livestock. In need of staples for his family and unable to break

HEART OF THE PROMISED LAND: AN ILLUSTRATED HISTORY OF OKLAHOMA COUNTY

This farm family survived the lean years of the early 1890s. The signs of prosperity include the well-built log cabin, cultivated land on either side of the cabin, the wooden fence, and blooming fruit trees. (OHS)

enough sod to raise a cash crop, Downing received 25 pounds of flour and meal, 10 pounds of bacon and beans, and five pounds of salt. Other hard-pressed farmers, too proud to seek the relief openly, accepted their commodities only under cover of night. Such assistance, although a last resort, helped many pioneers survive those first hard years in the new land.

By 1891 many farmers had cleared sufficient land to plant crops of wheat and cotton, the two most profitable cash crops. However, hard times would persist until 1897 because of drought, low market prices, and economic recession. Despite the financial difficulties, inventive farmers found ways to raise the cash they needed to buy farm improvements.

William H. Odor, a homesteader near Arcadia, constructed a hothouse during the bitterly cold winter of 1892. In his hothouse, which consisted of a tarp over an open trench heated with coals from a wood stove, Odor planted cabbage seed so it would be well developed by the normal planting time. By setting half-grown cabbages in the garden early in the spring, Odor had the first mature cabbages that season, an advantage he easily turned to profit.

Another farm family northeast of Arcadia had cows and chickens and sold eggs and butter for cash. They received four cents a dozen for

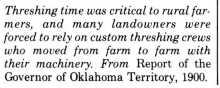

A crew of men and boys uses a combination of animal and mechanical power to bale cut prairie grass. Agriculture was the primary economic activity in Oklahoma County during the 1890s, and hay was the first crop to produce income for most farmers. (OHS)

Threshing time was critical to rural farmers, and many landowners were forced to rely on custom threshing crews who moved from farm to farm with their machinery. From Report of the Governor of Oklahoma Territory, 1900.

eggs and five cents a pound for butter. Matthew Reynolds, a native of Iowa who had claimed a homestead on Chisholm Creek southwest of Edmond, set out 200 grapevines and 13 acres of fruit trees in 1890. In 1891 he earned $103 from his grapes alone, enough cash to have more land cleared and planted.

Clearing land of sod and stumps required either back-breaking labor or cash to hire workers. In the western sections of the county, where thick bluestem grass grew shoulder high to a man, sod could be broken and turned only with several teams of sturdy oxen or mules. It took two men to handle such teams, for one man had to guide the animals while the other man handled the bulky plow. In the timbered sections of the county, this problem was compounded by the presence of stumps. It took days of cutting, burning, and pulling to rip the roots from the ground. Because both tasks required several men and at least two sets of animals, many farmers had to hire help.

HEART OF THE PROMISED LAND: AN ILLUSTRATED HISTORY OF OKLAHOMA COUNTY

Not all assistance from outside the family was hired. In most rural communities people generally were ready to lend a helping hand to hard-pressed neighbors. For example, one farmer who had claimed a homestead near present Nicoma Park suffered a lengthy illness in the fall of 1891, just as his crops needed to be harvested. Six of his neighbors appeared the next Saturday with their teams. While they cleared his fields, their wives helped with the kitchen chores and children.

Neighborliness, like rural life in general, had its humorous side as well. A story handed down through three generations of Oklahoma County farmers reveals this attitude: "One man in the neighborhood always helped when someone else was moving. When he was asked why, he replied, 'Well, I always like to help if they were good neighbors, and if they were bad neighbors, I helped to get them out of the community.'"

Despite a strong sense of community, the hard times of the early 1890s forced most frontier families of Oklahoma County to be largely self-sufficient. A few items, such as shoes, utensils, and implements, had to be purchased in town, but most food was homegrown and processed. As the granddaughter of a homesteader later wrote: "Grandfather raised both hogs and cattle, so they had meat by butchering and salting away or canning pork and beef. After slaughter, the carcass would be hung to 'cool' and then it would be skinned and cut into strips of meat. Grandmother would have already put a black iron kettle over a wood fire in the yard on to boil. It contained a smelly mixture of water and brown sugar and salt and salt peter and herbs. . . . That brew was what they used to cure the bacon and hams. And it was so good! When they made the sausage and lard, Grandmother fried those sausages in patties and packed them layer by layer into big stone crocks. Between each layer she poured new lard which would harden and seal the sausage air tight. Then when she wished, she would remove a layer, melt the lard, and the sausage was ready to serve."

Farmers needed oversized plows and equipment to break the thick prairie sod of the central Unassigned Lands. (OHS)

This open, flat field was typical of the terrain in the western part of Oklahoma County, where wheat was the primary crop. (OHS)

In addition to meat, frontier families canned vegetables from their gardens. Enough fresh green beans, beets, cabbage, corn, and tomatoes could be stewed and canned to feed a large farm family of eight persons for a year. To preserve perishable goods such as butter, milk, and fresh meat, most settlers used wells or springs. One family near Edmond lowered two barrels into a cold spring on their homestead and safely stored their food. The only inconvenience was the necessity of running to the spring before and after each meal.

Settlers could even enjoy fresh ice cream during the hot days of summer. Made at home primarily from milk and eggs, which were produced on the farm, the only ingredients to be purchased were sugar, vanilla, and ice. If not stored in a cellar, ice usually was available at any depot when a freight train stopped. The depot employee would open a refrigerated car and remove the required blocks of ice. Wrapped in a blanket and set in a shady place, the ice usually survived the wagon trip home.

Most rural farmers produced enough garden crops, fruits, and preserved meat to warrant trips to market in Oklahoma City. The largest concentration of truck farmers in the county lived along the fertile banks of the North Canadian River east of Oklahoma City. During the 1890s several trails or roads led from this region to Oklahoma City.

One set of wagon ruts followed a "hogback" (the highest elevation between two drainage basins) along what is now Northeast 10th Street in Oklahoma City. It veered south at a point near present-day Interstate 35, and entered the business district on Northeast 4th Street. There farmers sold their produce either to wholesalers or directly to the public.

The Fairchild Winery

Fairchild's wine vault from the south side. From Sturm's Magazine. *Courtesy, LeRoy H. Fischer.*

During the hot, dry summer of 1890, Edward B. Fairchild staked a claim to a 160-acre relinquishment eight miles northeast of Oklahoma City. Little did he know that he soon would construct one of Oklahoma County's most important historic sites.

A native of New York's wine-producing district, the middle-aged man planted 40 acres to fruit trees, 20 acres to grapes, and the rest to fodder and pasturage for his horses. He also constructed a 60' x 100' reservoir, a windmill, and a small frame house. His master plan for all this activity was to produce and sell wine.

By late 1892 Fairchild knew that his grapes would soon produce a bountiful harvest, so he constructed a wine vault similar in design to those used in his native New York. The structure was totally constructed of rough-hewn sandstone, and the two-foot thick walls and ceiling were arched, using the ancient wedged-mass concept. At one end of the 40' x 14' room was an entrance, and at the other end was a spring, which ran through the vault and maintained a constant temperature. Fairchild also piled dirt on top and beside the structure to insulate aging wine from the heat of summer.

That next year Fairchild produced more than 60 tons of grapes. He and his laborers built a screw-type press, which separated the juice from the hulls, and he stored the juice in barrels, where the fermentation process began. When fully fermented, the wine was siphoned from the original barrel to remove all sediment. Stored in the vaulted cellar and cooled by spring water, these barrels of wine were then allowed to age.

Fairchild preferred to store his wine for at least one year, but rarely could he age it the full period, for customers in Oklahoma City developed a demanding taste for Fairchild wine. Customers oftentimes would drive to the winery, where they could fill their containers and in blissful serenity enjoy a quiet rest at the tables surrounding the sandstone structure. Others paid Fairchild to deliver wine by wagon, much like milkmen who delivered dairy products. Fairchild was so successful that until 1907 and prohibition, no competing winery operated in the Oklahoma City market.

In 1907 Fairchild closed the winery and sold the 160-acre farm for $10,000. After that time ownership of the old winery changed hands 17 times, until 1973 when George Shirk purchased the decaying structures. Shirk, president of the Oklahoma Historical Society and a dedicated preservationist, restored the winery to its original condition. Today, it stands as a monument to farmers and businessmen who, like Fairchild, tamed and worked the land of Oklahoma County.

A typical farm family during the 1890s might make two or three wagon trips into Oklahoma City each year. On the road by 4:00 A.M., most farmers could be in Oklahoma City by 8:00 A.M. After selling their butter, eggs, cheese, meat, and produce at the market along Reno Avenue, they would leave their wagons and teams at a livery, such as the Perrine or Hales stables.

For the rest of the day, the men of the family probably would look at new plows at the Kingman-Moore Implement Company, shop for hardware at DeBolt's, or have a piece of machinery repaired at the Sherman Iron and Machine Works plant on East Main. The women would browse through Lyon's Store for yard goods and look longingly at the finery. The children would run in all directions, fascinated by the movement and variety of the "city." By 4:00 that afternoon, filled with memories of their day in town, they all would be in the wagon bound for home.

Life on the farm was not as fast-paced as in Oklahoma City, but most rural communities enjoyed an active social life. The most important social event, other than a church gathering, was the "literary." Organized and located at rural schools or in individual homes, the literary society sponsored singing, recitations, debates, and speeches. Early rural settlers of Oklahoma County attended literaries at Red Top School, Oak Hill School, Council Grove School, and scores of other one-room schoolhouses. Such gatherings provided the necessary social contact that farm families needed to break the isolation of homesteading.

Literaries, church socials, and a regional tradition of westward migration reflected the dominant culture of rural Oklahoma County. However, there was one exception to this pattern: the Polish community at Harrah. The original Polish homesteaders entered the county during the second land run on September 22, 1891, which opened the Potawatomi and Shawnee reservations to white settlement. Typically, one male member of each family participated in the run. After claim-

Fruit was a good cash crop in central Oklahoma Territory, especially in the eastern sections of Oklahoma County, where the North Canadian River and good soil combined to produce bountiful harvests of cherries, apples, and peaches. From Report of the Governor of Oklahoma Territory, 1900.

ag homesteads in the rich North Canadian valley, they returned home or their families and possessions. That winter 10 Polish families from Iarche, Arkansas, entered the promised land, less than 20 years after ney had arrived in the New World.

Like their native-born neighbors, these naturalized citizens suffered uring the early years after the run. Many Polish families lived in neir covered wagons, while a few constructed dugouts. The owakowski family lived underground for more than a year before the ead of the household, Olejniczak, erected a sizeable tent. The family emained in these quarters for another two years, after which they loved into a log cabin measuring 10′ x 10′. If the land had not provided ild fruits, crab apples, and rabbit, those first years would have been ır more difficult.

For the first three or four years the Polish settlers had other prob- ms in common with most 89ers, especially a scarcity of cash. To raise ie funds needed for staple foods, several men from the community ined Santa Fe railroad construction crews. After a week away from ome, the men would return with enough money to buy flour, salt, and offee. Meanwhile, the settlers who remained on the farms cleared the elds for the first crop.

Slowly this ethnic community prospered and grew as more Polish milies came to the region, lured by the rich land and the camaraderie ' fellow immigrants. Their communal settlement pattern caused them › retain their ethnic culture. Instead of cornbread and beans, Polish imilies served *kielbasa* (sausage), *kluski* (noodles), *maciek* (lambs' ver), and *czarnina* (duck-blood soup spiced with prunes, raisins, and negar). Instead of square dancing, they did the polkas, waltzes, and hottisches of Europe. Drawn together by these cultural ties, the olish community by 1907 consisted of 40 to 50 families.

Like their Polish neighbors, the native white and black rural settlers ` Oklahoma County suffered through the financially plagued 1890s,

Above
In 1892 Broadway Avenue in Oklahoma City was filled with farmers from the surrounding countryside. Without the productivity and success of farmers in the rural sections of the county, cities such as Oklahoma City would have lacked the early economic activity necessary for urban development. (OHS)

Right
Rural farmers relied on bridges to cross rivers and creeks. This bridge spanned the North Canadian River near Jones. Courtesy, Harrah Historical Society.

HEART OF THE PROMISED LAND: AN ILLUSTRATED HISTORY OF OKLAHOMA COUNTY

urviving by a combination of hard work and sense of community. The
conomic outlook for farmers began to change in 1897 and 1898,
owever, when more rainfall and improved prices for their crops
shered in the "golden age" of agriculture. Fortunately, the rainfall
nd high prices coincided with the time when Oklahoma County farm-
rs had cultivated their land to its most productive stage.

The census of 1900 reflected this prosperity. The rural population of
he county had increased from 7,297 in 1890 to 14,913 in 1900, while the
ollar value of land, machinery, and buildings had risen from $1,986,-
50 to $6,483,920 during this decade. The most dramatic changes were
een in the total crops produced in the county. In 1890, less than one
ear after the first land run, census takers reported only 3,907 acres of
ay as the only produce of farms in Oklahoma County. By 1900 the
ounty's farmers reported 60,048 acres in wheat, 54,116 acres in corn,
6,888 acres in cotton, and 12,782 acres in hay, in addition to more than
82,320 fruit trees. When combined with 21,000 cattle, 10,000 horses,
,800 mules, and 116,617 chickens, the ingenuity and productivity of
klahoma County farmers after only 10 years reflected their hard
ork, frontier grit, and grim determination.

The present generation of Oklahoma County residents owes a great
ebt to those rugged pioneers. Their productivity stimulated new
ailroad construction, attracted new businesses, and prompted the cre-
tion of more than a dozen crossroads towns. Moreover, the economic
uccess of the rural population built a financial base for the growth of
klahoma City and other towns in the county. From 1889 to 1907 the
armers of Oklahoma County survived untold hardships in order to
ransform a raw frontier into a productive "Heart of the Promised
and."

Above
An important part of community life for many pioneers was church. This Catholic church in Harrah reflects the size and prosperity of the Polish community in the eastern part of the county. Courtesy, Western History Collections, University of Oklahoma Library.

Left
Weddings were a time to gather friends and family in the Polish community near Harrah. This group celebrated with the aid of two musicians in 1913. Courtesy, Western History Collections, University of Oklahoma Library.

5

Oklahoma City, Territorial Town

As the train approached Oklahoma Station from the south young Frank Harrah looked at his watch. It was a little after 2:00 P.M., two hours since the land run had started. Looking through the window of his coach, Harrah viewed a sea of tents alive with the movement of men and animals.

As the train slowed, the young Missourian jumped from the car's exit, threw his luggage beneath the depot platform, and ran east toward the nearest unoccupied land. Before running 20 feet a soldier told him he was in a military reserve. Wheeling around Harrah then ran four blocks west until he found an unclaimed lot. At that location he drove his stake into the soft ground and merged his life with that of Oklahoma City.

For the rest of the day, Harrah remained on his recently won property, determined to protect it from lot-jumpers. When night descended, he found a neighbor willing to share his tent—if Harrah brought his own straw. Harrah asked his bunkmate what business he intended to pursue. When the gentlemen replied that he was in the restaurant business, Harrah asked if he needed a partner. The man, W.O. Church, answered, "Sure."

The two men rose early the next morning, cleared the straw

66

W.O. Church and Frank Harrah used the earnings from their restaurant to purchase a lot near the railroad, where they constructed this frame building for a feed and coal business. (OHS)

Missourian Frank Harrah, third from right, and his partner sold thousands of biscuits and gallons of coffee from this makeshift restaurant at the site of Oklahoma City during the land run, circa 1889. (OHS)

from the tent, and positioned a board countertop across two tree stumps. Without running water or utilities, the partners prepared their entire bill of fare—biscuits and coffee. Despite the limited menu the tent cafe was a success, drawing crowds at all hours and long into the night. Church and Harrah served thousands of homemade biscuits and gallons of hot coffee during the next 10 days, after which they used the profits to open a store selling flour, feed, and coal. Success in this venture later led to real-estate development, town promotion, and agricultural investments.

As typified by Frank Harrah, the economic lifeblood of early Oklahoma City depended on property and money carried in from other cities and states. The town had no industry, no agricultural clearing-houses, and no source of mineral or extractive wealth. It was a boom-town with no economic boom. Instead, the economy of Oklahoma City was based on potential or future wealth, a commodity that attracted enough people to generate a boom by virtue of their spending and investments. Henry Overholser was another good example of this phenomenon.

Born in 1839, Overholser was a businessman from Wisconsin who had succeeded and prospered during 40 or more years in diverse business endeavors. At the age of 50, when most men contemplated retirement, Overholser decided to try frontier life in David Payne's "promised land." Like many of Oklahoma City's early residents, Overholser arrived by rail several days after the opening. With him he brought several boxcars full of sections for prefabricated buildings, enough capital for investments, and a thirst for success.

Soon after his arrival, Overholser purchased eight lots on Grand Avenue just west of Robinson, and hired cash-hungry men to assemble his partially completed buildings. When they finished, he had six two-story frame buildings in the center of the town's busiest commercial district. Previously acquired wealth also enabled Overholser to build

other structures, most notably the Overholser Opera House, and to invest in various business ventures from cotton gins to railroads. By using his money to generate more wealth, the civic leader created many jobs. By investing in capital improvements, he attracted new industry. By building cotton gins and flour mills, he attracted the trade of farmers. Men like Overholser, who brought talent and wealth to the new land, formed the economic base of early Oklahoma City.

Pioneer businessmen fostered economic growth through aggressive optimism, and the most optimistic of all the schemes in early Oklahoma City was the "Grand Canal." Billed as the "most gigantic undertaking in Oklahoma Territory," the proposed canal was to be six miles and 320 feet long, have a total fall of 32.6 feet, and provide water power for mills and utilities in downtown Oklahoma City. The first dirt was removed on December 9, 1889, and work progressed throughout the winter, employing hundreds of men who otherwise might have left the city.

The next spring a new gristmill and a generating plant awaited the opening of the canal, ready to tap a steady flow of water. When the gates were opened, water from the North Canadian flowed as expected and the city rejoiced. By the second day, however, the water level began falling. By the third day the water was gone, absorbed into the sandy soils of the substrata. Vision, money, and energy could build a canal; it could not change nature. After six months of heartbreaking failures to correct the problems, all hope was abandoned. The "grand canal" had become the "grand illusion."

Despite temporary setbacks such as this, optimism remained the basic wealth of Oklahoma City during the early part of the decade. Much of this unflagging hope revolved around two series of events: land openings and railroad construction. Early in 1890, anticipating the opening of adjacent Indian lands to white settlement, the federal government opened a land office in Oklahoma City. This institution served as a magnet to attract adventurers and land-seekers, men who carried money with them to buy supplies and pay for services and entertainment.

In September 1891, as expected, thousands of men registered at the land office for the upcoming land run into the Sac and Fox, Iowa,

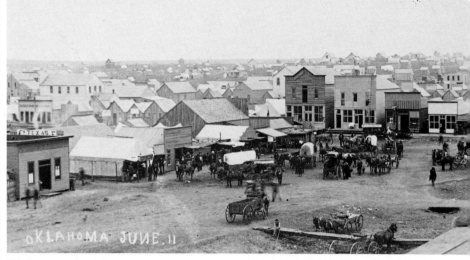

Kickapoo, and Potawatomi reservations. With 865,000 acres of prime farmland at stake, this run attracted more than 20,000 people, three times the number of claims available. While in Oklahoma City, these pioneers purchased goods and equipment and paid for hotel rooms, food, and entertainment. After the run, many of the unsuccessful participants returned to Oklahoma City.

In April 1892 an even larger land opening provided a new boost to Oklahoma City's economy. The run into the Cheyenne and Arapaho reservation, with 3,500,000 acres available for homesteading, attracted another 25,000 people. Many of these land-seekers disembarked in or passed through Oklahoma City in their quest for a new life, providing customers and clients for the town's struggling businessmen.

New railroad construction, whether real or only planned, also served to promote investment and economic activity. Within a year of the land opening in 1889, the Choctaw, Oklahoma, and Coal Railway Company laid the first east-to-west track into Oklahoma City. Completed in May 1891, this rail line later was continued west to the Texas border and east to McAlester, giving Oklahoma City merchants and businessmen easy access to vast farm markets and numerous small towns.

In 1894 city fathers Henry Overholser and C.G. "Gristmill" Jones initiated plans for bringing yet another rail line to Oklahoma City. After

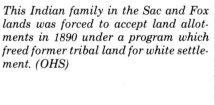

OKLAHOMA CITY

INDIAN TERRITORY.
1890.

raising $40,000 from local interests, the businessmen entered into an agreement with officials of the St. Louis and San Francisco Railway Company (Frisco) to build an extension from Sapulpa, Indian Territory, to Oklahoma City, for a total of 103 miles. Completed in 1895, this construction meant business for Oklahoma City merchants, employment for residents, and new speculative investment.

Oklahoma City's four banks provided financing for many of these early projects. One was the Citizens' Bank, located on the southeast corner of Main and Broadway. Another was the First National Bank, established by T.M. Richardson on a $300 lot just west of Broadway on Main Street. Richardson's bank failed within one year, a victim perhaps to over-expansion. J.B. Wheeler, after whom Wheeler Park later would be named, organized the Wheeler Bank. The fourth financial institution in the young community was the Bank of Oklahoma City, later renamed the Farmers' National Bank.

Bankers and merchants represented most, but not all of Oklahoma City's businessmen during the first years of the decade. A minority group, but one which was highly visible, consisted of gamblers and prostitutes, the city's "purveyors of vice." As one rhetorician characterized this class, they included "sentimental blacklegs, surething grafters, confidence sharks, get-rich-quick Wallingfords, brace game sharpers, slippery devils, audacious sharpers, unctuous swindlers, bunco steerers, wire-tippers, door-mat grafters, professional beggars, hopheads, white line artists, and blown-in-the-glass stiffs."

Actually, only a handful of gambling rooms and dance halls ap-

This aerial sketch of Oklahoma City shows the limits of the original townsite, which extended from South 7th to North 7th and from Walker Avenue to the Santa Fe right-of-way. In 1890, the year of this map, the population of the city was approximately 4,000. From the I.N. Phelps Stokes Collection. Courtesy, The New York Public Library; Astor, Lenox and Tilden Foundation.

peared in early Oklahoma City, but they were all concentrated in one area, known as "hell's half acre," along Broadway just west of the Santa Fe station. Gamblers and prostitutes operated openly during the first 11 months of settlement, for no federal law prevented such activities. Moreover, no local government existed to interfere. Captain Stiles and his men closed the gambling dens on Sunday, but otherwise such operations continued unhampered.

Although free-spending men could find prostitutes and gambling in the rough section of town, liquor was unobtainable during the first 11 months of settlement, for federal law prevented the introduction of distillates into Indian Territory. Not until territorial organization would residents of Oklahoma City have legal liquor and saloons.

Confronted with insufficient law enforcement, few public improvements, and nonexistent local services, most residents of the Unassigned Lands favored and promoted territorial organization. Besieged with requests for governmental status, Congress passed the Organic Act on May 2, 1890, providing for the organization of Oklahoma Territory. The act divided the new territory into seven counties, including Oklahoma County, and located the territorial capital at Guthrie, 45 miles north of Oklahoma City.

President Benjamin Harrison promptly appointed George W. Steele the first territorial governor. This Republican official from Indiana then named county commissioners, authorizing them to accept petitions for municipal incorporation. On July 15, 1890, after a hasty petition drive garnered 647 names, north and south Oklahoma were consolidated into the town of Oklahoma City.

Three weeks later, on August 9, the voters of the new town elected their first legal municipal government, naming lumberman W.J. Gault the first mayor. Gault, a "strong mayor" under the aldermanic form of city rule, then appointed officials to run the day-to-day operations of his government. One of his most fortunate appointments was Charles Colcord as the first chief of police.

"Flour and Feed," basic necessities for survival on the frontier, were the products offered by this enterprising man in early Oklahoma City. (OHS)

HEART OF THE PROMISED LAND: AN ILLUSTRATED HISTORY OF OKLAHOMA COUNTY

Charles F. Colcord: From Cowboy to Oilman

Charles F. Colcord. (OHS)

Few people in the history of Oklahoma City could have filled the demanding positions of pioneer lawman, real-estate developer, oilman, banker, historian, author, civic leader, and builder — one such individual was Charles F. Colcord.

Born in 1859, Colcord fled war-torn Kentucky for the open spaces of Texas, where he was educated on the back of a horse. At the age of 17 he started a ranch in Kansas, but once again the frontier called, this time from the heart of Indian Territory.

As the dust from the land run settled, Colcord rode into Oklahoma City and joined forces with the dominant townsite company. He was appointed the first provisional lawman, named the first official chief of police after territorial organization, selected as one of the first United States deputy marshals in Oklahoma City, and elected as the county's first sheriff.

Meanwhile Colcord invested in real estate and used his earnings to organize the Commercial National Bank of Oklahoma City. Five years later he entered the oil business, only to strike it rich in the Red Fork, Glen Pool, Healdton, Loco, and Duncan fields of Oklahoma, and in the South Bend field of Texas.

With oil profits Colcord expanded his interests in Oklahoma City. He organized and managed the Local Building and Loan Association, built the now-famous Colcord Building, and financed and constructed the Biltmore Hotel. In addition to his financial successes, Colcord served as president of the Chamber of Commerce and president of the Oklahoma Historical Society. He also found time to write his autobiography, which was published after his death.

Colcord was the embodiment of the pioneer Oklahoman, a blend of adventurer, gambler, fighter, businessman, and civic leader. He was one of the early builders who transformed a shanty town into a vibrant, metropolitan urban center. Modern Oklahomans owe much to gifted Charles Colcord.

A Legacy of Law and Order :
The Oklahoma City Police Department

This was probably the first jail in Oklahoma City, where Charles Colcord and his deputies confined the most unruly lawbreakers. (OHS)

Near high noon on June 30, 1895, Chief of Police Milton Jones and two officers stood at the corner of Broadway and Main, surveying their domain of wooden shanties, brick buildings, and dusty streets. Meanwhile, convicted murderer Jim Casey and the Christian brothers overpowered a guard at the city jail and escaped.

The jail was located between Grand and Main just west of Broadway, so the outlaws headed east, supposedly making for the livery stables and horses. When they approached Broadway, however, they ran into Chief Jones. As the startled lawman went for his gun, Casey fired, hitting the chief in the throat only seconds before the other officers killed Casey. When the smoke cleared, the pioneer lawman was found lying in the street, the first of Oklahoma City's policemen to give his life in the line of duty.

At the time of this gun fight, the Oklahoma City Police Department consisted of only eight men, each of whom had to enforce the law with fists and guns. As the town grew and prospered, the danger still existed, but increased manpower made the task easier. After the economic boom of 1898 and the attending population explosion, the force grew quickly to 12 men in 1901, 22 men in 1903, and 29 men in 1906.

Other than the suppression of violent crime, the major target for the police force at the turn of the century was vice. In 1907, encouraged by a committee of outraged citizens, Chief Charles Post organized a "flying squadron" of officers to raid gambling dens, houses of prostitution, and bootleggers. The crusade for social cleansing resulted in 7,112 arrests, including 1,962 for intoxication and 1,173 for prostitution. This was in addition to 431 arrests for assault, 92 for carrying concealed weapons, and a variety of other offenses such as six counts of allowing chickens to run loose.

During the next 20 years the OCPD reorganized and improved capabilities to confront new threats to law and order. Increased use of automobiles forced leaders to organize a traffic squad, and by 1936 this unit numbered 41 men, 18 stationed at intersections and 23 equipped with motorcycles. Other innovations included mounted patrolmen, Bertillon investigation, and the use of radios in patrol cars. Such adaptations kept the OCPD at the forefront of police efficiency.

After World War II the force entered an era of unprecedented expansion and specialization. Manpower increased to 277 in 1955, 600 in 1976, and 1,000 in 1981, while a succession of police administrators created new units whose personnel ranges from narcotics agents and liquor-raiders to antiterrorist specialists and bomb details. Today the OCPD fulfills the duties originally assigned to the first chief of police and his four men — to preserve the peace in Oklahoma City.

Colcord appointed a force of four men, one for each ward. The first officers were William Gill, F.M. "Bud" Reynolds, Abner J. Day, and John Hubatka, a man who would remain in the Oklahoma City Police Department for the next 40 years. Colcord and his men enforced a growing list of ordinances. One of the first city statutes forbade carrying concealed weapons, a law Colcord often cited for the relative peace enjoyed in the city. The policemen also collected taxes for the young government, especially the $250 tax on saloons. The city financed many of its early projects with revenues from "sinners."

With law and order secured, the city government turned to improving the quality of life in Oklahoma City. One means of achieving that goal was to promote and encourage the construction of utilities. During the first few years after the run, Oklahoma City residents obtained water from privately dug wells in town or from one of several creeks running south to the river. A safe water system was desperately needed, however, for creek water was unhealthy and well water was inadequate. Confronted with this pressing dilemma, one of the city government's first acts was to grant a water system franchise to the Oklahoma Canal and Ditch Company.

Unfortunately, the company failed to provide water, so in 1892 another franchise was granted to the D.H. Scott Company. Scott, who hired workers to dig a well near the North Canadian River, hit a good flow at a depth of about 30 feet in what later would be named the Garber sands. Despite some success, private ownership of the town's water supply ended in 1893 when the city purchased the well and 30 miles of water mains. Public demand for this service was reaffirmed in 1894 when citizens approved a bond issue of $80,000 to provide a better water system.

The city council granted a franchise for an electric system on November 26, 1890, to the Oklahoma City Light and Power Company, which promptly constructed a small generating plant at the intersection of Robinson and Frisco streets. The Colorado Light Company later purchased the facility and converted it to steam. Meanwhile, homeowners and businessmen of early Oklahoma City could opt for gas

Firms such as the Zylite Water Company, located at 1419 West 16th Street in Oklahoma City, provided water to many families of the county at the turn of the century. Courtesy, Joan Keys.

This ditching machine crew helped expand the water distribution system in Oklahoma City, circa 1906. This crew laid ceramic pipe, but the first lines laid in the city were wooden. Courtesy, Oklahoma County Metropolitan Library.

OKLAHOMA CITY, TERRITORIAL TOWN

Carpenters, merchants, and real-estate dealers formed the economic base of early Oklahoma City. In June of 1889, when this photograph was taken, the business community of Oklahoma City included 34 groceries, 5 furniture stores, 29 real-estate firms, and 27 lumberyards. (OHS)

power after 1893, when a company began manufacturing gas from oil. Due to insufficient demand, however, the gas plant failed in 1895 and did not reopen until 1902.

Many of Oklahoma's 5,000 or so citizens could have requested water, electricity, or gas service by telephone after 1892, when the first telephone system was installed in the city. Within two years the Missouri-Kansas Telephone Company network included almost 200 telephones. With the conveniences of electricity, gas, and telephones only a few years after the run, the residents of Oklahoma City enjoyed many of the amenities of more settled urban life.

Residents of Oklahoma City expected other public services, especially schools for their children. The only schools in town during the first year of settlement were subscription schools, which charged families one dollar to two dollars per month for each child. Operated in tents, business establishments, and even under blackjack trees, these free enterprise schools offered a temporary solution to the absence of a governmentally sponsored education system.

The first Oklahoma City public school was organized in the fall of 1890. Although Superintendent R.A. Sullins had inadequate public funds for his system, he hired a few teachers and continued instructing the city's children in tents and shacks. The town's four elementary schools were located at N.W. 4th and Broadway, Main and Broadway, California and Broadway, and on California near Santa Fe. That first year approximately 700 children were taught by 20 teachers, seven of whom were men.

The school system received a boost in 1893 when $45,000 was made available by a bond issue for school buildings. In 1896 the school fund was supplemented by the sale of lots in the old Military Reservation district. During the next few years the school board authorized the construction of Washington, Emerson, Jefferson, Lincoln, and Garfield schools, as well as Irving, the old high school. As the decade progressed the school system expanded, with total enrollment rising to approximately 2,000 children by 1898.

To foster education, the Philomathea Club in 1897 initiated a drive to build a library. By May of the following year, the club had organized the Public Library Association, purchased $500 worth of books, and opened the collection to the public in an office above the Farmers' National Bank at Grand and Robinson. The Philomathea Club, like many of its sister organizations, combined such community service with study programs. Other clubs, such as the Ladies Relief Club, devoted energies to worthy projects such as aid to the destitute.

The churches, which had organized soon after the opening, also provided assistance to the needy. On April 28, the first Sunday in the "Promised Land," a soldier walked through the downtown business district of Oklahoma City with a bugle, much like the Pied Piper, blowing a call for church. At the end of his route, Reverend James Murray and a Methodist gathering awaited. That same day Presbyterian minister Charles Hembree convened a street meeting at the corner of Main and Broadway.

Within a year several permanent church buildings had been constructed in Oklahoma City. Members of the First Methodist Episcopal Church built a meeting hall on two lots at 4th and Robinson. A Catholic congregation erected a house of worship at 4th and Harvey. The Baptists, who met initially above a hardware store on Grand Avenue, built their first permanent structure at 2nd and Robinson early in 1890. These and other church groups brought religious education to the people of Oklahoma City and provided a necessary social element for orderly development.

Most churches were located near the central business district where the largest concentrations of residential housing were found. Charles Colcord, for example, at first lived on 3rd and Robinson, where he built

First Methodist Episcopal Church at 4th and North Robinson is shown here before the neighborhood was engulfed by commercial expansion. (OHS)

Irving, the first high school in Oklahoma City, was constructed after the sale of lots in the old Military District in 1896. By 1898, 2,000 children attended Oklahoma City schools. (OHS)

J.L. Marrinam's home typified housing in the Military Addition east of the Santa Fe tracks. By 1898, the first "exclusive" residential district was home to many of Oklahoma City's most prosperous businessmen. (OHS)

a frame house for himself and his wife. The first "exclusive" residential district in Oklahoma City was the Military Addition, carved from the old Military Reservation east of the Santa Fe tracks and north of Reno. The 160-acre site was platted and subdivided in 1892 with large lots, basic street improvements, and a tree-lined avenue running diagonally through the neighborhood. By 1898 the addition was home to many of the city's most prosperous businessmen.

Although Oklahoma City was a small community with fewer than 10,000 population as late as 1898, its residents enjoyed an active social life. For example, less than one year after the opening, a choral association was organized, the Weaver Hotel emerged, and theatrical troupes arrived in town periodically. Even during the tumultuous summer of 1889, the people of Oklahoma City managed to provide community entertainment. The occasion was a congressional visit to the recently opened district and the plan was to celebrate with horse races, games, and amusements on the Fourth of July. The festivities ended in tragedy, however, when hastily constructed bleachers collapsed, injuring several people and killing one child.

Entertainment and diversion were important during the early stages of settlement, for businessmen and laborers worked diligently just to survive the lean years of the early 1890s. James L. Wyatt, who opened a market soon after the run, serves as a good example of this early work ethic. When he arrived in Oklahoma City, Wyatt purchased a $300 lot located between Robinson and Harvey on Main Street. Low on cash, the businessman then traded his horse to a carpenter in exchange for his services. Wyatt then hired himself to the carpenter for $1.50 a day. When the 18' x 24' building was completed, he still had $65 to invest in trade goods. Wyatt's business survived those early years to become Crescent Market.

Another demanding business was the newspaper profession. By 1890 Oklahoma City was home to four dailies: the *Oklahoma City Times*, the

Oklahoma Times, the *Daily Oklahoman*, and the *Evening Gazette*. The first paper printed in Oklahoma City was the *Oklahoma Times*, published by Angelo and Winfield Scott. Winfield served as the business manager while Angelo fulfilled the duties of reporter and editor. Together, the Scotts and their fellow publishers helped promote the early economic development of their chosen city.

Journalism in the pioneer city during the 1890s was focused primarily on local affairs and personalities. Vitriolic editors, using their positions to espouse personal beliefs, often generated as well as reported news. In one instance, Hamlin Sawyer of the *Oklahoma City Times* mounted an editorial attack against Captain D.F. Stiles, whom Sawyer considered a puppet for the Seminole Townsite Company. On a hot afternoon that first summer the two men exchanged inflammatory comments on the street. Sawyer, accustomed to the safety of his office, lashed out at the soldier, screaming, ''I would thrash you if you didn't have that uniform on.'' Pleased to have an opportunity to respond, the fiery captain tore off his coat, threw it to the ground, and retorted, ''Don't worry about the uniform!'' Sawyer quickly decided he was better with his pen than his fists and fled the scene.

When not distracted by personal feuds and local politics, most newspaper editors of early Oklahoma City dedicated themselves to the town's growth. Many of those early papers promoted Oklahoma City as an oasis of opportunity and success. Realistically, economic growth came slowly during the 1890s, advancing only as fast as the surrounding farmers cleared their fields and began producing good crops.

By 1894, after rebounding from the financial panic of 1893, businessmen of Oklahoma City reacted to the farmers' increased production. Typical of the business directly related to the agricultural upturn was the Acme Milling Company, organized by Kansan George Sohlberg in 1894. The mill, with a capacity of 500 barrels of flour and 100 barrels of

Oklahoma City's first baseball field was located at Stiles Park. The grandstand bleachers, shown here, collapsed on July 4, 1889, under a holiday crowd. Courtesy, Oklahoma County Metropolitan Library.

The Oklahoma City Band supplied entertainment in early Oklahoma City, providing a welcome diversion for businessmen and laborers who worked diligently to survive. (OHS)

meal per day, attracted farmers to Oklahoma City where they deposited their earnings, shopped, and enjoyed a brief respite from hard work on the farm.

While farming conditions in Oklahoma Territory improved gradually, more land openings were conducted, railroad construction continued, and industries such as the Acme Milling Company took up residence in Oklahoma City. The combination of these elements resulted in a moderate rate of economic growth for the town. In 1896 an evaluation of property in Oklahoma City determined the total wealth of the populace at $1,047,513. In the list of personal possessions, the assessor reported 504 horses, 46 mules, 138 cattle, 3 sheep, 7 hogs, 223 carriages, 292 gold watches, 35 silver watches, and 114 pianos. Although still a small hamlet by modern standards, Oklahoma City by 1896 was a growing community.

In 1898 Oklahoma City was the most prosperous town in Oklahoma Territory. Despite this comparative status, the growth had been slow and agonizing. Agriculture, although improved over the disastrous years of 1889 and 1890, still suffered from depressed markets and drought. Merchants, although optimistic and aggressive, still lacked the expanding markets needed for profits high enough to justify heavy investments. The unspectacular growth, however, was overshadowed by cultural, physical, and civic advances. The people of Oklahoma City had banded together to survive the first years on the frontier. After 1898 their patience would be rewarded.

6

A City Emerges

I n 1897 Oklahoma City looked like any other rural village of few thousand people. The streets were unpaved and mudd much of the time. The central business district, confined t Grand and Main streets between the Santa Fe tracks and Robin son, had the rough appearance of a frontier town with woode sidewalks and false fronts. Even the residential districts, wit the exception of the new Military Addition, reflected the boom town origins of the city. To a visitor passing through town, th spirit of '89 apparently had faded.

Despite this outward appearance, Oklahoma City was poised a a turning point in its brief history. In 1897 the young town sti was locked in a stagnating five-year economic depression; by th end of 1898, the town again would be alive with the sounds o hammers and saws. There were several reasons for this trans formation. One was an agricultural upturn after 1898; anothe was the arrival of a new generation of talented and energeti men. The real catalyst for the phoenix-like economic resurgenc however, proved to be the completion of the St. Louis an Oklahoma City Railroad.

Organized in 1895 by C.G. "Gristmill" Jones, Henry Overholse

Frisco Station was constructed soon after the St. Louis and Oklahoma City Railroad was built into Oklahoma City. Eventually the Municipal Building was erected at this site. Courtesy, Oklahoma County Metropolitan Library.

and officials of the St. Louis and San Francisco Railroad (Frisco), the St. Louis and Oklahoma City line was to extend from Sapulpa, Indian Territory, to Oklahoma City. After more than two years spent raising $40,000 subscription fee, gaining federal permission to cross Indian lands, and financing the construction of 103 miles of track, the Frisco's first locomotive pulled into Oklahoma City on October 21, 1897.

This southwest-to-northeast rail connection linked Oklahoma City merchants with markets in Tulsa, Kansas City, and St. Louis, and drove a commercial wedge into territory previously controlled by Guthrie wholesalers. This was an important development, for after 1898 rural communities prospered as never before. With wheat prices rising daily and cotton selling for 11 cents a pound, farmers could buy more goods and services from Oklahoma City merchants.

Angelo Scott, who lived in Oklahoma City in 1898, recognized a greater effect of the Frisco's arrival: "Most of all there was a new psychology, or shall I say the returning of the old psychology. The old hope, the old expectation, and the old spirit came back, and with redoubled strength." As a result of this rekindled fire, Oklahoma City entered an economic boom that tripled the population in just three years.

The Oklahoma Cotton Compress Company was typical of the manufacturing and wholesale distribution firms that relocated in Oklahoma City after 1898. Constructed during the summer of 1898, the plant's facilities covered seven acres and ginned and pressed up to

1,200 bales of cotton each day. Located east of the Santa Fe tracks near the Frisco and Choctaw lines, this clearinghouse for cotton was the largest in the Southwest.

Other large firms that opened plants in Oklahoma City were Anheuser-Busch, which opened an ice plant at 3rd and Santa Fe, William-Halsell-Frazier Company, a wholesale grocery concern that grossed one million dollars during its first year, and Plansifter Mills, which produced 200 barrels of flour and 75 barrels of meal per day. All three of these companies located in Oklahoma City during the pivotal year 1898.

This phenomenal economic transition was reflected in a published listing of industrial plants that opened in Oklahoma City in 1898 and 1899. It included a cotton compress, a cottonseed oil mill, an ice factory, an electric light plant, two iron foundaries, two flour mills, two door and sash factories, two machine shops, four cigar factories, a shirt manufacturer, a harness and saddle factory, a marble works, a candy factory, two carriage and wagon works, and four brickyards.

Just as manufacturing and wholesale companies followed railroads, people followed jobs. In 1898 the population of Oklahoma City barely exceeded 4,000 people; in 1900 the official United States census listed Oklahoma City as a town of 9,990. By 1901 that number had increased to 14,369. This three-year population explosion, from 4,000 to 14,000, represented a remarkable burst of economic and physical growth.

Industrial and population expansion also generated renewed construction in the central business district. In 1900, two years after the boom began, construction of new commercial buildings in Oklahoma City was valued at more than $1.2 million. By the end of 1900 the town's business streets were fronted by 7,900 feet of brick or stone buildings, while wooden structures survived only on the outskirts of the commercial district.

Above
Oklahoma Furniture Manufacturing Company was an industry attracted to Oklahoma City just after 1898. Producing furniture and mattresses on the east side, these plants were only blocks from two railroad depots. Courtesy, Oklahoma County Metropolitan Library.

Left
The Oklahoma City Cotton Compress Company, located on East Reno, typified the industrialization of Oklahoma City. Constructed in 1898, the compress baled millions of pounds of cotton each year. Courtesy, Oklahoma County Metropolitan Library.

By 1909 Oklahoma City was the "jobbing center of the Southwest." Its excellent rail connections and central location in the state made the city attractive to business. From Sturm's Magazine.

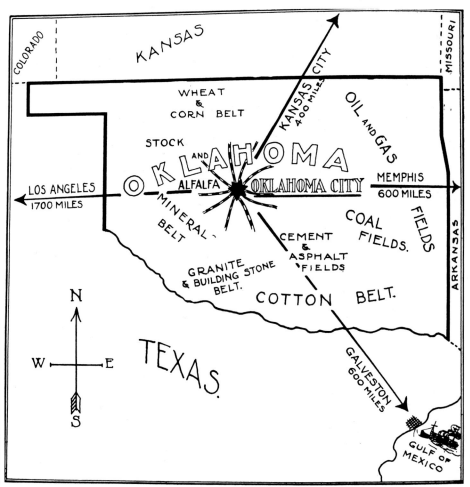

Constructed in 1900 by Oscar G. Lee, the Hotel Lee was the most ornate hotel in Oklahoma City. Theodore Roosevelt attended a banquet and ball at the hotel shortly after it was completed. Courtesy, Oklahoma County Metropolitan Library.

The growth of industry and construction, as well as the population explosion, reflected the newfound aggressiveness and self-confidence of the people of Oklahoma City. It was appropriate, therefore, that in 1900 the city was host to one of America's most dynamic figures, Theodore Roosevelt.

Roosevelt, at that time governor of New York and the Republican candidate for Vice President, was Oklahoma City's guest of honor at the national reunion of the Rough Riders. On the first night of his visit in town, Roosevelt attended a banquet and ball at the ornate Lee Hotel, to the delight of the city's social elite. The following day's activities were for everyone.

That eventful day, which was unseasonably serene and cool for July 3, began with a grand parade. Advancing down Broadway amid the color of the decorated city, the parade was spearheaded by a marching band. Then Roosevelt followed, mounted on a black charger and leading his friends. Company after company, the veterans of the Spanish-American War filed by carrying their battle flags. Then came a heterogeneous multitude of Civil War veterans, Indians in full dress, cowboys in their western regalia, and a host of others on horseback and on foot. In all, it was a colorful pageant matching the exuberance of the period.

From the parade Roosevelt and the crowds proceeded to the fair grounds west of town, where he continued the emotional tempo. When he stood to deliver his speech the crowd sank into utter silence. "Men and Women of Oklahoma," he yelled, and the crowd roared with delight. When the frenzy subsided, he continued, "I was never in your country until last night, but I feel at home here. I am blood of your blood, and bone of your bone, and I am bound to some of you, and to your sons, by the strongest ties that can bind one man to another." That eventful day, Roosevelt expressed the community spirit of Oklahoma City in 1900.

Roosevelt's positive traits—aggressiveness, self-confidence, and determination—were shared by a new generation of business and community leaders in Oklahoma City after the turn of the century. Three of the most exemplary men of this class were Anton Classen, John Shartel, and Charles Colcord.

Above
Onlookers crowded the streets of Oklahoma City during the Rough Riders parade on July 3, 1900, in which Theodore Roosevelt rode on a black stallion. (OHS)

Left
Governor of New York Theodore Roosevelt visited Oklahoma City in 1900 to attend a reunion of the Rough Riders. He attended a banquet and ball at the ornate Hotel Lee and participated in a parade on July 3. (OHS)

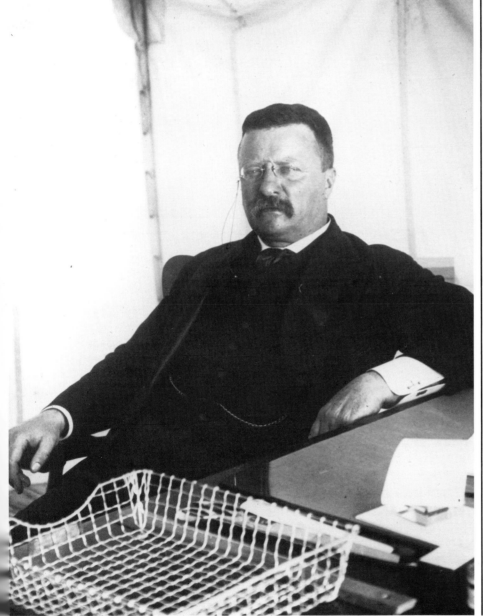

Anton Classen, a pioneer city leader who arrived in Oklahoma City in 1897, was elected president of the Commercial Club (Chamber of Commerce) in 1899. He became involved in property development, a savings and loan company, and mass transportation. (OHS)

Classen, a native of Illinois, participated in the land run of April 22, 1889. The young attorney settled first in Guthrie, where he was soon embroiled in a contested claim suit. Although he won the court case, Classen sold his lot and moved to Edmond, where he practiced law, bought and sold property, and published the *Edmond Sun*.

Arriving in Oklahoma City in 1897 as Receiver of the United States Land Office, Classen quickly assumed a position of leadership in his new hometown. In 1899 he was elected president of the Commercial Club (Chamber of Commerce), a position he would hold for three years. Meanwhile, he became active in property development, a savings and loan company, and mass transportation.

Like Classen, John W. Shartel was a lawyer who had made the run into Guthrie in 1889. He, too, relocated in Oklahoma City during the early rumblings of the new economic boom. Active in real-estate development, he joined Classen in numerous projects. In this effective partnership, Classen was the builder and organizer while Shartel was the promoter. As one contemporary said of Shartel in his role of promoter, he "had to be one of two things: a diplomat or a fighter. He chose to be a fighter."

HEART OF THE PROMISED LAND: AN ILLUSTRATED HISTORY OF OKLAHOMA COUNTY

Charles F. Colcord, who had earned a reputation as a tough lawman in Oklahoma County from 1889 to 1891, returned to Oklahoma City in 1899. Having prospered in Perry, Oklahoma Territory, Colcord used his considerable wealth to buy land and property in the expanding city. After 1899, if there was a beneficial project underway to promote Oklahoma City, Charlie Colcord was involved. For the next 30 years he would be instrumental in the construction of the city's finest buildings, the operations of the Chamber of Commerce, the luring of railroads and industry, and the acquisition of the state capitol.

Classen, Shartel, and Colcord arrived in Oklahoma City during the second boom, and all three men entered the land development business. Yet, unlike many of their contemporaries, they went beyond mere purchasing and selling of land. Colcord entered the oil business, becoming a leader in developing the Glenn Pool and Healdton fields, both of which boosted the economy of Oklahoma City and the state. Classen and Shartel channeled their energies into another important project affecting the history of Oklahoma City—the streetcar system.

John Shartel first proposed streetcars for Oklahoma City in 1898. The city council, however, took no action on the franchise request. By 1902 three other proposals had been submitted, involving prominent Oklahoma City businessmen Henry Overholser, Anton Classen, and Charlie Colcord, and a group from New York City. On January 30, 1902, the city council finally granted the franchise to the Metropolitan Street Railway Company, a firm that eventually included Anton Classen, W.W. Storm, S.L. Alton, John Threadgill, and Edward H. Cooke. John Shartel, the secretary and treasurer, was to manage construction and operations.

With right-of-way secured from the city, the company began laying track. The ribbon of metal progressed north on Broadway to 13th

Men construct rails in the residential neighborhoods east of the Santa Fe tracks. This line probably extended east and north to Stiles Park. Courtesy, Oklahoma County Metropolitan Library.

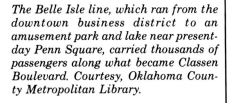

Crews began laying streetcar track in 1903. From the corner of Grand and Robinson, shown here, the ribbon of steel proceeds west on Grand. Courtesy, Oklahoma County Metropolitan Library.

The Belle Isle line, which ran from the downtown business district to an amusement park and lake near present-day Penn Square, carried thousands of passengers along what became Classen Boulevard. Courtesy, Oklahoma County Metropolitan Library.

Street, west on Main Street to Western Avenue, north on Walker to 13th Street, and east on 4th Street to Stiles Park. Within nine months the company was operating five cars along 6.5 miles of track.

The electric-powered cars made their first runs on February 2, 1903, beginning service that would continue for more than 40 years. Each morning thereafter cars began running at 5:45 A.M. and returned to the shop at midnight. Each car, furnished with a vestibule, gate, seats, and a heater, could make a two and one-quarter mile trip in 10 minutes.

As in any new venture, troubles developed. One problem was the reaction of frightened horses. As Shartel counseled horse owners, "Every owner of a private convenience (horse and buggy) ought to get his animals inured to meeting the passing cars. . . . This is a precaution which no owner of a horse ought to disregard!" Another troublesome inconvenience was the noise of the cars. Between the rumbling of the metal wheels and the grinding of the gears, streetcars did much to disturb the peace and quiet of Oklahoma City.

The streetcar system, reorganized in 1904 as the Oklahoma Railway Company, radically altered the development of Oklahoma City and influenced the quality of life of its residents. One result was access to

wo parks along the North Canadian River. The smaller of the two was Wheeler Park, located directly south of the city on the banks of the river. The site consisted of 44 acres of grass and timber, a picnic area, nd eventually a zoo.

The other park was Delmar Gardens, a 140-acre amusement center ocated farther west and north on the river just beyond Western Avenue and south of Reno (near the present location of the Public Market). The land was owned by Charlie Colcord, while the concessions nd amusements were operated by John Sinopoulo and Joseph Marre, ho had worked at Delmar Gardens in St. Louis.

Featured attractions at the social center included a 1,200-seat heater, a scenic railway, a dance hall, a hotel, a restaurant, a swiming pool, and an outdoor refreshment and picnic area. Other than eneral relaxation, visitors to the park attended car races, horse races, ramatic presentations, and vaudeville. The success of both Wheeler ark and Delmar Gardens was due in large part to the streetcar ystem, on which residents of Oklahoma City could ride to the parks for five cent fare.

The Oklahoma Street Railway Company also was the catalyst eeded to attract Epworth College (Oklahoma City University) to

Located at 18th and Classen, Epworth College helped draw residential development to the northwest side of Oklahoma City. The brick structure, shown here circa 1904, included schools of medicine and law. Courtesy, Oklahoma County Metropolitan Library.

Oklahoma City and to develop more than a dozen new residential additions. This significant turn of events began in 1902 when the Methodist Episcopal Church and the Methodist Episcopal, South, officially stated a desire to locate a church-sponsored college in Oklahoma. Classen and Shartel, who owned extensive tracts of land north and west of the city, conceived a scheme through which all parties would profit.

The offer, which guaranteed 50 acres of land and a $100,000 endowment fund for the school, was made by the Oklahoma Commercial Club and its president, John Shartel. The terms of the pledge were to be fulfilled by the University Development Company, of which Classen and Shartel were the dominant directors.

The development company began by consolidating 480 acres of land located almost a mile northwest of town. The directors then platted the eastern 320 acres, extending east and west from Walker to Indiana Avenue, and north and south from 16th to 23rd streets. Named the University Addition, the area had enough lots to be sold to raise the $100,000 endowment, while 50 acres were to be donated to the school. The remaining lots would be sold for a profit. To make the entire project successful, Classen and Shartel agreed to construct a streetcar line to the new addition.

By controlling the public transportation network, the two entrepreneurs raised more than $100,000 for the church and attracted a college to Oklahoma City, all while earning a profit through free enterprise. With the land and endowment fund, Epworth College built a brick structure, organized schools of law and medicine, and provided a full curriculum for a college degree. Although it would be reorganized, renamed, and disbanded temporarily, the college would remain in Oklahoma City for the next 80 years.

Many leaders recognized the benefits of transportation and fought for improvements. The image of Oklahoma City as a transportation mecca was enhanced in 1902 and 1904 by the arrival of two more rail lines, both of which were part of the Missouri-Kansas-Texas Railway (KATY) system. One line stretched 146 miles from Oklahoma to

Bartlesville; the other, laid in 1904, extended from Oklahoma City to Atoka, 136 miles to the southeast.

Paved road construction within the city limits was another transportation improvement after the turn of the century. On November 19, 1900, the city council enacted an ordinance providing for the paving of the busiest commercial streets. The city let a contract in 1901, and by 1902 crews had paved Main, Grand, and First Street between Santa Fe and Harvey, and Broadway and Robinson streets from California north to the Choctaw tracks at 2nd Street. By 1907 the city would have 12.3 miles of asphalt road, 1.2 miles of brick streets, and .44 miles of macadam-covered avenues. This was in addition to 38 miles of graded roadway within the city limits.

Although such accomplishments would have been impossible without strong and determined individuals, most public improvements required the strength of group efforts, especially that of the Oklahoma City Chamber of Commerce. Organized on May 25, 1889, this association of

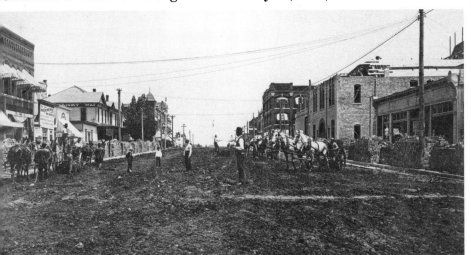

During the early years of settlement, the Oklahoma City Chamber of Commerce, shown here circa 1910, became an important and essential group that supported the growth and development of city services such as highways and water supplies. (OHS)

merchants and businessmen operated for several years under a variety of names—the Board of Trade, the Commercial Club, the Merchants Club, and the Oklahoma City Club—before emerging as the Oklahoma City Chamber of Commerce in 1902. The Chamber attracted industry, encouraged railroad construction, and supported civic improvements. The results were seen in successes such as the Cotton Compress Company plant, the Frisco Railroad, and Epworth College.

The Chamber of Commerce served as a non-elected governing body concerned with development and progress, for it was a stable, conservative institution with the perspective needed for long-range planning. Whereas the Chamber dealt with promotion and the economy, the city government was responsible for more immediate needs.

The first legally elected city government assumed office in 1890 and established the first city hall at 13 N. Broadway in a two-story brick building, which also housed the Black and Rogers Saloon. The city office, police headquarters, police court, and jail remained in this building until 1893, when city hall was moved to the corner of Grand and Broadway. Soon after 1900 the city borrowed $30,000 from Henry Overholser and built a three-story brick structure, which would house city hall until the 1930s.

During the first 16 years of city government, the dominant issue was law enforcement. Repeated cries of "reform" became the slogans of both Democrats and Republicans every year at election time. In 1897, for example, the Democratic-aligned *Press-Gazette* waged a fight against the Republican administration of C.G. Jones. "The honky-

*Oscar G. Lee was an early day business-
man and Oklahoma City's chief of
police. During the first 16 years of city
government, the dominant issue was
law enforcement against gambling
dens, saloons, and brothels. (OHS)*

Overholser Opera House, located on Grand Avenue, was constructed in 1903 by Henry and Ed Overholser. Reflecting the prosperity of Oklahoma City, the playhouse cost more than $100,000 and seated up to 2,500 people. (OHS)

Colcord Mansion is shown here under construction in 1903. Built by Charles F. Colcord, the ornate house was located on North 13th Street between Hudson and Harvey. Such residential development, a mile and one-half from the business district, was made possible by extension of the streetcar line. Courtesy, Oklahoma County Metropolitan Library.

tonk," the paper's editor cried, "is a thoroughly Republican institution. Our city government and the *Times-Journal* are Republicans. Let's run the rascals out of town."

Despite such rhetoric, neither Republicans nor Democrats cleansed the city of the "trinity of evils—the saloon, the gambling den, and the bawdy house." Directed by able leaders such as Big Anne Wynn, "Kid" Bannister, "Old Zulu," "Big Mitt," and Tom Cook, brothels and gambling establishments survived and prospered in Oklahoma City during the territorial years.

The lurid conditions described by moral crusaders and politicians were exaggerated. The contributions of streetcars, Wheeler Park, and Delmar Gardens joined other cultural improvements, including the Carnegie Library, constructed in 1900; the Overholser Opera House, built in 1903; a professional baseball team, organized in 1904; and St. Anthony's Hospital, constructed in 1900, to substantially improve the quality of life after 1900.

These advances were matched by improved city services, better utilities, and residential development. By 1907 residents of Oklahoma City proudly pointed to 15 miles of paved streets, 13 miles of storm sewers, 42 miles of sanitary sewers, 35 miles of streetcar track, 116 miles of sidewalks, 35 miles of gas mains, 50 miles of water mains, and a telephone system serving more than 5,000 families and businesses. This development was reflected in the hundreds of beautiful homes that were built in all sections of the city. To the people of Oklahoma City, their community had finally reached the "Promised Land" status envisioned by David L. Payne 20 years earlier.

Bucket Brigade to Firefighters:
The Oklahoma City Fire Department

On September 3, 1889, less than five months after the land run, a small shanty on the edge of the young boom town burst into flames. As word of the potential disaster spread, Andy Binns and his handful of volunteer firemen rushed to their makeshift headquarters at 100 W. First Street, grabbed their hand-drawn, converted beer wagon, and raced to battle the city's first recorded fire. With that important beginning the impressive record of the Oklahoma City Fire Department (OCFD) was underway.

During the first decade of operation, the OCFD was a volunteer organization only partially supported by the city. In 1891 the city council purchased the first hook and ladder wagon for $570 and a 50-gallon chemical fire engine for $1,750. Both were pulled by the department's two horses, Jumbo and Babe. A year later the city built the first central fire station, a distinctive two-story frame building at Main and Robinson with a 65-foot tower where "watchmen" could see the entire town. If a fire erupted, the man on duty would shoot a gun and ring a bell until volunteer firefighters responded.

As Oklahoma City expanded and prospered, the OCFD became larger and better equipped. In 1893 the force consisted of four paid firefighters and 13 volunteers who were paid 50 cents for each fire fought. Their equipment consisted of a Holloway Chemical Engine, a combination Rumsey Hose Wagon, and a hook and ladder wagon. During the territorial era, the OCFD added five fire stations to keep pace with the growing city.

Although the department purchased its first motorized fire truck in 1910 — an American LaFrance Type 5 hose and chemical vehicle — firemen continued to maintain a stable of 40 fire-trained horses that were still pulling most of the rolling stock as late as 1917. It was not until 1921 that the last horse-drawn vehicle was eliminated from the department.

At the end of World War I firefighters in Oklahoma City worked a six-day week, 24 hours a day. In 1919 the two-platoon system was adopted, whereby the day shift was on duty 10 hours a day and the night shift was on duty 14

Fire fighters pose in front of Oklahoma City's Central Fire Company Station at the turn of the century. (OHS)

hours. Not until the 1950s would a three-platoon, 40-hour work week be implemented.

Between the two world wars, the department improved training and equipment. In 1921 Chief George Goff and one assistant attended the New York City Fire Department Drill School in order to learn current fire-fighting tactics. The department also added new American LaFrance and Seagrave motorized apparatus, many equipped with two-way radios.

Since World War II the OCFD has grown even more dramatically. Aided by several bond issues and the city sales tax, approved in 1965, the department has increased the number of stations to 30, and all of the older stations have been upgraded. The sites of these stations have been carefully chosen so firefighters can reach any fire within three to six minutes, a scientific distribution which makes the most efficient use of the department's staff of 786 men and women. Another improvement has been the new Central Fire Station at N.W. 5th and Shartel, which houses one of the nation's only computer-aided dispatch systems.

Chief Jimmie Catlege and his staff continue to improve the services of the OCFD. Through fire prevention, arson investigation, educational programs, and fighting fires, the department protects property and saves lives, a tradition that dates to 1889 and those first volunteers.

7

Packing Plants, Politics, and Prohibition

On the morning of November 16, 1907, more than 1,000 people from Oklahoma City traveled to Guthrie to celebrate the recently won status of statehood. Leading the delegation was C.G. Jones, who would represent the bridegroom in the symbolic marriage of Oklahoma and Indian territories. For Oklahoma City the ceremony would mean the beginning of statehood and an era of prosperity; for Jones, a founding father of Oklahoma City, it would be another eventful day in a life full of such honors.

Born November 3, 1856, in rural Illinois, Charles Gasham Jones was a descendant of a pioneer farm family. Like many young men from the Midwest during the 1870s and 1880s, Jones made the transition from farming to business. In January 1890, hungry for new accomplishments, Jones brought his business and agricultural background to Oklahoma City, where he constructed the first flour mill in Oklahoma Territory.

For the next seven years Jones fought for and supported Oklahoma City, even when the town's future seemed limited. He served as a member of the First Territorial Legislature, as Speaker of the House in 1891, and as mayor of Oklahoma City for two terms from 1896 to 1897 and from 1902 to 1903.

Above
C.G. "Gristmill" Jones came to Oklahoma City in 1890 and became a driving force in the economic and political life of the young town. He served as mayor of the city for two terms. (OHS)

Above right
The original State Fair of Oklahoma took place on 160 acres on Eastern Avenue near 10th Street in Oklahoma City. The grounds included a grandstand, a racetrack, and other facilities. Courtesy, Oklahoma County Metropolitan Library.

During his administration as mayor, Jones was instrumental in attracting the St. Louis and Oklahoma Railroad, an accomplishment that rekindled the potential of his chosen city. He continued his interest in transportation after 1900, organizing the Oklahoma and Southwestern Railroad and constructing a belt line around Oklahoma City.

In 1901 Jones again was elected mayor. During his third term, the city government built the city hall at Grand and Broadway, improved the sewer and water systems, and funded additional road construction. After leaving office in 1903, he remained active in business and civic affairs and worked diligently to attract new industry.

Jones considered one of his greatest contributions to Oklahoma City to be the State Fair of Oklahoma, organized in 1907 with him as president. Located on 160 acres of school land near 10th Street and N. Eastern Avenue, the first permanent fair grounds included a grandstand, a racetrack, a music hall, a large exposition structure, and several exhibit buildings for farm products and machinery.

The expansion of Belle Isle Park was another cultural and social addition to Oklahoma City after 1907. Located five miles north of town near a natural spring (just north of present-day Classen Circle), the park was owned and operated by the Oklahoma City Street Railway Company. The transportation company constructed the lake for a generating plant, and added the park as a magnet for passenger traffic on the Classen Boulevard line.

Recognizing the profits that could be made in the entertainment field, especially with the new silent pictures being produced, many Oklahoma City entrepreneurs invested in theaters. Among the new amusement establishments were the Lyric Air Dome, opened by Peter and John Sinopoulo on the corner of First Street and Robinson; the Folly Theater, opened in 1907 at 125 W. Grand; the Metropolitan Theater, constructed on W. Main; and the Colonial Theater, erected in 1909.

The expanding telephone system was yet another investment that served the public and improved the quality of life in Oklahoma City. The Arkansas-Kansas Telephone Company installed the first telephones in the young town in 1892. Nine years later the Citizens Independent Telephone Company entered the market, forcing many businessmen and homeowners to keep two telephones, one for each system. In 1905 this problem was solved when the Pioneer Telephone Company consolidated the two exchanges.

With headquarters in Oklahoma City, the communications firm grew even more rapidly than the population. By 1907 Pioneer employed more than 150 workers and maintained thousands of miles of telephone lines. To house new exchange boards, operators, and office workers, company officials constructed a new building. Designed by William A. Wells, the Pioneer Building at 5th and Broadway was an "enduring monument" and "the handsomest building in the state," according to the *Daily Oklahoman.*

The momentum of Oklahoma City's economic and physical growth accelerated after 1907, for statehood removed many of the legal and political disadvantages of territorial status. Increased investments, new companies, and more people followed the new political stability. The best example of this growth was the arrival of the meat-packing plants.

The boardwalk and pavilion at Belle Isle are shown here soon after the park was constructed in 1907. Visitors could travel to the park on the Oklahoma Railway Company Classen Boulevard line. Courtesy, Oklahoma County Metropolitan Library.

Dreamland Theatre, located in the lower right corner of this street scene, showed silent moving pictures and staged vaudeville productions. Upstairs was the Dreamland Hall, with "Dancing Every Night." Such establishments provided entertainment for the growing Oklahoma City population. Courtesy, Western History Collections, University of Oklahoma Library.

In October 1908 an official of Nelson Morris & Company, a Chicago packing house, arrived in Oklahoma City on a fact-finding mission. Attracted by the geographic location and the rail connections of the young community, the official told directors of the Chamber of Commerce that he wanted to build a $3 million packing plant in their town. In return, he asked for a $300,000 cash bonus and several concessions. Recognizing the potential benefits of such a plant, Chamber leaders Sidney Brock, Anton Classen, John Shartel, and E.K. Gaylord agreed to the terms.

The following May, Chamber of Commerce officials called a meeting of the city's leading businessmen. When the plea for subscriptions began, Anton Classen shouted that he would pledge $10,000. Oscar G. Lee, Charlie Colcord, and C.G. Jones each matched that amount. Then, from the back of the crowd, department store owner Sidney Brock interrupted, ''Gentlemen, I am not a rich man, but I know what this means to all of us and I want to make my subscription $25,000!'' Suddenly, Classen raised his pledge to $40,000, and the others followed. When the frenzy subsided, Chamber officials announced the total exceeded $400,000.

The subscription fund was used to purchase a 575-acre block of land southwest of Oklahoma City. From the sale of lots in this district, later referred to as Stockyards City, the directors raised the $300,000 bonus

Oklahoma City National Stockyards, located south of the North Canadian River and just east of May Avenue, add to the economic health of Oklahoma City and County. Courtesy, Oklahoma Historical Society.

required by the packing firm. Within months Nelson Morris & Company was constructing the $3 million plant.

One year later another packing firm, Schwartzchild and Sulzberger, announced that it too would construct a plant in Oklahoma City if a $300,000 cash bonus could be raised. Again, the businessmen of Oklahoma City responded. By 1910 the two packing houses and the attendant holding yards were employing more than 4,000 people.

The effects of the packing plants were evident even before construction began. Within 24 hours of the first pledge in May 1909, the telephone company announced new investments exceeding $2 million, and the Oklahoma Gas and Electric Company announced it would double the output of its generating plant with an investment of $600,000. Within months the fever of optimism and progress had infected the entire city, and a new boom was underway.

Almost all of Oklahoma City's business and commercial enterprises reaped the benefits of new investments. From 1908 to 1910, for exam-

The Livestock Exchange Building, at the National Stockyards near the packinghouses, served as headquarters for the purchasing and selling of thousands of livestock each year. The Spanish-style structure burned in 1980. (OHS)

Edward "E.K." Gaylord, communications czar of Oklahoma City for more than 50 years, was instrumental in luring the packing plants to his hometown. As a member of the Chamber of Commerce in 1908, he agreed to strike a deal with packinghouse Nelson Morris and Company that aided the firm in moving to Oklahoma. From Sturm's Magazine, 1909.

The renovated and restored Oklahoman Building, located at 4th and North Broadway, was constructed in 1909-1910 during the building boom. Classical in design, the structure features stained-glass panels on the fifth floor which are illuminated from behind. From Sturm's Magazine.

ple, the value of goods manufactured in Oklahoma City increased from $7 million to $17 million; retail sales spiraled from $16 million to $25 million; and bank clearings soared from $52 million to $122 million.

Another, more visible result of the economic boom was a wave of major construction. In 1909 the City of Oklahoma City issued more than $6 million in building permits, a $4 million increase over the previous year. Leading the way was Charlie Colcord, who announced plans for a $300,000 office tower at Robinson and Grand.

As crews broke ground for the Colcord Building, other workers moved onto construction sites to erect the Baum Building, the State National Bank Building (Hales Building), the Huckins Hotel, and the American National Bank Building. Before the year ended, contractors also had started construction on the Insurance Building, the Herskowitz Building, the Terminal Building (for the streetcar system), the International Harvester Building, and the Stock Exchange Building.

The construction frenzy continued into 1910, when investors expended almost $7 million on new buildings. Some of the major projects included the Skirvin and Kinkade hotels, the Patterson Building, the Levy Building, and the Miller Brothers Building. The pace did not slacken until the winter of 1911, when construction returned to a more normal level.

While brick and stone structures rose above the skyline, Oklahoma City leaders were winning yet another battle—the fight for the state capital. The location of the capital had been an issue as early as the meeting of the First Territorial Legislature, but not until June 11, 1910, was the question presented to a vote of the people. As a result of active campaigning and a population advantage, Oklahoma City won

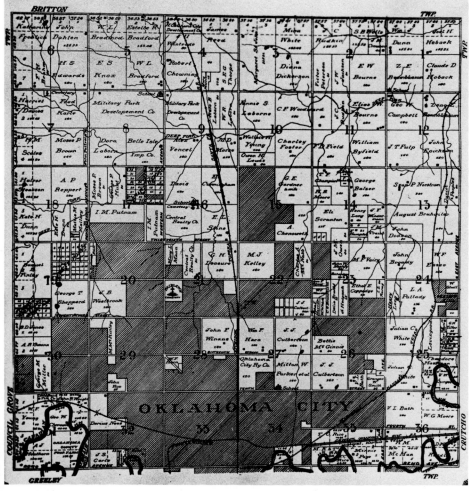

Residential construction expanded during the first decade of the century, especially toward the north and west where developers such as I.M. Putnam, Anton Classen, and G.A. Nichols platted new additions. In 1907, when this map was drawn, the city had moved as far north as 36th Street. From Standard Atlas of Oklahoma County, 1907.

the election with 96,261 votes to 31,301 for Guthrie and 8,382 for Shawnee.

With the election results in, Governor Charles Haskell left for Oklahoma City and ordered the official state seal removed from Guthrie. The next day, on Huckins Hotel stationery, the governor wrote a proclamation declaring Oklahoma City the official capital of Oklahoma. A series of court injunctions and suits followed, but the result of the June 11 election was never changed. Oklahoma City was the capital of Oklahoma.

The next step was to determine a site for the capitol building. I.M. Putnam and John Shartel offered the state 1,600 acres of land and $1.7 million in cash if the building would be located on their land northwest of the city on the interurban line (the future Putnam City). Another offer was extended by William Fremont Harn and J.J. Culbertson, who owned land northeast of the city between 13th and 23rd streets. The selection committee chose the Harn-Culbertson offer, for it was closer to the central business district. The Capitol Building was completed on the site seven years later.

While the capital fight was being waged, the citizens of Oklahoma City approved a $400,000 bond issue for development of a park system and a "grand motor raceway" encircling the city. A series of greenbelt parks was planned, but the only significant result was Northeast Park

Constructed in 1910, the Skirvin Hotel was one of the many buildings in Oklahoma designed by Solomon Layton. Located within blocks of three railroad depots, the famous hotel soon became a popular spot for travelers. (OHS)

Completed in 1917, the Oklahoma State Capitol Building attracted new development to the northeastern quadrant of Oklahoma City. It was built on land offered by William Fremont Harn and J.J. Culbertson. (OHS)

(Lincoln Park), located on 700 acres of land southeast of the intersection of 50th and Eastern Avenue. The motor raceway, although partially completed and referred to as Grand Boulevard, would never fulfill expectations.

Although plans for the superhighway fell short, electric traction made substantial advances after 1907. The Oklahoma Railway Company, with its own power plant in 1908, purchased 29 pieces of rolling stock and built two locomotives in the company shop. By 1909 the system included 32 miles of track and 46 passenger cars.

In 1910, encouraged by the economic activity in Oklahoma City, the Oklahoma Street Railway Company purchased the rolling stock and tracks of the Oklahoma City & Suburban Railway Company, a transportation firm which had built 20 miles of track to outlying sections of town. One year later the firm acquired the holdings of the El Reno Interurban Railway Company, which had constructed a streetcar system in El Reno and had initiated an interurban track between that town and Oklahoma City. On December 3, 1911, the Oklahoma Street Railway Company completed the interurban line and opened the 29 miles of track to traffic.

The investments proved successful, for gross revenue from operations rose from $440,846 in 1909 to $623,887 in 1910. Shartel still was not content, so he constructed interurban lines to Britton and Edmond in 1912, and to Capitol Hill, Moore, and Norman in 1913. With the opening of the interurban to Norman, the company operated 103 miles of track, 95 passenger cars, 22 freight and dump cars, and serviced Oklahoma City, Putnam City, Britton, Edmond, Moore, Norman, Bethany, Yukon, and El Reno—in short, all parts of Oklahoma County and beyond.

The transportation giant reached a peak of prosperity from 1913 to 1918. During that period the interurban was extended to Guthrie, the company purchased 50 new cars, the amusement centers of Belle Isle, Briarwood, Fair Grounds, and Wheeler Park were drawing good crowds, and the company was earning a substantial profit by selling excess electricity to utilities. The nerve center for this sprawling system was the terminal at Grand Avenue and Hudson. Constructed in 1911, it had four through tracks and four stub tracks. Interurban cars left the terminal for their respective routes every hour, and streetcars usually left every 20 to 30 minutes.

The streetcar system expanded to accommodate a growing population. In 1900 the population of Oklahoma City was 10,000; by World War I it exceeded 60,000, a 600 percent increase. This extraordinary rate of growth fueled the economy, but it taxed public services, especially the water system.

Since the earliest days of settlement, water for Oklahoma City had been provided through a system of wells. Subterranean water could supply a town of 10,000, but it was inadequate for a city of 60,000. With new industry consuming thousands of gallons of water each day and with residential needs increasing with the population, the water problem intensified each year. During a dry spell in October 1914, domestic water consumption was limited to two hours per day.

The shortage grew worse the next two years, as periodic drought and increased consumption brought on a series of near disasters. Led by Ed Overholser, concerned citizens recognized the problem and fought for a city-funded reservoir. On May 20, 1916, their dreams were realized when the citizens of Oklahoma City approved a $1.5 million bond issue

PACKING PLANTS, POLITICS, AND PROHIBITION

Above

Edward Overholser, mayor of Oklahoma City from 1915 to 1919, was the prime mover in the construction of Overholser Lake west of the city. The lake, completed in 1918, was developed as a solution to periodic droughts and increased water consumption. (OHS)

Right

The headlines of the Daily Oklahoman *on December 4, 1907, announced that the state legislature had begun to formalize a segregated society. Blacks had lived in Oklahoma since the land run of 1889, and they resisted the moves toward segregation.*

for a lake on the North Canadian River.

Completed in 1918, the eastern end of the lake began on the North Canadian just north of 10th Street, where a natural gorge in the river valley required a dam of only 1,110 feet. Within four years, runoff and the flow of the river had filled the lake, providing 17,000 acre feet of water for Oklahoma City, enough for years of expansion.

As proven by the water shortages, growth and prosperity after 1900 resulted in problems as well as benefits. City services lagged behind demand, schools suffered from overcrowding, and housing shortages occurred. The most divisive issue of the era, however, was racial tension over segregated housing.

Racial coexistence had been a part of Oklahoma City since 1889, when approximately 200 blacks made the run shoulder-to-shoulder with their white neighbors. By 1910 the number of blacks in the community had increased to more than 7,000, approximately 10 percent of the total population.

Until 1910 the majority of blacks in Oklahoma City lived in three loosely segregated neighborhoods: South Town, between Washington and Choctaw avenues south of town; West Town, on W. First Street; and Sand Town, along the river east of the Santa Fe tracks. All three districts were near the railroad tracks or the river, neighborhoods that were undesirable due either to rail traffic or periodic flooding.

After 1910 the economic shackles confining black families to these "slum" areas were removed. Suddenly, new companies and warehouses moving to Oklahoma City needed labor, providing better paying jobs for blacks. With newfound purchasing power, many blacks who had wanted to move out of the depressed areas could do so. But when they purchased houses in previously all-white neighborhoods, racial prejudices were stirred and demands for forced segregation followed.

The white outcry for separation of the races peaked in 1916, when the Oklahoma City Board of Commissioners enacted an ordinance making it illegal for a person of either race to move into a block on which 75 percent of the structures were occupied by persons of the opposite race. This plan, which would prevent blacks from moving into white neighborhoods, also legally segregated schools, churches, theaters, and dance halls.

Local opposition to the ordinance centered around the *Black Dispatch*, a newspaper founded in 1915 by Roscoe Dunjee. In addition to his editorial attacks against the new law, Dunjee personally helped break the barrier between white and black housing east of the Santa Fe tracks. William Floyd, a black shoemaker, purchased a house at the corner of N.E. 2nd and Central Avenue, an all-white block. Four times Floyd tried to occupy his new home; four times he was arrested and dragged to jail; four times Dunjee paid bond and encouraged Floyd to return. When the case finally reached court, a federal judge stated that Floyd had the right to move into his property, based on a United States Supreme Court decision of 1916 declaring such ordinances unconstitutional.

Segregation would continue under other forms, and civil rights advocates would continue the fight for social and legal equality. Roscoe Dunjee usually led the charge. The son of a former slave, Dunjee received a basic education from his father, a black minister. In 1892 the Dunjee family immigrated to the recently opened Oklahoma Territory, where the elder Dunjee eventually enrolled at Langston College. In 1903 he died, leaving young Roscoe to provide for the family.

Twelve years later Roscoe left home for Oklahoma City, where he sold vegetables on streetcorners. In 1915, when he had accumulated enough savings, he purchased a small print shop and began publishing the *Black Dispatch*. Through its editorial pages he encouraged blacks to register and vote, supported black businesses, and fought an unceasing battle for racial equality. For more than 50 years Dunjee would be a strong force in the development of Oklahoma City.

The period from 1907 to 1917 was a time of change for whites as well as for blacks. A dominant theme of the era was reform, especially reform of social ills such as child labor, unsafe working conditions, and widespread poverty. But the cause that stirred the greatest burst of

The Black Dispatch, *published by Roscoe Dunjee, provided a voice for the black community of central Oklahoma. The paper served as an organ of protest against encroaching segregation laws in the 1910s.*

reform activity in Oklahoma City proved to be the war for law and order.

Vice, in the form of gambling and prostitution, had existed in Oklahoma City since the land run. But with statehood and the victory for constitutional prohibition, a new crime evolved that would stir social crusaders to new levels of righteousness. The social evil was the illegal sale of liquor—bootlegging.

On November 16, 1907, the 70 saloons of Oklahoma City served the last legal drinks in town. The "reign of Bacchus," however, did not end that night, for an army of entrepreneurial bootleggers rushed in to serve the demand for liquor, dispensing their profitable contraband at "joints" such as Two Johns Saloon, the Southern Club, and the Athletic Club. At these social spots, the nighttime crowd could relax, enjoy a drink, and gamble away the evening.

Pressured by a growing force of moral reformers, city officials after 1907 periodically tried to rid the city of these "dens of vice." In 1907 Chief of Police Charles Post organized a "Flying Squadron" to strike bootleggers quickly and without warning. Two years later Chief of Police John Hubatka, a member of Charlie Colcord's first police force, conducted a series of raids. Despite these occasional strikes against the underworld, bootleggers and gamblers survived and even prospered during the first few years of statehood.

In 1913, with the purveyors of vice profiting from population growth and increasing prosperity, moral crusaders from the churches of Oklahoma City organized the Central Hundred, a committee of men and women who "entered militantly into a campaign in behalf of law and order, public morals, and public decency." Thereafter, church leaders in Oklahoma City became a political force that determined the outcome of several elections. The Central Hundred used this power in a war on bootleggers.

In 1915 the Central Hundred helped elect a slate of city officials who had pledged themselves to reform and law and order. Ed Overholser,

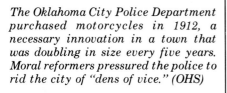

The Oklahoma City Police Department purchased motorcycles in 1912, a necessary innovation in a town that was doubling in size every five years. Moral reformers pressured the police to rid the city of "dens of vice." (OHS)

HEART OF THE PROMISED LAND: AN ILLUSTRATED HISTORY OF OKLAHOMA COUNT

Oklahoma City in 1916, as viewed from the junction of the Santa Fe tracks and Grand Avenue, boasted high-rise buildings. A billboard, center, advertises Owl cigars for only five cents. (OHS)

the mayor and son of former leader Henry Overholser, appointed W.B. "Fighting Deacon" Nichols as chief of police. Soon after his appointment, Nichols announced to the vice peddlers, "You'd better get your dens closed or I'll chop 'em to kindling and put all of you on the rockpile for the rest of your lives."

Nichols was aided in his struggle by John Embry, the Oklahoma County Attorney. Embry, who had earned a reputation as a tough United States District Attorney, was the leader of the Central Hundred. When Nichols raided clubs and bootleggers, he knew Embry would prosecute to the full extent of the law.

Embry used various tactics in his holy crusade. He sued property owners who rented space to gamblers and whisky peddlers; he investigated express offices, which reportedly transported whisky; but most importantly, he attacked William J. Creekmore, the kingpin of a statewide bootlegging empire.

On December 20, 1915, Embry convicted Creekmore and several co-conspirators on several counts, initiating legal proceedings that eventually would place the underworld "boss" in federal prison. By 1916 the Southern Club, the Olympic Club, the Arlington, the Monte Carlo, and a host of other "joints" had been closed, victims of the moral reformers of Oklahoma City.

The spirit of reform remained strong in Oklahoma City until 1917 when America entered World War I. Suddenly, a new cause, "to make the world safe for democracy," displaced social reform. "Go to work, go to war, or go to jail" became the new spiritual battle cry. Oklahoma City responded overwhelmingly. More than 7,000 men from the city registered for the draft, Liberty Bond drives raised more than $5 million in less than one year, families gave up sugar and meat for the "boys on the front," and more than 10,000 families in town planted victory gardens. Two years later, the city would surface from the conflict, ready for a new era of progress and expansion.

PACKING PLANTS, POLITICS, AND PROHIBITION

Kate Barnard: Oklahoma's Joan of Arc

Courtesy, Oklahoma Historical Society.

In 1907 Oklahoma was one of the nation's most progressive states. Compulsory education, labor reform, social welfare, and the protection of individual liberty — all were advanced by the State Constitution. One of the leading activists in the fight for these reforms was a frail, dark-haired woman from Oklahoma City, Kate Barnard.

Born in Nebraska in 1879, young Kate moved to Oklahoma Territory soon after the land run of 1889. She stayed on her father's 160-acre claim until the turn of the century, when she moved to Oklahoma City. During her early years in the territory's largest city, Kate attended St. Joseph's Academy, taught school, temporarily worked for the city government, represented the state at the St. Louis World Fair, and served as director of the United Provident Association, an organization dedicated to caring for the homeless and needy. During this period, she also served as recording secretary of a local union which was affiliated with the American Federation of Labor.

During the late territorial era, Kate joined other progressive reformers across the nation to attack poverty, crime, and inhumane treatment of workers. She wrote numerous articles for the *Daily Oklahoman*, spoke before groups in all regions of the nation, and supported local charities. Then she extended this crusade to the upcoming elections for delegates to the State Constitutional Convention. Tenaciously she campaigned for candidates who supported her causes and battled those who opposed reform.

In 1906, when delegates met at the Constitutional Convention in Guthrie, Kate was there to broaden her influence for social and labor reform. She helped mold an alliance between leaders of the labor and farmer groups, a political bloc that would dominate the Constitutional Convention and early state government. Largely through the lobbying efforts of the 27-year-old woman, the State Constitution included a series of progressive labor laws. Kate also promoted provisions to help orphans, mental patients, and inmates in the state's prisons, and she helped create the State Department of Charities and Corrections.

In 1907 Kate resigned her post in Oklahoma City and entered the political race for commissioner of the new department, an unprecedented move in a state that still did not allow women the vote. Despite this handicap, she won the election and took office on November 16, 1907, as the first commissioner of Charities and Corrections — one of the first women in the nation to be elected to a state office.

During her two terms, the energetic firebrand entered battle after battle. In April 1908 she forced Oklahoma County officials to hire female nurses to care for women patients in local hospitals. She investigated the hospital for the insane in Norman, where, as she wrote, "Hell has reigned for 20 years undisturbed." Then she turned her attention to prison reform. She toured county and city jails, helped break a contract with the State of Kansas for the care of state prisoners, and initiated the move to construct a state penitentiary at McAlester.

She also directed her wrath at the ill treatment of Indian orphans, who were systematically being defrauded of their land-rights and inheritances. By 1912 she had helped recover more than $2 million, which had been illegally taken from Indian wards of the state. Kate would continue her struggles for Indian civil rights long after she left office.

Although she was effective, two controversial terms in state government created powerful enemies for the female reformer. During the fourth legislature, Kate's political opponents successfully attacked her department and withheld funds for operations beyond her own salary and office expenses. Confronted with this obstacle, she declined to run again in 1915.

Out of office, Kate continued her crusade for the poor, sick, and needy. She made speaking tours throughout the East, fought to protect Indians, and raised money for charitable causes. Only poor health slowed her pace in 1922, when she grew ill and required hospitalization. Eight years later the 51 year old reformer was found dead in her Oklahoma City apartment, alone with a half-finished autobiography on her desk.

During her eventful life, Kate Barnard publicized controversial and sensitive issues, touched the social conscience of a generation, and initiated reforms which we now take for granted. Kate had the vision to see potential changes, the intensity and perseverance to fight for what she believed, and the keen mind and political ability to achieve her goals.

8

Towns Rise from the Soil

Facing page
Frank Harrah was the pioneer of
Oklahoma City who platted and
developed the town of Harrah near the
eastern edge of the county. (OHS)

From 1889 to 1917 the pioneers of Oklahoma City transformed a railroad watering stop into a metropolis of 60,000. The same forces that contributed to the growth of the state's largest city also stimulated the development of towns in the rural regions of the county.

Other than Oklahoma City, Edmond was the only town in the county to experience real growth before the onset of agricultural prosperity in 1898, for, like its neighbor to the north, Edmond was viewed as a potential "boomtown" prior to the land opening. The site was midway between Oklahoma City and Guthrie; it was in the heart of rich farming land; and it was the only coaling station in the future county, thus assuring promoters that it would have a depot after settlement.

As anticipated, Edmond Station attracted hundreds of pioneers on April 22, 1889, and by September more than 30 businesses lined Broadway and a half-dozen side streets. With no economic base to support this activity, however, development relied on the boomtown mentality generated by the land opening. This spirit of optimism and aggressiveness did not persist unaided; men such as Milton W. "Kicking Bird" Reynolds nurtured and promoted it.

114

Edmond Station on the Santa Fe tracks was the magnet which attracted hundreds of settlers during the land run of 1889. Courtesy, Central State Museum, Central State University, Edmond.

Reynolds was a newspaperman who had migrated west in 1857. After serving in the Nebraska Legislature, he was appointed by the Secretary of the Interior to council with the Cherokees for land on which to settle the Sac and Fox and Potawatomi Indians. He also attended the Treaty of Medicine Lodge as a news correspondent.

An effective booster for the opening of the Unassigned Lands, Reynolds was aboard one of the first railroad cars entering the "Promised Land" on April 22. At first he settled in Guthrie, where he established the *Oklahoma State Herald*. The town was overcrowded with newspapers, however, so he moved to Edmond. On July 18, 1889, housed in a small frame building at 109 N. Broadway, Kicking Bird published the first issue of the *Edmond Sun*.

With his newspaper for a pulpit, Reynolds hammered away at the successes and the greater potential of his new hometown. He reported every civic improvement, featured new businesses in town, and supported progressive politicians. It was this kind of promotion that kept the fires of early growth burning.

Even with the support of men like Reynolds, the boomtown spirit of Edmond soon collapsed, forcing merchants to look for other means of economic survival. In a pattern that would remain constant until the 1920s, this economic safety margin for small towns in the region proved to be agriculture. Farmers needed financing to buy land, machines to plant and harvest their crops, and mills and gins to market their wheat and cotton; they could find these services and goods only in towns such as Edmond.

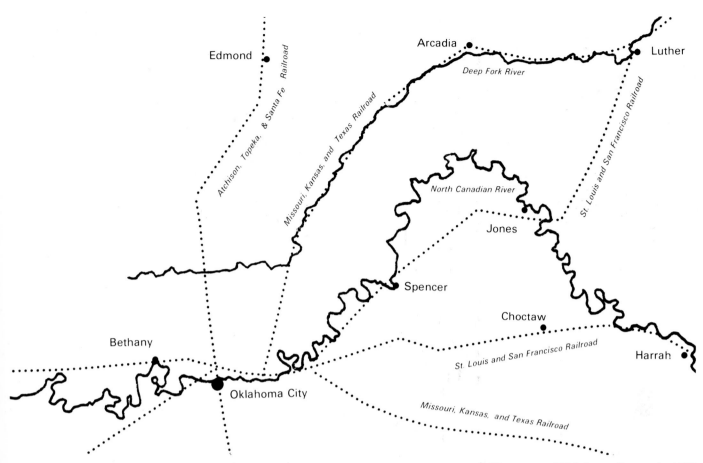

The positive effects of agricultural prosperity were readily apparent in the brisk business enjoyed by implement and machinery suppliers in Edmond. In 1894, merchants in the young town sold 69 twine binders, 103 farm wagons, 7 threshing machines, 17 mowing machines, 61 buggies, 14 railroad cars full of barbed wire, and 87 sets of wagon harness.

This economic stimulus became more important as the decade progressed, especially after 1898 when the ''golden age'' of agriculture began. As cotton and wheat prices soared to record levels, farmers made more money, which they in turn spent in towns such as Edmond. By 1910 the value of farm property in Oklahoma County exceeded $29 million, directly affecting the prosperity of towns.

Even with the gradual improvement of farming conditions, agriculture alone could not have supported a town of more than 500 people. In Edmond the added fuel for prosperity was the Territorial Normal School. Established by the First Oklahoma Territorial Legislature in 1890, the Normal (or teachers') College conducted its first classes in 1891 in the Methodist Episcopal Church on the southwest corner of Broadway and Hurd.

Meanwhile, the Normal School Commission advertised for property to be used as a permanent campus. The accepted offer, extended by Anton Classen, provided 40 acres east of town. Original architectural plans for the school building called for a three-story structure with a central section, two wings, and a bell tower in the front. The first classes, consisting of three teachers and 80 students, met in the new building for the first time on January 2, 1893.

The towns of Oklahoma County in 1907 were located either on a railroad line or along a river, the two most important factors determining the location of rural towns. Courtesy, Bob Blackburn.

The Normal School provided the additional economic stimulus that Edmond needed for expansion and development. Courtesy, Central State Museum, Central State University, Edmond.

For several years thereafter the Territorial Legislature provided thousands of dollars for new construction and expansion of curriculum. In 1894 the appropriation was $15,000, followed by another $3,000 in 1895. In 1898 construction crews completed final details on the building, which included 15 classrooms and an assembly hall with a seating capacity of 500. By 1907 the student population exceeded 600.

With the school generating more business each year and the farming population prospering as never before, the town of Edmond gradually expanded. Between 1898 and 1907 five new housing additions were platted and businessmen constructed a new generation of buildings downtown. By 1902 the commercial district of Edmond consisted of 79 structures, 10 of which were of stone or brick. This physical growth was matched by an ever-increasing population, which had swelled to 1,833 by 1907.

Whereas in Edmond the school generated new business, encouraged investments, and provided a sense of security, all factors needed by towns to survive recurring cycles of agricultural prosperity and depression, in Choctaw the catalyst for economic growth proved to be the railroad. The community of Choctaw had existed since the first year of settlement in the county, but with agriculture as the only means of economic survival, the crossroads village remained small. After two years it still consisted of only a school, a post office, and two churches. The rural community changed suddenly in 1893, when the Choctaw Coal and Railway Company constructed tracks through the rich farming region. In league with railroad officials, C.G. ''Gristmill'' Jones, Angelo Scott, and Moses Neal platted an 80-acre townsite along the tracks near the school and named it Choctaw City. Two years later an adjoining 80-acre plat was filed and the two sites were combined and renamed Choctaw.

From 1895 to 1897 town promoters encouraged settlement in Choctaw, painting a picture of prosperity and opportunity. By 1897 the business district of the town had grown to 31 frame buildings and the

In this photograph of Edmond, circa 1900, the wide street in the foreground is Broadway, and the Normal School can be seen in the background. Courtesy, Central State Museum, Central State University, Edmond.

population had increased to 200. But, like the rest of the county, Choctaw enjoyed its greatest growth after 1898. By 1910 the town had two cotton gins, a stockyard and shipping pens, a hotel, and a variety of businesses from grocery stores to harness shops.

Jones was another town dependent on rail connections. Platted by C.G. "Gristmill" Jones on the Frisco route on June 1, 1898, 18 miles east of Oklahoma City, the site was ideal, combining the advantages of transportation with good water and rich farming land. In 1901, after three years of steady growth, the town even had a newspaper, the *Canadian Valley News*.

By 1903 Main Street in Jones was lined with the McCutcheon Hardware Store, the Jones Livery and Feed Stable, the Kreps Hotel, a blacksmith shop, a harness shop, the Wykerts' general store, the Stone Pharmacy, a bank, a lumberyard, and a saloon. A cotton gin was located near the Frisco tracks. These businesses supported a population of 163 in 1910.

Nine miles northeast of Jones, where the Frisco crossed the Deep Fork River, the town of Luther was platted in March 1898 by Luther Aldrich. One of the first businessmen attracted to the town was W.J. Arthur, who bought several lots on the northeast side of town to construct a flour mill and a cotton gin.

These processing plants attracted farmers, so other businessmen rushed to Luther. On April 1, 1899, the First National Bank of Luther opened, and soon the town also had a hotel, a lumberyard, a hardware store, a newspaper, a drug store, a livery stable, a blacksmith shop, and a grocery store.

Loman's Grocery was typical of the shops opened in Luther. Jake Loman had immigrated to the United States from Lebanon in 1899. After reaching Chicago and a Syrian colony, the 26-year-old Loman borrowed money to buy a peddler's backpack. With his meager possessions, he earned enough to pay his debts and buy a horse and cart. After years of peddling he married a German girl and began looking for a town where he could open a store.

Cotton production was important to the development of towns in the eastern sections of Oklahoma County. Farmers ginned their cotton in town, marketed it there, and spent the revenues for needed supplies. The cotton market remained strong from 1898 to 1921, coinciding with the peak years of growth for towns in rural areas. (OHS)

Frame business buildings, men on horseback, muddy streets, and wooden sidewalks made up a typical scene in the small towns of Oklahoma County after the turn of the century. Courtesy, Oklahoma County Newspapers, Incorporated.

By 1910 the population of Jones had reached a plateau that would remain steady until the Depression. Not until the postwar era would small towns such as Jones again enjoy population increases. Courtesy, Oklahoma County Newspapers, Incorporated.

Loman heard about the "promised land" in the former Indian Territory. After a visit he moved his bride and merchandise to Luther, where he opened a grocery. Gradually, his business grew with the town. By 1907 Luther was home to more than 400 people and Loman was the owner of a new building on the east side of Main Street.

For towns such as Choctaw, Jones, and Luther, railroad connections and agriculture provided the economic base for the growth of local businesses. Such was not always the case. Munger, for example, was platted on the Choctaw Railroad near the head of Nine Mile Flat, one of the most fertile farming regions in the North Canadian River Valley. The town consisted of a post office and a grocery store, and it even had railroad connections; still, the town did not survive. The missing element for growth was promotion, the intangible force needed to attract the first generation of businesses.

Meanwhile, one-half mile upriver from Munger, the Canadian River Water Power Company developed plans for another townsite on the rail line. The company improved an 11-year-old dam, constructed a mill and elevator, and successfully lobbied to have the post office transferred from Munger to the new townsite of Spencer.

The promoters built upon the foundation of land, water, and transportation by manufacturing a spirit of boomtown expansion. In early 1901 the townsite company invited a party of Oklahoma City businessmen to the site for an outing. The next week an Oklahoma City newspaper carried an article with the headlines, "Building a New Town—Spencer, Oklahoma County—With Water Power, Mills, and Factories." The article extolled the virtues of the townsite and predicted a population exceeding 1,000 people. As a result of the promotion and development, Spencer attracted a general store, a hardware store, and a grocery store. By 1920 the town also had the *Spencer Star*, a bank, a Ford dealership, and a population of 250.

The town of Harrah, another example of aggressive promotion, was founded, nurtured, and named after Frank Harrah, a young man who had staked a claim in Oklahoma City on April 22, 1889. Harrah's new venture began in 1899 when he purchased an 80-acre piece of land about 20 miles east of Oklahoma City where the Choctaw, Oklahoma, and Gulf Railroad crossed the North Canadian River. Harrah then platted a town, created the Harrah Mercantile Company, and began building a cotton gin, a general store, and a lumberyard.

His next objective was to sell town lots, so he printed handbills stressing the advantages of settling in his town: "Harrah, Oklahoma Territory, twenty miles east of Oklahoma City, offers an excellent opportunity for parties looking for a location as Merchants, Doctors, Mechanics, and others . . . with good roads in all directions, Harrah Railroad has built a fine freight and passenger depot . . . a fine four-stand, seventy-saw cotton gin is now on the ground. . . ."

Harrah also made arrangements with officials of the Frisco Railroad to recruit immigrants. As their cooperative advertisements read, "We have over 300 farms to select from, besides residence and business property and mercantile lines to suit any customer." The enticements succeeded. By 1901 the town of Harrah included 13 buildings and a population of about 300.

In Spencer and Harrah town promotion was initiated by men from outside the original communities; in Arcadia, the "booster" role was filled by local families such as the Odors. William H. Odor was a Kansan who had migrated to Oklahoma Territory in 1892. He and his wife rented a farm, lived in a log cabin, and grew cotton and cabbage as cash crops. By 1896 the couple had earned enough money to buy their own farm. At that time Arcadia was a community with a school, a church, a blacksmith shop, and a combination general store and post office.

Flooding was a problem common to all the towns located on the North Canadian River. This shot, taken from the railroad right-of-way in Harrah, illustrates the extent of one such natural disaster. Courtesy, Harrah Historical Society.

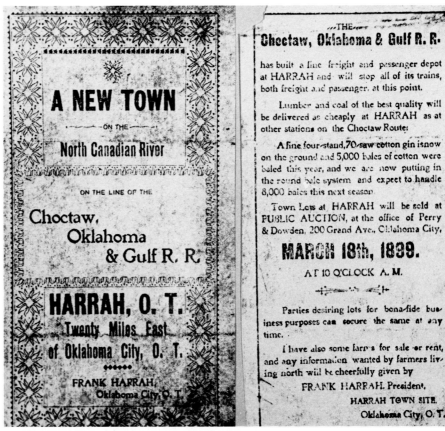

The Odors were one of the most prosperous families in the Arcadia vicinity when the Missouri-Kansas-Texas (KATY) Railroad put down tracks through the community in 1902. Seizing upon the opportunity, Odor and two other local men met with KATY officials about platting a townsite. Odor donated the land for the site and in return he received title to several lots. He and Ed McMinimy opened a hardware store, and in 1905 he helped organize the First State Bank of Arcadia. As president of the bank, Odor provided the financing and capital necessary for town growth.

Like other towns in the county, Arcadia experienced its greatest expansion during the first decade of the century. By 1906 the town had 27 commercial buildings, including two cotton gins, three grocery stores, two general stores, a furniture outlet, and a combination barber shop-pool hall. With three churches and two schools (one for whites, one for blacks), Arcadia by 1910 was one of the most prosperous towns in the county.

Britton was another town established and promoted by local residents. During the land run of 1889, George H. Light had staked claim to a 160-acre tract surrounding a Santa Fe station seven miles north of Oklahoma City. On October 23, 1890, Light platted the townsite of Britton around his claim.

With visions of an urban oasis on the prairie, Light promoted his townsite. He opened a general store and successfully applied for a post office. He tried to attract a church school, offering 40 acres for a proposed college. He even pushed a bill through the Territorial Legislature prohibiting the sale of liquor within three miles of his proposed town. Despite these efforts, Britton by 1900 consisted of only a combination general store-post office, two homes, and a derailed boxcar which served as a makeshift depot. Discouraged, Light sold his townsite for $3,000 and returned to Missouri.

The first real growth in Britton occurred after 1908, when the Oklahoma Railway Company extended an interurban line through town and on to Edmond. Suddenly, residents of Britton could easily commute to Oklahoma City, which was expanding at a phenomenal rate following statehood. The spirit of expansion and optimism spread to Britton, where developers opened eight housing additions within a few years. Then a pearl button factory was built and other businesses followed. By the end of 1909 Britton was a town of 700 people, with a commercial district of 32 business establishments.

While Britton evolved from a whistle-stop on the rail line to a suburban community, the El Reno Interurban Railway Company was laying track in the western part of Oklahoma County. To encourage business along its route, and to sell land next to the tracks, the interurban company offered 10 acres of land to the Church of the Nazarene, which was looking for a site to establish a school. C.B. Jernigan, district superintendent of the church, accepted the offer and quickly platted the townsite of Bethany.

In the city charter Jernigan included restrictions forbidding the sale of liquor and tobacco or the establishment of theaters, dance halls, and pool rooms. Church leaders intended the town of Bethany to be as conducive to religious training as their school, the Oklahoma Holiness College. With similar determination, the first school building was completed during the fall of 1909.

Initially, most residents of Bethany were associated with either the school or the church, so the population remained small. This changed during the 1920s, after the college merged with the Peniel Nazarene

On Main Street in Harrah on a Sunday afternoon, circa 1900, horses and wagons are parked in front of stores while neighbors pause to visit. Courtesy, Harrah Historical Society.

TOWNS RISE FROM THE SOIL

Britton Station, or stop number nine, was located on the interurban run to Edmond and Guthrie. The trolley car in the picture is traveling north. Courtesy, Oklahoma County Metropolitan Library.

College of Texas, and U.S. Highway 66 was extended through town. With excellent transportation the town became a residential suburb of the capital city. By 1930 Bethany was a town of 2,032.

Of the towns that eventually became suburbs of Oklahoma City, Nicoma Park was the most unique. Located east of Oklahoma City on N.E. 23rd Street, a major thoroughfare, Nicoma Park was a planned suburban community organized by officials of the KATY Railway Company, the Oklahoma City Chamber of Commerce, and G.A. Nichols, one of Oklahoma City's most active developers.

The concept was to combine ''country living'' with a second income for financial support. After visiting several planned communities in other regions of the country, Chamber of Commerce officials determined that the answer was to establish a poultry colony. As the advertisements read, ''Your family can enjoy country living while having the advantages of the city close at hand . . . (The sale of) poultry and eggs alone will make your payments.''

Nichols enthusiastically began the project by purchasing 2,000 acres of undeveloped land adjoining the KATY tracks. He then contracted Hare and Hare of Kansas City to landscape the townsite. Streets were established, lots were marked off, trees were planted, and a community center building was constructed. During the first six months of 1928, Nichols constructed 96 houses in the community, each with an identical chicken coop in the backyard.

Initially, the concept worked. People moved to the community, bought houses from Nichols, and raised chickens, selling eggs and meat through the Nicoma Park Cooperative. The co-op hired a poultry expert, the KATY provided shipping, and the marketing association

handled sales. In one month the sale of 800 chickens allegedly produced a profit of $300.

The dream of a chicken colony crumbled overnight when a chicken wholesaler shipped a diseased flock to Nicoma Park. Within a few days the disease had spread to every chicken house in the colony, while attempts at halting the epidemic proved futile. The catch phrase of "a few months from eggs to dollars" suddenly became "a few days from disease to disaster." All that was left of the poultry colony were empty chicken huts, a few hundred homes, and a community of disillusioned investors.

Other than Nicoma Park, most towns in Oklahoma County expanded and matured during the first two decades of the century, reaching plateaus of population growth and economic prosperity before 1920. This leveling effect was due to a depressed agricultural economy, which declined steadily after 1920 and reached its nadir during the early- and mid-1930s.

The only towns in the county to experience growth from 1920 to 1940 profited from economic activity other than agriculture. For the people of Edmond, Bethany, and Britton, jobs were found in Oklahoma City, which could be reached over improved routes of transportation. By 1930 all three towns were located on both a direct interurban line and a hard surfaced highway into the central business district of Oklahoma City.

By the time of America's entry into World War I, nine towns, excluding Oklahoma City, dotted the landscape of Oklahoma County. Most had evolved from crossroad communities, their growth occurring in response to a variety of factors. After the war, these towns again would be thrust into a world of transition.

Chicken coops and suburban homes were constructed side-by-side in Nicoma Park, the "poultry community." Courtesy, Oklahoma Publishing Company.

G.A. Nichols: A Man of Vision

Thousands of residences, such as these along Northwest 16th Street in 1908, were constructed on the fringes of Oklahoma City after the development of the streetcar system. G.A. Nichols recognized the possibilities of expansion related to transportation. (OHS)

In some of Oklahoma City's most distinctive pre-1941 neighborhoods, visitors are often surprised to find a rich variety of architecture. Airplane bungalows, mission-style houses, and columned colonials are seen side by side along tree-lined streets once intended to attract middle-income families. In other, more exclusive neighborhoods, stately mansions financed by oil riches share the same sense of variety and individuality. The driving force behind much of this architectural and entrepreneurial creativity was Dr. G.A. Nichols.

Born in 1876, Nichols spent his youth on a farm near Guthrie in Oklahoma Territory. He then attended dental college and moved to Oklahoma City in 1904, just as the city was changing from a compact walking city to a sprawling suburban metropolis. After four years as a dentist, the 32-year-old Nichols invested in his first speculative house, a small bungalow near present-day Heritage Hills.

Looking to the northwest quadrant of the city, where streetcar lines were piercing the flat prairie fields, Nichols bought land, platted additions, and built homes. His first major development was the University Addition, a housing development adjacent to streetcar lines and more than two miles from the downtown business district. Then came Winan's Addition, located between Broadway and Robinson just south of N.W. 23rd Street. Again, his medium-size bungalows were less than a block from a streetcar line.

By the early 1920s Nichols had broken ground for the housing additions of Military Park, Central Park, Nichols University Place, Gatewood, and Harndale. He moved into townsite promotion by founding Nicoma Park, a "poultry colony" offering rural living for middle-income families. And he developed small, Spanish-style suburban shopping centers at N.W. 24th and Robinson, N.W. 16th and Indiana, and along Paseo Drive.

With the economy of Oklahoma prospering during the mid-1920s, Nichols turned his attention to additions with larger, more expensive homes. First came Lincoln Terrace, a neighborhood of large two-storied homes located south of the recently completed State Capitol. Then in 1928 came his most ambitious project, Nichols Hills, a 2,780-acre development spread across rolling, timbered land located more than six miles from the downtown business district. The stately mansions and landscaped elegance of the exclusive addition made it one of the region's most beautiful neighborhoods.

During Nichols' career he provided affordable, quality housing for middle-income families as well as for rich clients; he created two of the city's most renowned neighborhoods; and he influenced the direction of urban growth in central Oklahoma. His legacy was a rich tapestry of architectural creativity that has long improved the quality of life in Oklahoma County.

New Era of Growth

From 1920 to 1941 Oklahoma City experienced phenomenal population increases while smaller towns in the county reeled under the impact of agricultural depression. After World War II Oklahoma City continued its rapid expansion, but this time many of the surrounding towns kept pace and even surpassed the growth of the urban center. Populations of towns such as Edmond exploded from 4,002 to 34,637; Choctaw went from 289 to 7,520; Bethany grew from 2,590 to 22,130; and Nichols Hills expanded from 942 to 4,171.

This redistribution of population was the result of developments typical to hundreds of metropolitan areas throughout the nation. First, new jobs were available in Oklahoma City after the war as service and light industries gravitated toward the town's large labor force and favorable climate. Just as new jobs became available, super highways radiated from the inner city in all directions, providing a convenient means of commuting from small towns to jobs in the city. Broadway Extension, I-35, I-40, and I-240, when combined with 30-cent gasoline, made commuting to work a way of life.

Families with increasing purchasing power also found that new houses were cheaper and more accessible in and around small towns. Low interest loans, often guaranteed by the federal government, and cheap land distant from other development enabled middle-income families to buy 1,000 to 2,000 square-foot houses in residential additions 10 and 20 miles from the downtown business district. Builders and developers rushed to meet this demand.

With these factors converging after World War II, the populations of the county's small towns mushroomed. The following chart, with a decade-by-decade growth of selected towns, illustrates this transition:

	1930	1940	1950	1960	1970	1980
Choctaw	242	289	355	623	4,750	7,520
Del City	—	—	2,504	12,934	27,133	28,424
Edmond	3,576	4,002	6,086	8,577	16,633	34,637
Harrah	693	620	741	934	1,931	2,897
Jones	288	260	476	794	1,666	2,270
Luther	613	425	409	517	836	1,159
Midwest City	—	—	10,166	36,058	48,212	49,559
Oklahoma County	221,738	244,159	325,352	439,566	527,717	568,933
Oklahoma City	185,389	204,424	243,504	322,355	361,567	377,003

As these figures illustrate, the county is not one large metropolitan area, but rather a patchwork of towns surrounding Oklahoma City. Each town, with its own schools, public services, and downtown business districts, adds a touch of variety to life in Oklahoma County and continues the traditions of small towns begun in 1889.

This view looks north across Edmond, circa 1900, before the town's population boom of 1940-1980. Courtesy, Central State Museum, Central State University, Edmond.

9

A City of Two Hundred Thousand

At 2:15 A.M. on November 11, 1918, sirens disrupted the nighttime peace of Oklahoma City. World War I, "the war to end all wars," was over. News of the victory spread quickly to all corners of the community, sending thousands of jubilant revelers onto the streets. They fired guns, blew automobile horns, and shouted at the tops of their lungs to express their relief after two years of wartime restrictions.

By 3:00 A.M. a crowd of celebrants had gathered around the Lee-Huckins Hotel, where Governor R.L. Williams slept. While the throngs chanted for a speech, a tall soldier on leave began singing the "Star Spangled Banner." The crowd joined him. Then the governor appeared on the balcony. In a few words he expressed the feeling of relief shared by the swelling crowd. The "delirium of joy," as a reporter described the scene, continued for two days.

The signing of the Armistice ended the fighting in Europe, but it did not end the economic upheaval created by war. Prices still were inflated, certain consumer items still were in short supply, and wages still were spiralling upward. Shoes that once had sold for $7 now cost $20; beef prices soared from $.10 to $.18 a pound

This Armistice Day parade is reminiscent of the celebrations which erupted on the streets of Oklahoma City at the end of World War I. Courtesy, Oklahoma Publishing Company.

This view of Oklahoma City, circa 1920, shows Robinson Avenue, with the Baum Building on Grand Avenue, facing south. Courtesy, Western History Collections, University of Oklahoma Library.

rent for hotel rooms increased from $1 to $5 a night; and the average rent for a house rose from $25 to $60 a month.

Rampant inflation, profiteering, and speculation were intensified by a wild spending spree as a reaction to wartime inhibition. As a contemporary writer described the local scene in 1919, "this was an era of silk shirts, two-bit cigars, $3000 motor cars, short skirts, and the immodest exhibition of feminine limbs."

The postwar exuberance of Oklahoma City made the city election of 1919 one of the wildest on record. Called the "Jazz Campaign" by newspaper columnist Walter Ferguson, the political race pitted the usual slate of businessmen and moral crusaders against one of the most controversial political figures in city and state history, John Calloway "Jack" Walton.

Born in Indiana in 1881, Walton migrated to Nebraska with his parents during the depression years of the early 1890s. There, Walton may have developed much of the political philosophy that later earned him the support of the Farm-Labor League coalition in Oklahoma. At the turn of the century he resettled in Oklahoma Territory, where he found employment first as a railroad construction worker, then later as a railroad engineer. In 1913 Walton organized a sewage system and water plant installation firm and moved to Oklahoma City.

In 1917 Walton entered the political arena. Despite the vehement opposition of the local press, he easily won the election for Commissioner of Public Works. In 1919 he declared for the mayor's office. Usually accompanied by a crowd-pleasing jazz band, Walton frequented the city's busiest corners in his search for votes. During these excursions he made informal speeches on the plight of the common laborer, attacked "Bolshevism and autocracy at home," and lambasted the "tentacles of wealth squeezing Oklahoma City Democracy to death." Again, despite the opposition of the newspaper establishment in Oklahoma City, Walton won the election.

HEART OF THE PROMISED LAND: AN ILLUSTRATED HISTORY OF OKLAHOMA COUNT

In 1919, when Walton took office, the Oklahoma City municipal government still operated under the "strong mayor" system, an appellation Walton took literally. He fired the chief of police, named his own chief, and ran the police department from his office. He quarreled with the county attorney, the county sheriff, and the Chamber of Commerce. Then, during the winter of 1921-1922, he supported the meat-packers' strike, furnishing police protection for the strikers and helping them raise $800 for their relief fund.

While mayor, Walton also battled the Ku Klux Klan, especially during the summer of 1921, when he learned that half his police force belonged to the secret order. He abruptly ordered his chief to fire any officer associated with the hooded order, all to little avail. In a show of force, the Klan marched through the streets of Oklahoma City on the night of February 20, 1922, an event that drew more than 2,000 hooded Klansmen.

In 1922 the controversial Walton ran for the office of governor. Riding to victory on a surge of farm and labor unrest, he treated his supporters to an open inaugural celebration in Oklahoma City. In the best Jacksonian tradition, Walton replaced the usual formal ball with an open-air barbecue at the state fair grounds. More than 20,000 people attended what would be the high point of Walton's troubled tenure as governor.

After Walton vacated the mayor's office, a group of civic leaders initiated a petition drive to change the structure of the municipal government to a nonpartisan city manager plan. On November 2, 1926, the citizens of Oklahoma City voted by a margin of 3 to 1 to adopt the progressive system. Under the plan, the mayor and council would establish policy, while a professionally trained city manager would run the daily affairs of city government.

John "Jack" Walton was an Oklahoma City businessman who became mayor in 1919 and governor of Oklahoma in 1922. (OHS)

During his tenure as mayor, Walton closely controlled both the fire and police departments. The Oklahoma City Fire Department was photographed in 1923. (OHS)

This radical change in the structure of local government was made necessary by the growth and complexity of the city. From 1918 to 1926 the population of Oklahoma City increased from 91,000 to 150,000, compounding the problems of providing city services such as police protection, public works, parks management, and fire protection. This rapid growth, however, did not begin in earnest until 1921, following a postwar economic depression.

In 1920 the national economy suffered a recession following an end to wartime production. In Oklahoma the economic instability became a true depression, for the most severely affected sectors of the economy were the oil industry and agriculture. During the war high prices and strong demand had convinced many farmers to expand operations, which they did only by going heavily into debt for land and machinery. When demand suddenly dropped, prices declined sharply, forcing over-extended farmers into bankruptcy.

The effects of the financial and agricultural depression quickly spread to Oklahoma City. By the early months of 1921, bread lines had lengthened at St. Anthony's Hospital, real-estate prices had plunged, and a record number of wholesale and mercantile firms had declared bankruptcy.

The young automobile industry was another severely affected sector of the economy. In January the state labor commissioner announced that the ranks of the unemployed had increased by 4,000 people, a majority of whom had been employed by automobile manufacturers or dealerships. In Oklahoma City, where 95 percent of the state's automobiles were distributed, the loss of jobs and income was immediately felt.

In this map of Oklahoma, the highway system reflects the growing importance of automobiles. By 1925 all the main arteries in Oklahoma County were paved. Courtesy, Oklahoma Department of Transportation.

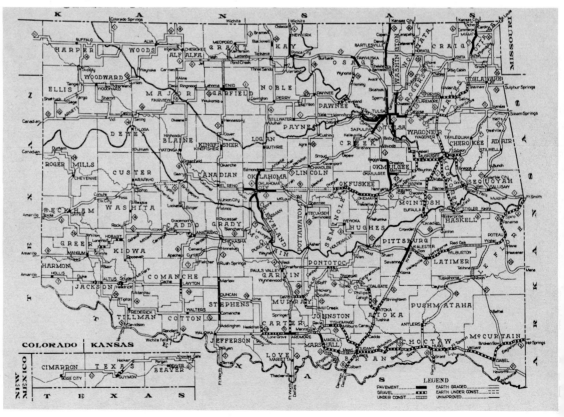

HEART OF THE PROMISED LAND: AN ILLUSTRATED HISTORY OF OKLAHOMA COUNTY

The Buick Building, constructed in 1910, was one of the many automobile sales outlets along Broadway Avenue, known as "Automobile Alley." By 1920, 52 of the city's 76 dealerships were located on this important street. Courtesy, Oklahoma County Metropolitan Library.

The automobile industry had been one of Oklahoma City's fastest-growing enterprises prior to the war. In 1905, for example, only five distributors offered cars in the city; by 1910 the number of dealerships in Oklahoma City had increased to 34. The importance of the industry to the local economy mounted in 1915 when Henry Ford constructed a Model-T assembly plant on W. Main. One year later residents of Oklahoma City registered more than 1,900 "horseless carriages," outnumbering horses for the first time in city history. By 1920 and the postwar depression, the number of dealerships in the capital city had climbed to 76, 52 of which were located on N. Broadway Avenue, known by that time as "Automobile Alley."

By the latter months of 1921, the economy of Oklahoma City was showing signs of recovery. The construction industry was helping to lead the charge back to prosperity. In 1922 several housing additions were opened, with most building concentrated south of the State Capitol Building in the Harndale Addition and west of Classen Boulevard between 16th and 23rd streets in the Gatewood Addition. The most active builder was G.A. Nichols, a former dentist who would be responsible for more than a dozen housing additions in Oklahoma City.

Commercial construction rebounded even more quickly. Although bank financing was limited from 1919 to 1921, several companies continued plans for new construction. In 1919 the Magnolia Petroleum Company, the Southwest's largest oil pipeline/distribution firm, constructed a five-story office building at 7th and Broadway. Another major addition to the city skyline was the Terminal Building, constructed by the Oklahoma Railway Company.

During the early years of the next decade, the tempo of construction quickened. Grain dealers invested more than $2 million in storage and milling facilities; the Tradesman's National Bank erected a 10-story limestone building at Main and Broadway; and James W. Mann constructed the Cotton-Exchange Building at First and Harvey. Designed

Constructed originally in 1911, the Skirvin Hotel was expanded during the late 1920s with an additional wing on the east and two additional levels. Courtesy, Daily Oklahoman.

by the architectural firm of Hawk and Parr, it housed the operations of 23 cotton companies. The most celebrated building completed during this period was the Federal Building and Post Office on 3rd Street.

As the decade progressed, other buildings rose above the streets of Oklahoma City. The 10-story Braniff Building was constructed in 1923 by Thomas E. Braniff, insurance tycoon and founder of Braniff Airlines. Another impressive structure was the India Temple Shrine, financed by the 16 Masonic lodges of the metropolitan area. The $1.3 million edifice, designed by the architectural firm of Layton, Hicks, and Forsythe, featured classical styling and included an ornate auditorium with a seating capacity of 2,062.

Other structures erected during the mid-1920s included the Elks Lodge (ONG) Building, the Harbour-Longmire Building, the Montgomery Ward Building, the Perrine (Cravens/First Life Assurance) Building, and the Medical Arts Building, which was financed by a group of physicians. The list of new structures lengthened each year, with the additions of the OG & E Building, the Hightower Building, the Telephone Building, the Petroleum Building, the Mid-Continent Life Building, the Public Market, and the ornate Biltmore.

This unprecedented burst of major construction reflected the "bullish" economy of Oklahoma City. The spirit of optimism, which encouraged investment, was buoyed by reports of growing sales and mounting prosperity. From 1922 to 1928 retail firms increased sales from $85 million to $146 million; the number of retail establishments rose from 1,516 to 2,110; and bank deposits soared from $40 million to more than $100 million.

Constructed in 1923 by the Masonic lodges of Oklahoma City, the India Temple Shrine Building was an ornate addition to the downtown business district of Oklahoma City. Courtesy, Record-Journal Publishing Company.

Southwestern Bell Telephone Building, constructed in 1928 just north of the Pioneer Building, added to the city's skyline. Courtesy, Daily Oklahoman.

The growth of the petroleum industry in Oklahoma also contributed to this era of expansion. Oil had been a longtime preoccupation with the people of Oklahoma City. In 1890 the first wildcatter arrived in town convinced that the soil of the county floated on a sea of black gold. The unidentified driller erected a derrick at 4th and Santa Fe, rigged his cable tools, and started sinking hole. His efforts proved fruitless, however, and at a depth of 600 feet he abandoned the site.

From 1890 to 1928 more than 20 test wells were drilled in Oklahoma County, none of them striking oil. Meanwhile, drillers found petroleum in other sections of the state. Glenn Pool, the Healdton Field, the Osage Field, and the Greater Seminole Field all pushed Oklahoma to the top of the oil-producing states. Although the closest field was more than 60 miles distant, more than 100 oil firms established offices or headquarters in Oklahoma City. By 1928 the capital city already was in the mainstream of the state's petroleum industry.

In 1928 the Indian Territory Illuminating Oil Company (ITIO) turned its attention to Oklahoma County, hoping to find the cache of oil that had eluded so many drillers. The reason for returning to the region was the surface geology, which indicated that the Mid-Continent oil field extended south to the Oklahoma-Cleveland County line. With this lead, company geologists mapped a southward projecting nose of the larger field. Then the company unleashed an army of lease-hounds, who secured drilling rights on more than 6,000 acres of land.

With the test site protected for miles in all directions, ITIO roughnecks erected a derrick for the first well at what is now S.E. 59th and Bryant. Drilling commenced on June 12, 1928. Anticipation mounted as the crew pushed the hole deeper and deeper below the surface. At 4,000 feet it hit a show of gas, which flowed at 47 million cubic feet daily. But gas was only a secondary concern, so the drillers continued their vigil.

Working in 12-hour shifts, the roughnecks kept the rotary rig busy day and night. Finally, on December 4, with the hole partially filled with oil, the drillers tried to pierce a cement plug at 6,355 feet. Before it could be completed, the well blew in, forcing the tools up the hole where they lodged at 2,500 feet. For an hour and a half the well ran wild, but the Oklahoma City Oil Field had been discovered.

Ten days later the Oklahoma City No. 1 was deepened and cased. During its first 27 days of open flow, the well produced 110,496 barrels of 40-gravity oil, which sold at that time for $1.56 a barrel. Such profits attracted an army of leasemen, drillers, roughnecks, and suppliers, as well as the usual horde of prostitutes, gamblers, and con-men who followed oil play.

Oklahoma City quickly became the nation's newest oil boomtown, a distinction reinforced on June 20, 1929, when the field's second producer came in. Lease by lease, drillers advanced northward, erecting a forest of derricks, convinced they were sinking a gusher each time. By

September, 12 wells were producing 60,000 barrels a day, and crews were drilling another 19.

By March 1930 the field had expanded to 135 completed wells and 173 drilling rigs on location, while estimated production totalled 14,500,000 barrels annually. Despite this record of success, problems arose. The most damaging was strong gas pressure, which blew sand up shafts, cutting control fittings and making drilling more dangerous. On the morning of March 26, 1930, the gas problem erupted into a crisis.

At about daybreak, a tired drilling crew was leaving the Sudik No. 1 after a grueling 12-hour stint. The well, which was located in the southern part of the field, had just reached the top of the oil-laden Wilcox Sand. Suddenly the workers heard a deafening roar as the unleashed fury of oil and gas rushed toward the surface. The pressure blew tools and mud from the hole as if shot from a cannon; then came a stream of oil, gas, and sand, blowing the traveling block and cable about as if they were toys. Frantically, the crew returned to the well, only to find that the pressure had ripped all control valves from the pipe; only a short piece of surface pipe remained. For the next five days, while the gusher sprayed the surrounding countryside with 20,000 barrels of oil a day, workers feverishly prepared a master gate that could be swung onto the opening. The gate was lowered into place, but it could not stop the fury of the blowing well.

The crew that capped the "Wild Mary Sudik" poses on a drilling platform for this photograph in 1930. Courtesy, Cities Service Oil Company.

For another seven days the "Wild Mary Sudik" raged untamed as news of the event circled the world. Oklahoma winds whipped a spray of oil in all directions, spreading a layer of crude from Oklahoma City to Norman. Then, on April 6, a crew of engineers and mechanics from the American Iron and Machine Company cut new threads on the surface pipe and lowered a control valve into place. Surprisingly, it held.

Two months later another well, the Gas-Slick No. 1 Sigmon, blew wild. Then in October, Morgan Petroleum's No. 1 Stout broke loose about a mile south of the central business district. For three days "Stout Fella" sprayed Oklahoma City with as much as 60,000 barrels of oil per day, drenching more than 1,000 residences. The disaster reached a climax when the oil-covered waters of the North Canadian River caught fire. The blaze spread five miles downriver before it was brought under control.

These wild wells received worldwide publicity and damaged thou-

The city ordinance allowing oil rigs into the city limits stipulated that companies could place only one derrick on a block and that each property owner would share equally in the royalties. (OHS)

sands of dollars worth of property, but they did not slow the pace of drilling in the Oklahoma City field. Even "Black Thursday," the day of the Stock Market Crash in 1929, did not interrupt the race for crude.

As drilling moved northward at startling speed, the Oklahoma City Council passed an ordinance limiting wells inside the city limits to a "U" zone where drilling could be closely controlled. One arm of the zone extended along E. Reno; the south edge skirted the southern edge of the city. Within these limits, only one well was allowed in each block, and every lot owner in a block where oil was produced shared in the royalty payments.

Although oilmen chafed under city restrictions and others suffered from blowouts, the most destructive problem confronting oil companies was overproduction. By 1931 the Oklahoma City field was producing more oil than the nation could consume. Then the East Texas oil field blew in, adding to the oversupply. When the price of a barrel of oil dropped to a low of $.16, Governor William "Alfalfa Bill" Murray acted to save the ailing oil industry.

On August 4, 1931, he declared a state of emergency in the oil fields of the state, ordering the militia to shut down all production until the price of a barrel of oil returned to $1.00. For the next two years Murray maintained a varying control over oil production until the Legislature enacted a proration law, a conservation measure which would serve as a model for other oil-producing states.

Murray's actions were harsh, but he achieved his goal of raising the price of crude. Again receiving more than $1.00 a barrel, oilmen resumed the quick pace of drilling. In October 1935 oil was discovered on the grounds of the Governor's Mansion, just east of the State Capitol Building. After a bitter struggle with the Oklahoma City Council over placement of wells inside the city limits, Governor E.W. Marland ordered militia to protect drillers on state property. Within a year, derricks appeared in the Northeast quadrant of the city.

By the mid-1930s the Oklahoma State Capitol grounds and surrounding neighborhoods were pierced by derricks. The Oklahoma Historical Society Building, right of the Capitol Building, was surrounded by wells on three sides. (OHS)

By 1935 the Oklahoma City oil field extended from the Cleveland County line through the Southeast quadrant of the city, through the Capitol Grounds between 13th and 23rd, and north and east of the capitol. Then the field skipped to the far northwest part of the county to the West Edmond Field, which had been discovered in 1930. By 1935 the 1,713 wells of the county had produced 290,730,062 barrels of oil; five years later that total exceeded 475,000,000 barrels.

This enormous production had a profound influence on Oklahoma City and County. The Indian Territory Illuminating Oil Company alone pumped more than $69 million into the local economy in less than eight years. This included $11 million in payrolls, $21.5 million to contractors, $11 million in leases and royalties, $23 million in supplies, and $2.6 million in direct taxes.

The wealth generated by oilmen such as H.V. Foster, Tom Slick, Harry Sinclair, and Frank Buttram proved more beneficial to the local economy than all the public relief projects during the Great Depression. The wealth of the Oklahoma City oil field provided capital for future investments, energy for expansion, and the incentive to open new frontiers, elements needed during the 1930s and 1940s as Oklahoma City faced depression and war.

Oklahoma City experienced a decade of spectacular growth apparent in this 1929 view. (OHS)

Miss Edith Johnson, Pioneer Journalist

"The world doesn't owe you a living . . . it is up to you to fit yourself to earn a living . . . the world owes opportunity to everyone who is willing and eager to work industriously and efficiently."

"No woman shall be safe and no woman's husband or child until there shall be established a basis of justice for all peoples." These are but two examples of the common sense philosophy of Oklahoma City's pioneer woman journalist and humanitarian, Edith Johnson.

In 1903, at the age of 24, Edith moved to Oklahoma City, where she raised her sisters and took care of her widowed father. In 1908, freed from her family obligations, she applied for a writing job that had recently been vacated at the *Daily Oklahoman* newspaper. Publisher E.K. Gaylord sent her to editor Roy Stafford, who decided to give her a chance.

Her first article, a humorous story about a YWCA biscuit-baking contest, appeared on the society page on December 15, 1908. During the next decade "Miss Edith," as her readers called her, filled a variety of roles at the paper. She was the staff critic for art, music, books, and drama, and she often interviewed visiting celebrities such as Theodore Roosevelt.

In 1915 she created a woman's page for the Sunday edition, and three years later she earned her own column on the editorial page, a distinction which gave her a place at the editorial conference each morning. In her columns Miss Edith combined folksy common sense with the values of love and kindness. Her writing ability and sensitivity were justly rewarded. Her column was syndicated by the Republic wire service; a book of her essays was published in 1920; and her book entitled *Women of the Business World* was published by Lippincott in 1923.

After years of expressing her philosophy of everyday life, Miss Edith was showered with honors. In 1935 she was elected to the Oklahoma Hall of Fame, and a decade later she was chosen Woman of the Year by the Business and Professional Woman's Club. In 1950, near the end of her career, Miss Edith was one of seven newspaper women awarded certificates of achievement by the Women's National Press Club.

Edith Johnson. (OHS)

In 1958, after 50 years on the staff of the *Daily Oklahoman*, Miss Edith did not write her column. The hardworking and compassionate woman was ill. Her daily advice and encouragement was gone, but her philosophy survived in the hearts of her readers. As one minister described Miss Edith after her death in 1961, she was "our dear little mother of brotherhood . . . an apostle of compassion and good will."

10

A New Skyline, Then Depression and War

While oil gushed from the ground, bankers and businessmen in Oklahoma City speculated about the effects of the stockmarket crash on Wall Street. Many assumed it was merely a natural downturn in the capitalistic system, which expanded and contracted in cycles. Others thought it was a localized crisis generated by manipulative money merchants. After all, the economy of Oklahoma City was surging ahead at an unprecedented pace.

Indeed, Oklahoma City looked like a boomtown during the winter of 1929-1930. Fifty-eight new industries and more than 400 smaller firms opened for business in the city; building permits exceeded one million dollars each month; and oil companies raced to sink more wells and buy more leases. For nine years the economy had been growing at a hectic pace and the people of Oklahoma City expected more of the same.

As during the mid-1920s, the most outward sign of prosperity was to be the construction industry. The First National Bank, recently strengthened by a merger with the State National Bank led the way downtown by announcing plans for a $5 million, 31 story skyscraper on Robinson Avenue. Meanwhile, a block north

The construction boom of the late 1920s combined with the effects of oil production to keep the economy of Oklahoma City healthy after the stock market crash on Wall Street. This view of Walker Avenue facing south shows the Montgomery Ward Building under construction. (OHS)

oil millionaire W.R. Ramsey began construction of the Ramsey Tower, another 31-story behemoth, which cost $3 million. Other major construction projects in the business district were the Black Hotel and the Skirvin Tower.

Residential construction also raced ahead, seemingly unaffected by the easterly march of the Depression. The most successful housing project during this period was Nichols Hills, conceived as an "exclusive housing community" by veteran developer G.A. Nichols. Located north of present-day N.W. 63rd Street, the 2,780-acre addition catered to the wealthier residents of Oklahoma City with large lots, professional landscaping, and a $300,000 clubhouse. According to one account, Nichols sold in excess of one million dollars' worth of lots during the first week they were on the market.

Oil production developed rapidly, and the economy of Oklahoma City expanded well into the 1930s despite the growing national depression. (OHS)

The combined boost of continued construction and oil development only temporarily muted the early shock waves of the financial collapse advancing from the East. While skyscrapers and oil derricks rose above the streets of the city, casualties from the snowballing Depression mounted. By 1931 the Emergency Employment Committee reported that more than 4,200 families in Oklahoma City were in dire need of financial assistance.

With no federal programs to aid the destitute, public service organizations and local government tried to help victims of the spreading disaster. The Community Fund organization pledged $338,092 of its $450,000 annual budget for relief. With these monies, the Salvation Army, the United Provident Association, and the Red Cross bought and distributed food, clothing, and supplies to more than 46,000 men, women, and children during the first six months of 1931.

The Oklahoma City Council appropriated $250,000 for make-work projects. City Manager Albert McRill used this and other resources to provide work for the growing ranks of the unemployed. One of the projects he initiated was straightening the North Canadian River channel from Pennsylvania Avenue east to the Santa Fe right-of-way. The make-work employees dug a 3,600-foot channel with 14-foot levees and opened the river bottom to development.

Locally, organized public works crews also improved and equipped 15 parks in the city. Formerly unemployed men converted an old brick pit on N. McKinley Avenue into McKinley Park and transformed river bottom wasteland into Wiley Post Park. Both would provide recreation for years to come.

The riverbed reclamation projects also focused public attention on the growing blight of "Hoovervilles." Communities of ramshackle dwellings usually found around public dumps, along highways, and on

During the 1930s soup lines helped many women, children, and men survive the immediate crisis. Charitable organizations such as the Red Cross, the Salvation Army, and the United Provident Association provided food, clothing, and supplies to needy people. Courtesy, Oklahoma Department of Libraries.

Despite the effects of oil and construction, the Depression took a heavy toll in Oklahoma County after 1930. Many families, without means of support or assistance, gathered along highways and along the riverbed. Courtesy, Oklahoma Department of Libraries.

the banks of rivers, Hoovervilles were inhabited by dispossessed, unemployed, and migratory persons uprooted by the Depression.

In Oklahoma City more than 6,000 poverty-stricken people had settled in Hoovervilles by 1931, most of which were located along the banks of the North Canadian. Although city officials had legal authority to level these camps, City Manager McRill found a temporary solution to the problem by organizing what he called the Community Camp. McRill began his "noble experiment" by leasing 52 acres of land on S. Pennsylvania Avenue, part of which had been included in the old county poor farm. The city engineer surveyed the land, platted small lots, and established streets. City workers employed by the make-work program installed utilities, water lines, and sewage facilities. Crews then used old lumber belonging to the city to construct one- and two-room houses, a community building, and a schoolhouse.

Before workers destroyed the Hoovervilles, city-owned trucks provided free transportation to the Community Camp. Once in the public community, penniless people were assigned houses, which they rented for a nominal fee. To help them buy food and clothing, McRill made city jobs available to all able-bodied men. Thus the experiment in public welfare provided housing, better living conditions, and jobs for victims of the Depression.

Governor William "Alfalfa Bill" Murray also improvised to help the 10,000 unemployed and impoverished people in Oklahoma City. In one instance, he wrote letters addressed to grocers and restaurant owners, asking for food that could be salvaged but not sold. He then requisitioned state highway trucks to gather the supplies and used state militia to prepare and dispense huge vats of stew and coffee. To pay for this type of public welfare, Murray levied a one and one-half percent tax on the salaries of state employees and contributed $5,700 of his own money.

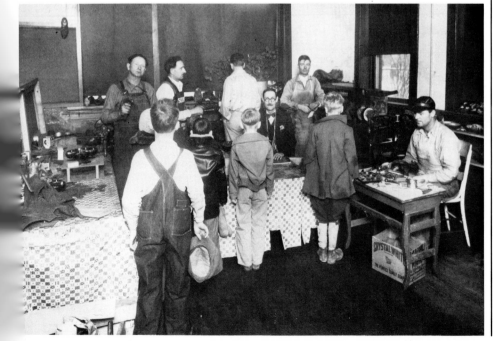

In March 1933 President Franklin D. Roosevelt initiated his "New Deal." During the next six years the most effective federal efforts to help the unemployed were the Public Works Administration (PWA), the Civilian Conservation Corps (CCC), and the Works Progress Administration (WPA). These agencies expanded public aid far beyond what had been possible through local government.

In 1935 the new city manager of Oklahoma City, Orval "Red" Mosier, saw an opportunity to utilize federal assistance. The city owned a broad strip of land through the heart of the downtown business district, which had been the right-of-way for the Rock Island and Frisco railroads. The tracks had been removed in 1930 after the city purchased the property for $4 million. Mosier's idea was to construct a new government complex on this land, using bond issue monies to match federal funds.

Since 1890 the business district of Oklahoma City had been divided by the Frisco and Rock Island tracks, which impeded growth and posed a safety hazard for automobile and pedestrian traffic. (OHS)

This shoe shop at Franklin School was funded by a federal relief program to repair shoes for schoolchildren in 1936. Federal programs such as this expanded public aid far beyond what had been possible through local government. Courtesy, Oklahoma Department of Libraries.

The Municipal and County Complex is shown here at night from the east in 1940. The Oklahoma County Courthouse (right), the Municipal Building (center), and the Municipal Auditorium (back) were built with both local and federal funds. (OHS)

Enlisting the enthusiastic support of city leaders E.K. Gaylord and Stanley Draper, Mosier presented a bond issue for $1,787,500 to the voters. It was overwhelmingly approved. The federal government then matched the fund with $1,462,500, much of it in the form of PWA labor assistance. By the end of the year, crews had broken ground on the "bargain of the century," and by 1937 the former railyard included the County Courthouse, the City Hall, the City Police Headquarters, and the Municipal Auditorium.

By 1935 the federal government had committed more than $250 million to relief in the state, much of which was distributed in Oklahoma City. This was ensured by the location of regional and state agency offices there. Among the New Deal agencies with state headquarters in Oklahoma City were the CCC, the PWA, the National Recovery Administration, the Rural Rehabilitation Administration, the Home Owners Loan Corporation, and the Federal Housing Authority.

Efforts to ease the Depression also produced the effect of enhancing the cultural life in Oklahoma City. The Municipal Auditorium, completed with PWA assistance in 1937, was used for plays, concerts, and other programs. For the next 40 years the acoustically superior auditorium would host numerous ballets, Broadway productions, and musicals.

The WPA also assisted in constructing amphitheaters at Will Rogers and Lincoln parks. Built of native red sandstone, the Lincoln Park Amphitheater became the site of the annual Easter Sunrise Pageant. The program drew thousands of visitors each spring until the outbreak of World War II. Both theaters have since been used for concerts, lectures, and various forms of entertainment.

The WPA likewise supported actors, writers, artists, and musicians in Oklahoma City. The WPA Theater, established in 1935, was one of the most successful of these projects. Supervisors searched the city for unemployed actors, then held rehearsals at 21 W. Main. The troupes staged dramas, comedies, and musicals at a variety of locations, and even performed on radio.

A similar contribution was made by the WPA Writers' Project, which put unemployed playwrights, poets, and historians to work. The historical phase of the project was supervised by Grant Foreman. By 1939 he and his army of writers had assembled 116 volumes of Indian-Pioneer interviews, hundreds of town histories, and thousands of short historical narratives. Other contributions to the arts in Oklahoma City were the WPA Music Project, which created the Oklahoma City Symphony in 1937, and the WPA Art Project, organized by Nan Sheets in 1935.

Entertainment, whether drama, art, or music, was just as important to the people of Oklahoma City during the Depression as it had been prior to 1929. One of the most popular new forms of entertainment during the 1930s was radio. The first radio station in Oklahoma City was WKY, founded by Earl Hull in his garage in 1922. In 1928 the Oklahoma Publishing Company purchased the station, and it became an affiliate of the National Broadcasting Company.

By 1939 other radio stations in town were KOMA, established as an affiliate of the Columbia Broadcasting System in 1932; KTOK, founded in 1937; and KOCY, organized in 1939. Families in Oklahoma City would gather around their radios and tune into shows such as "The Shadow," "Lum and Abner," "Mr. District Attorney," "The Bob Hope Show," "Stella Dallas," and "Dr. I.Q." These national programs were supplemented with local shows featuring live bands and drama.

Men employed by the Works Progress Administration (WPA) were assigned tools for a project at Brock Park on January 31, 1934. The WPA also employed people to construct amphitheaters at Will Rogers and Lincoln parks. Courtesy, Oklahoma Department of Libraries.

The stage and interior design of the Midwest Theater reveal the cost and imagination expended on early motion picture houses in Oklahoma City. Courtesy, Oklahoma Publishing Company.

Motion pictures were another form of entertainment that matured during the 1930s. As the decade progressed, the quality of pictures improved, culminating in 1939 when moviemakers released such classics as *Gone With the Wind, The Wizard of Oz, Casablanca,* and *Stagecoach*. The people of Oklahoma City watched these products of Hollywood's golden age in ornate theaters such as the Orpheum (originally the Overholser Opera House and later the Warner), the Liberty Theater, the Midwest, and the Victoria (the first suburban theater in town). Th showpiece of theaters in Oklahoma City, however, was the Criterion.

Located on the south side of Main Street between Robinson and Broadway, the Criterion was a "symphony in brick and stone." It was five stories tall, cost $700,000 to construct, and featured a $25,000 pipe organ. The entryway on Main Street was covered by a massive marque and the interior was enriched by a liberal use of velvet carpets, walnut panelling, and original paintings. This landmark theater survived until 1973, when it was destroyed by the Urban Renewal Authority.

Residents of Oklahoma City also could seek entertainment at a number of dance clubs in town. Several bands were based in Oklahoma City including Clarence Tackett's Toe Teasers, the Bonnie Spencer Orchestra, and the Blue Devils. But for contributions to the evolution of music, Oklahoma City will undoubtedly be best remembered for Charles "Charlie" Christian, the "greatest of the jazz guitarists."

The Christian family had migrated to Oklahoma City during the early 1920s when Charlie was still a child. It was not surprising that the young black man turned to music, for his father played guitar and sang, his mother played piano, his oldest brother played violin and bass, and his other brother was a pianist-arranger and bandleader. By age 15, Charlie was playing guitar at clubs such as the Goody-Goody Cafe on California Avenue and Ruby's Grill on Deep Second.

In 1937, at age 18, Charlie organized his own band in Oklahoma City and played lead guitar. As his skills improved, his fame spread, earning him a place in the Benny Goodman band. He later recorded with the Metronome All-Stars and with Lionel Hampton, before he died from tuberculosis in 1942. The musician was only 24 years old.

The regionally famous Criterion Theatre is shown here on opening night. Richly designed with elements of Mediterranean, classical, and Spanish architectural influence, the ornate structure graced Oklahoma City for more than 50 years. Courtesy, Barney Hillerman.

From Three-D Danny to Ida "B":
Local Personalities in Television

Ho Ho, John Harrison, Ida "B" Blackburn.

Courtesy, Ida Blackburn.

In 1949 television burst into the lives of Oklahomans, making national celebrities of stars such as Milton Berle, Groucho Marx, and Dinah Shore. To many Oklahomans, however, the most important new stars were local men and women who provided programming from the small studios of Oklahoma City. These people, from Danny Williams to Ida "B," represented television to thousands of viewers during the formative years of the media.

One of the earliest television personalities in the Oklahoma City market was Danny Williams. A native of Texas, Danny started his career in radio and made the transition to television in 1950 when he created an hour-long talk show on WKY-TV. That early show survived until 1953, when he changed directions and opted for a children's show — Space Science Center. With his robot, Bozark, "Dan D. Dynamo" fought the forces of evil in space for the next five years. Since that time Danny has been in and out of local productions, and he now stars in "Dannysday," seen daily on KTVY.

Another early big-timer on WKY-TV was Steve Powell, better known as Foreman Scotty. Like Williams, Powell began his career in radio before moving to television. In 1952 he created the "Foreman Scotty" show in Tulsa, and two years later he moved the show to Oklahoma City, where he established the "Circle 4 Ranch" with features such as audience participation, Woody the birthday horse, the magic lasso, and the golden horseshoe. A favorite segment of his long-running show was the adventure series; dramatic episodes produced by Powell which involved unseen villains, shootouts, and time travel. The show prospered until 1971, when an FCC ruling restricted advertising on children's shows.

Ed Birchall, better known as "Ho Ho the Clown" also enjoyed a share of the lucrative children's market in Oklahoma City. In 1959 Ho Ho aired his first show, "Ho Ho's Cartoon Circus," a Saturday morning show that included cartoons, live talent, and his own clowning antics. After this success the show became a daily production featuring a variety of cartoon series. In 1963 he began "Lunch with Ho Ho" with a new co-star, Pokey, a sassy puppet brought to life by Bill Howard. Ho Ho's show ran daily until 1975, when the American Broadcasting Company created the nationally aired show "Good Morning America," which preempted the morning time slot. Since that time Ho Ho has entertained another generation of mesmerized children on Saturday mornings.

"Kiddy" shows dominated local programming during the early years of television, and one of the most popular was "Romper Room," which launched the career of Ida Blackburn, known to thousands of preschool fans and grateful parents as Ida "B." In 1961, after "Romper Room" had moved to another market, Ida used her experience to create a new type of show for Oklahoma City. She adopted a magazine format with a combination of live entertainment, film features, and interviews. Through the years other elements she introduced into the popular show were movies, cooking instruction, and a strong theme of promoting Oklahoma City. The name of the show changed from "At Home with Ida 'B'" to "Dateline Hollywood," and finally to "The Ida 'B' Show." Like Ho Ho, Ida lost her time slot in 1975 when ABC initiated "Good Morning America." Since that time she has excelled as an account executive at KOCO-TV.

Others who helped establish early television programming in the region include Lola Hall, Tom Paxton, John Fields, Harry Vokeman, Frank McGee, Bill Fountain, Scotty Harold, Russel Pearon, "Miss Fran" Morris, Eddie Koonz, and a host of others. These people established a strong and progressive television market in Oklahoma City, and added a regional flare to broadcasting.

The decade also was memorable for the rising interest in all kinds of sports. The Oklahoma Indians baseball team, for example, had been organized in 1923, but did not enjoy its greatest success until after 1930. In 1935 the professional team captured the Texas League championship and went on to win the Dixie Series. Playing in Holland Stadium at N.W. 4th and Pennsylvania, the team at one time included Carl Hubbell, a southpaw who would go on to achieve fame in the National League.

Baseball also grew in popularity among the youth during the 1930s. During the early years of the decade, the American Legion organized a national baseball program, with several teams located in the metropolitan area. Later in the decade the YMCA of Oklahoma City initiated a youth baseball program, with two leagues divided by age groups, the peewees and the preps. Both programs still are popular today.

Football, too, enjoyed a high tide of popularity during the Depression. The Oklahoma City University Goldbugs, a football team organized during the early 1920s, achieved their greatest success in 1930 and 1931, when they lost only one game in two seasons. Following a perfect season, Goldbug enthusiasts organized the city's first professional football team. Composed mainly of former OCU players, the team won eight of ten games its first year and drew good crowds. Despite this initial success, the team folded after another season.

Played on December 3, 1934, this football game shows the intensity of sports during the decade of the Depression. Professional, college, and high school football became increasingly popular in the 1930s. Courtesy, Oklahoma Publishing Company.

Football fever spread even to the high schools. In 1933 the Capitol Hill Redskins won 12 straight games, including a 55-12 victory over the Chicago city champions. As the decade progressed, interest in high-school football mounted. In 1936 the Oklahoma City Junior Chamber of Commerce initiated a fund-raising campaign to build a stadium. After 10 percent of the cost was raised, the WPA took over the project and finished Taft Stadium at N.W. 25th and May Avenue in 1937. Area teams still use the facility.

Basketball also gained in popularity. Sponsored by the Milk and Ice Fund of the Oklahoma Publishing Company, the All-College Basketball Tournament was initiated in 1936. The first tournament, played on various courts around Oklahoma City, offered a slate of 16 teams, including Henry "Hank" Iba's Aggies from Oklahoma A & M. The legendary Iba, who would earn an international reputation through his many collegiate and Olympic achievements, had coached a championship team at Central High School only a few years earlier.

The "sports decade" in Oklahoma City also was a time of achievement in other events. In 1934 and 1935, Twin Hills Golf Course hosted the Western Amateur and the PGA Championship tournaments. In 1938 area boosters organized the Oklahoma City Fourball Tournament which has since become a major amateur golf event in the state.

Even bowling increased its following with the organization of the Oklahoma City Men's Singles Classic in 1933. And finally, in 1937, at the height of the sports craze, participants from throughout the state gathered in Oklahoma City for the Municipal Marble Tournament. Whether such events were merely a passing phase or attempts to lessen the effects of the Depression, the people of Oklahoma City showed their love of sports during the 1930s.

While the people of Oklahoma City, Oklahoma County, and the nation weathered the storm of Depression, clouds of war gathered in other parts of the world. During the early 1930s, Germany, Italy, and Japan launched campaigns of aggression, which embroiled three continents in war by the end of the decade. From 1939 to 1941 the United States followed a dual policy of aid to Britain, China, and the Soviet Union, while stressing preparedness at home.

Both policies—massive aid and national preparedness—fueled the American economy to new heights of productivity and ended the Depression. In Oklahoma City 123 manufacturers had secured more than $3 million in Defense Contracts by 1940. Within a year total federal expenditures in Oklahoma City would exceed $30 million. Two of the earliest projects prompted by the plan of preparedness were the Civilian Pilot Training Program and the expansion of Will Rogers Airport. By 1941, after expending $2 million on the airport, the Army Air Corps based a bomber squadron at the site.

In the mad scramble for defense installations, Oklahoma City had several advantages: mild climate, flat landforms, and a large work force. These same conditions, however, could be found in dozens of cities in other sections of the country. Oklahoma City succeeded where others failed because of an energetic and daring group of civic leaders. One of the most important men in this influential group was Stanley Draper.

The son of a tidewater farmer in North Carolina, Draper was born in November 1889, eight months after the land run into the Unassigned Lands. Benefiting from his father's successes, young Draper completed school and attended college before joining the army in 1917. As a lieutenant in the infantry, Draper commanded a unit in several campaigns in France.

After his release from the army, Draper received a letter from a friend stating that the Oklahoma City Chamber of Commerce needed a secretary to build membership. He applied for and received the job, which paid $2,100 a year. From 1919 to 1927 Draper learned from experienced Chamber leaders W.J. Pettee and Ed Overholser. In 1927, after eight years of work to increase membership, manage the Committee on Conventions, and promote industry, Draper was named executive director of the Chamber of Commerce.

Throughout the Depression years Draper struggled to lessen the effects of unemployment. One of his most important decisions was to assign R.A. Singletary, a Chamber employee, to Washington, D.C., where he could lobby for relief funds. After 1939, when the federal government began gearing for war, Singletary and Draper turned their sights to luring defense installations to Oklahoma City.

The All-College Basketball Tournament, shown here in the 1960s, was initiated in Oklahoma City in 1936. The first tournament, played on various courts around the city, offered a slate of 16 teams. Courtesy, Oklahoma Publishing Company.

B-24s were stored in this hangar at Tinker Air Force Base in 1943. The base was built on a 960-acre site and employed more than 3,500 workers. Courtesy, Tinker Air Force Base History Office.

As Draper knew, one of the prerequisites in the battle for Defense Contracts was the ability to acquire land. On October 16, 1940, Draper and 14 business leaders solved this problem by organizing the Industries Foundation of Oklahoma, a trust that could purchase land for sale to the federal government. The first acquisition was a 1,219-acre tract adjacent to Will Rogers Airport, which later was sold to the Army Air Corps.

This organization proved its worth during the early months of 1941, when Singletary heard rumors that the Army Air Corps was looking for a site in middle-America for a major air depot. In February these rumors were confirmed when the Air Corps asked the Chamber for information on Oklahoma City. With nothing more than speculation to go on, the Industries Foundation used its funds to buy options on land for the depot at two locations, one of which was on S.E. 29th Street.

On March 8, 1941, an Air Corps inspection team arrived in Oklahoma City. Draper, Mayor Robert A. Hefner, county officials, and a group of Chamber members heard their demands: a 960-acre site, 40 miles of gravel road, 10 miles of paved highway, a railroad spur, running water, complete utilities, and the removal of all pipelines from the site. Within two days the group had arranged to meet all the requirements. On April 8, 1941, the Assistant Secretary of War announced that Oklahoma City was to be the location of a $14 million air depot that would employ more than 3,500 workers. Within two years Tinker Field was completed.

With acquisition of the air depot still current news, Draper and his urban allies actively sought other defense industries. In January 1942 officials of the Douglas Aircraft Company arrived in Oklahoma City to announce their interest in locating a plant there. As before, the inspection team had a list of demands, all of which city hall and the Chamber of Commerce quickly agreed to meet. By 1943 the Douglas plant employed 24,000 people in producing C-47 cargo planes.

These preparations for war proved fortunate, for on December 7, 1941, the Japanese bombed Pearl Harbor. Suddenly, the fighting spirit of America turned from concentrating on the economy to fighting the enemies of democracy. Within days the country declared war on the member nations of the Axis, and the people of Oklahoma City reacted quickly to the crisis. Mayor Hefner closed critical installations to public access, postal authorities increased security measures, war-related industries stepped up production, the Red Cross pleaded for nursing recruits, and military officials at Will Rogers Air Field canceled all leaves.

While Americans mobilized for war, life in Oklahoma City quickly changed. With gas and tires rationed, twice as many people rode street-cars. Women who had never worked attended war industries training classes and secured jobs. A series of ''war loan'' drives were promoted in the press. And, as during the days of World War I, patriotic citizens observed ''meatless'' and ''sweetless'' days.

Oklahoma City made another contribution to the war effort—

AT-6 Advanced Trainers were housed in a hangar at Tinker Air Force Base during World War II. Construction and maintenance on such aircraft contributed to the war effort. Courtesy, Tinker Air Force Base History Office.

A NEW SKYLINE, THEN DEPRESSION AND WAR

157

Lieutenant General Raymond S. McClain (right) is shown here with Lieutenant General William Simpson (left) and British Field Marshal Bernard Montgomery (center). McClain, an Oklahoma City native, won distinction in World War II. Courtesy, Roy Steward.

General Raymond S. McLain. A native of Oklahoma City, McLain had been in the 45th Infantry Division since 1924. After the outfit was activated for combat, McLain saw early action in Sicily as a commander of artillery. At Anzio, commanding the combined artillery of the invasion force, he provided one of the most concentrated bombardments in military history up to that time.

During the Normandy invasion, McLain commanded the 30th Division artillery. Later, at the head of the 90th Infantry, he won major victories at Metz and Julich. As the commander of the XIX Corps of the Ninth Army, McLain was the first to cross the Elbe. Such success earned him the rank of lieutenant general, the first guardsman ever to receive such an honor.

With the leadership of men such as McLain, the fighting spirit of troops such as that found in the 45th Division, and the support of workers on the homefront, the Allies defeated the combined forces of Italy, Germany, and Japan. On August 15, 1945, news of Japan's surrender was announced. Reminiscent of 1918, the people of Oklahoma City danced in the streets. As one news reporter described the scene, "Oklahoma City was engulfed in a flood of hilarious happiness that swept through the streets in a wild torrent of joyful humanity." After 16 years of Depression and war, the celebration had been earned.

THE DAILY OKLAHOMAN EXTRA

On August 5, 1945, Oklahomans read of the Japanese surrender on the previous day in the Daily Oklahoman. *Courtesy, Oklahoma Publishing Company.*

PRESIDENT ANNOUNCES PEACE

War Over, Allies Win

WASHINGTON, Aug. 14.—(AP)—President Truman announced at 6:00 p. m. (Oklahoma wartime) Japanese acceptance of surrender terms.

They will be accepted by Gen. Douglas MacArthur when arrangements can be completed.

Mr. Truman read the formal message relayed from Emperor Hirohito through the Swiss government in which the Japanese ruler pledged the surrender on the terms laid down by th Big Three conference at Potsdam.

President Truman made this statement:

"I have received this afternoon a message from the Japanese government in reply to the message forwarded to that government by the secretary of state on August 11.

"I deem . : reply a full acceptance of the Potsdam declaration which specifies

U.S. Is Born Anew As Big Guns Cool

WASHINGTON, Aug. 14.—(AP)—The war clouds that now roll away reveal a tremendously changed United States —changed both in its relations to the world and in the problems it must face at home.

Seven nations were regarded as world powers when the guns began to roar in Europe six years ago: Great Britain, the United States, Russia, France, Germany, Italy, Japan.

Now that the guns are silent again, only two as major powers.

Army Cancels War Contracts

DAYTON, Ohio, Aug. 14.

News that World War II had ended on August 14, 1945, sent thousands of Oklahoma City residents into the streets for a massive celebration. Courtesy, Oklahoma Publishing Company.

11

A New Era Begins

In 1945 soldiers returning home found that the war had taken a heavy toll on Oklahoma County and its residents. Increased production and full employment had been offset by consumer shortages and rationing. The sweetness of victories had been offset by the loss of sons, brothers, and husbands. Life, however, had continued.

Those returning soldiers also discovered that Oklahoma County still offered myriad opportunities, especially in choices of entertainment. They could see a moving picture at one of 30 theaters, including the Criterion, the "showplace of the Southwest." For more traditional fare, it was only a short walk to the Municipal Auditorium, where the Oklahoma City Symphony performed regularly. In sharp contrast, boisterous crowds attended wrestling and boxing matches at the Stockyards Coliseum, a short trolley-car ride to the southwest.

During daytime hours, fun-seekers could ride a trolley car or one of the new motorized buses to any of the 68 parks in Oklahoma City. One of the most popular was Lincoln Park, which included a lake, a picnic grounds, and a recently constructed zoo and amphitheater. A mile south of Lincoln Park on Eastern

On the morning of April 26, 1949, WKY-TV transmitted this test pattern as the first regularly scheduled television signal in Oklahoma City. The pattern helped television installation technicians adjust pictures on new sets. Courtesy, Oklahoma Publishing Company.

One of the most popular new forms of entertainment in Oklahoma City after World War II was television, provided by a local station as early as 1949. These people are viewing the new communication miracle in a downtown showroom. Courtesy, Oklahoma Publishing Company.

Avenue was Springlake Park, where returning servicemen could take their dates to dances at the pavilion. The Springlake swimming pool also was a major attraction that August of 1945.

For less adventurous veterans of the war, entertainment could be found at home on the radio. Four local stations—WKY, KOMA, KOCY, and KTOK—carried music, soap operas, and variety shows. People also had the option of patronizing the Carnegie Library downtown or one of 12 branch libraries.

Entertainment and employment in Oklahoma County were only two of the varied opportunities awaiting returning soldiers. For many, a college education became possible. In 1945 the county was served by three colleges—Oklahoma City University, Central Teachers College, and Bethany Nazarene College.

After World War II, Oklahoma City entered a new era of prosperity and expansion. This view, looking west from Robinson, shows Main Street in 1956. Courtesy, Oklahoma County Metropolitan Library.

Founded as Epworth College in 1902, Methodist-affiliated Oklahoma City University had struggled for years, at times offering degrees in such diverse areas as fine arts, law, business, liberal arts, civil engineering, pharmacy, dentistry, and even medicine. Such ambitions, however, bankrupted the college by 1911.

In 1922, after two reorganizations, the college finally was moved to its present location at N.W. 23rd and McKinley. During the postwar era the school trimmed its programs to liberal arts, music, law, and business, and initiated a series of fund-raising drives for financial stability. The campus expanded during this period with a chapel, the Gold Star Building, the Fine Arts Auditorium, and the Library Building.

While Oklahoma City University narrowed its scope to a few areas of specialization, Central Teachers College and Bethany Nazarene continued in the roles originally developed by the schools' founding fathers. During the postwar era Central Teachers College, later renamed Central State College and still later Central State University, expanded its programs and enrollment. Today, the student population at the state's fourth largest college is approximately 12,000.

Bethany Nazarene, located along N.W. 39th Street in Oklahoma City, also grew during the prosperous postwar years. Beginning as a small campus with only a few hundred students, the college after 1945 added six new buildings. Today, more than 1,300 students are enrolled in liberal arts classes, education programs, business courses, and religion studies.

Gold Star Building, constructed during the period from 1949 to 1952 on the Oklahoma City University campus, serves as a distinctive landmark on the northwest side of Oklahoma City. Courtesy, Oklahoma City University.

Postwar prosperity and the progressive spirit of Oklahoma County attracted other colleges. In 1946 the Pentecostal Holiness Church established the Southwestern Bible College on N.W. 10th Street. Another religious school, Midwest Christian College, was founded in 1947. But the largest church school attracted to the county was Oklahoma Christian College.

Founded in 1950 in Bartlesville, Oklahoma, OCC in 1957 moved to a 200-acre site between Oklahoma City and Edmond. Since that time the college has pioneered dial-access learning modules while expanding curriculum to 45 major areas of study. In 1980 the campus included 30 buildings and enrollment exceeded 1,700 students.

Since 1960 three other institutions of higher education have located in Oklahoma County. One is the Oklahoma A & M Technical Institute opened in 1961. Relocated to a 60-acre campus on N. Portland Avenue in 1971, the school offered a variety of practical degrees from accounting to carpentry. In addition, South Oklahoma City Community College was established on S. May Avenue in 1970. Designed with open classrooms, the city-supported school offers general education courses and adult education. Oscar Rose Junior College, located in Midwest City, was organized in 1970. Today, its enrollment exceeds 10,000.

HEART OF THE PROMISED LAND: AN ILLUSTRATED HISTORY OF OKLAHOMA COUNTY

Colleges and universities have contributed to the quality of life in Oklahoma County since World War II. Similar accomplishments have been achieved in the field of health care. In 1945 Oklahoma County had only 14 hospitals, most of which were small clinics. The only large hospitals were St. Anthony's and the State University Hospital. University Hospital was part of the Medical Center on N.E. 13th Street, which also included the University of Oklahoma Medical School and the Crippled Children's Hospital.

In 1946 the Medical Center assumed greater significance when alumni and friends of the medical school launched a drive to raise funds to build a medical research center. That same year the federal government announced plans to construct a 500-bed, $15,000,000 Veterans Hospital across the street. By 1950 both were completed and serving the public.

The Medical Center was the site of more development during the 1960s when the Oklahoma City Urban Renewal Authority initiated plans for governmentally assisted redevelopment and expansion. In 1967, after five years of study, final plans were approved for a massive acquisition and clearing project involving the federal, city, and county governments, the University of Oklahoma, the State Highway Department, the State Health Department, the Board of Education, and the Capitol and Medical Center Improvement and Zoning Commissions. The ambitious project included approximately 250 acres of land between N.E. 8th and N.E. 13th streets and Durland and Stonewall avenues.

By late 1967 the Urban Renewal Authority was actively purchasing and clearing land, preparing it for new streets, utilities, and construction sites. Within a few years the Health Sciences and Basic Sciences Education centers were opened, and a headquarters building for the State Department of Public Health was dedicated. By 1973 more than $63 million had been spent on new development, including the $27 million Presbyterian Hospital.

Located east of Lincoln and south of 13th Street in Oklahoma City, the Medical Center Complex has become one of the region's most complete medical research and care centers. Courtesy, Oklahoma Department of Human Services.

From 1973 to 1980 new investments in the Medical Center Complex included the renovation of University and Children's Memorial hospitals and the construction of the $2.2 million Dean A. McGee Eye Institute. Other new facilities and programs included the College of Nursing, the Library and Learning Resources Center, the College of Pharmacy, the Child Study Center, the Dental College, the Clinical Sciences Center, and the Bio-medical Sciences Center. Today, the Medical Complex is one of the region's most advanced health care and research centers.

Improved health care between 1945 and 1980 was not confined to the urban renewal district. St. Anthony's Hospital, the oldest operating medical facility in the county, expanded and renovated its downtown site. Mercy Hospital, while still at its downtown location, also expanded and updated its facilities, financed by a $1,725,000 fund-raising drive.

Other hospitals were constructed during the postwar era. In 1956 Baptist Hospital was erected on Northwest Highway, only to be expanded 20 years later. Two new hospitals were the high-rise Mercy Health Center on Memorial Road and South Community Medical Tower on S.W. 44th. By 1979 there were 19 major hospitals in the metropolitan area, with approximately 5,000 beds.

Private donations and institutional investment for hospitals reflected the progressive attitude shared by the people of Oklahoma County. This spirit of reform and social improvement was evident in the programs of the Oklahoma City Urban Renewal Authority. While the Medical Center project was being developed, the Urban Renewal Authority was launching two other ambitious redevelopment projects: the John F. Kennedy Housing Project and the Downtown Urban Renewal Project.

The John F. Kennedy Housing project was designed to rehabilitate a depressed 1,258-acre neighborhood bounded by N.E. 23rd Street on the north, N.E. 4th Street on the south, the Medical Center on the west, and Interstate Highway 35 on the east. In 1967, with federal funding approved, Urban Renewal officials began to purchase land in the troubled neighborhood and to relocate families and businesses. Then reconstruction began. The 234-unit Collins Gardens Apartments were built; more than 1,000 new homes were constructed with federal financial assistance; and the 200-unit Marie Curie Plaza for the elderly was erected. Money also was made available for home renovation. Altogether, more than 2,000 living units were provided or upgraded during the urban renewal program, financed at a cost of $28.4 million.

The downtown business district was another target of the Urban Renewal Authority. In 1964, with financial support from the Urban Action Foundation, officials of the Authority hired the architectural firm of I.M. Pei and Associates to prepare a long-range plan for downtown redevelopment. The first product of the plan was Mummers Theater (now the Oklahoma City Theater Center), then the Myriad Convention Center.

Initiated in 1962, the Myriad was financed by two general obligation bond issues, one in 1962 for $5 million, the other in 1968 for $18 million. Extending over a four-block area, the 950,000-square-foot building in-

The Colcord Building, located at the corner of Grand (Sheridan) and Robinson, was spared the wrecking ball when urban renewal cleared three blocks during the early 1970s. Courtesy, Bob Blackburn.

The old Baum Building became a victim of urban renewal in the downtown business district after attempts to save it proved futile. (OHS)

cluded the Great Hall, the Arena, the Exhibit Hall, and numerous meeting rooms. In 1972 the massive complex was dedicated and opened for use.

During that same year the downtown urban renewal project was expanded when the Urban Renewal Authority received permission to purchase a six-block area bounded by Robinson, Grand (Sheridan), Walker, and Park avenues, to be used for a retail complex. In 1974, with $16 million in federal funds and $18.7 million from the city, the Authority began purchasing and razing property for a retail galleria.

After several delays caused by hesitant investors and the economic recession of 1974, an investment firm from Dallas, Texas, was chosen for the development. Construction began in 1979 on American First Tower, a $200-million, 14-story retail building at Main and Robinson. Then came the second and even larger First Oklahoma Tower, a 31-story office complex. Additional offices, department stores, one hotel, and numerous smaller retail shops will also be located in the galleria.

Another current project is Leadership Square, a $70 million office complex to be located between Robinson and Harvey from Park Avenue to Robert S. Kerr Avenue.

Another project envisioned in the Pei Plan was Myriad Gardens, located east of the Convention Center. In 1973, after land had been purchased and cleared by the Urban Renewal Authority, title was transferred to the city government. With a $4.9 million federal grant and additional city funding, the project began in 1977. Bulldozers attacked the site, forming retaining walls, clearing walking paths, and dredging a lake bed. After almost three years of sporadic work, city philanthropists led by Dean A. McGee raised $5 million for a botanical gardens which will be more than 300 feet long and seven stories tall, spanning the lower lake. Construction will begin in January 1982.

Although several significant buildings were destroyed during the evolution of urban renewal, the basic concepts of modernization and development never changed. The program was designed to attract millions of dollars in investments to a suffering inner-city area, to arrest the decline of the downtown environment, and to focus attention on the shortcomings of postwar America. The ultimate results of urban renewal will be judged by future generations.

Whether considered as unnecessary governmental intervention in local affairs or as a second chance for Oklahoma City, urban renewal was the product of a new social attitude that developed during the late 1950s and early 1960s, a belief in man's ability to change and improve his world. This same attitude fueled another movement to reform society—the civil rights movement.

In 1980 the downtown business district began to assume a new appearance. Courtesy, Oklahoma City Urban Renewal Authority.

The black struggle for civil rights in Oklahoma was as old as the state, but demands for social and political equality reached new heights of success during the late 1950s and early 1960s. These victories affected education, voting privileges, jury duty, public transportation, and housing, but the most celebrated episode in the civil rights movement in Oklahoma City was the sit-in movement.

Restaurants owned and patronized by whites long had been segregated in Oklahoma City. Even where blacks were served, they often had to consume their food and drinks outside. In May 1957, the local chapter of the National Association for the Advancement of Colored People (NAACP) organized a committee to contact owners and managers of restaurants about ending this injustice. One year later, after the efforts had achieved little success, black leaders turned to sit-ins, a new method of massive but nonviolent protest.

On August 19, 1958, the first group of black youths staged a sit-in at the lunch counter at Katz Drug Store, located at 200 W. Main. For the next two days the group sat quietly at the counter although they were not served. Then on August 21, after blacks occupied virtually every seat at the counter for two hours that day, the manager ordered his waitresses to serve the youngsters. The first racial barrier had been broken.

For the next six years the sit-ins continued, slowly dismantling the walls of segregation in Oklahoma City restaurants. Some of the victories were hard won. The luncheonette at the downtown John A. Brown Store, for example, resisted sit-ins and demonstrations for almost three years before blacks were allowed service at the store's luncheonette counter. Anna Maude Cafeteria and Bishop's Restaurant resisted until 1963, despite repeated sit-ins and protest demonstrations. In 1964, after years of organizing and suffering, civil rights leaders announced that not one restaurant could be found in Oklahoma City that would

HEART OF THE PROMISED LAND: AN ILLUSTRATED HISTORY OF OKLAHOMA COUNTY

Demonstrations by blacks in Oklahoma City continued throughout the early 1960s in a fight against discrimination. Restaurants in the city that were owned and patronized by whites had a long history of segregation. Courtesy, Oklahoma Publishing Company.

not serve blacks. The struggle for equality between the races continued well beyond the sit-in era, spreading to amusement parks, swimming pools, and the public school system. The efforts proved successful, for by the mid-1970s, public and legal segregation had been destroyed in Oklahoma City.

The black community of Oklahoma City wielded such influence partially due to its newly discovered consumer power. New jobs with better wages enabled black families to purchase better housing, to improve educational opportunities, and to attract the attention of businessmen.

One of the most important sources of employment after the war for both blacks and whites was Tinker Air Force Base. When World War II ended, Tinker was only one of many Air Force bases maintained in the continental United States. While other facilities were dismantled during the postwar era Tinker survived, for it was an air depot, not just an assembly plant. Providing parts and maintenance services for the nation's fleet of aircraft during the Cold War era, the base maintained a secure place in the defense structure.

From 1952 to 1958, however, the Air Force closed 23 bases in a move to economize. Tinker was saved only through the swift and effective action of city leaders such as Stanley Draper, who spent months in Washington, D.C., lobbying for its survival. Draper and his allies in Oklahoma County secured a 640-acre site for a base hospital, committed more than $5 million for the purchase of 12,000 acres of land around the base, and developed plans for a four-lane highway from the base to the downtown business district of Oklahoma City. Such action convinced federal officials to continue funding Tinker.

Throughout the 1960s and 1970s Tinker remained an active link in the nation's defense strategy. Training units were moved to the base, maintenance facilities were opened, and storage capabilities were ex-

This AWAC, a converted 707 with a radar scanner mounted on the fuselage, was assigned to the Tactical Air Command Wing at Tinker Air Force Base. This aircraft serves as part of the early warning defense system of the United States Air Force. Courtesy, Tinker Air Force Base.

panded. Then, in 1977, the Air Force assigned a Tactical Air Command Wing to the base. Converted 707s with large radar scanners mounted on the fuselages, the E3As brought new importance, more personnel, and increased investment to Tinker.

By 1982 the various units at Tinker employed more than 25,000 civilian and Air Force personnel and distributed more than $500 million each year in wages. The influence of the base on Oklahoma City, Midwest City, Del City, Choctaw, Spencer, Nicoma Park, Jones, and the entire section of central Oklahoma has been of unmatched importance since 1941.

As exemplified by Tinker Air Force Base, aviation has played a major role in the economic development of Oklahoma County. Private aviation in the county dates to the era of Orville and Wilbur Wright, a time when adventurous young men piloted their canvas-covered craft over the landscape of central Oklahoma. Later came barnstormers and airshows. Then private companies such as the locally organized and owned Braniff Airlines and the innovative Aero Design and Engineering Company blazed new paths in aviation history.

To accommodate the growing fleet of aircraft, the county has provided a number of airports, beginning in 1919, when the Chamber of Commerce leased an 80-acre site on the Oklahoma-Cleveland county line for a municipal airport. By 1930 Oklahoma City served as an air terminus for several commercial carriers, including Braniff Airlines, Bowen Airlines, Transcontinental Air Transport, and Western Air Express, as well as the growing fleet of private planes.

In 1931, confronted with the limitations of a small air field on May Avenue, the people of Oklahoma City approved a bond issue to purchase a 640-acre site for a new airport. Located southwest of the

A tornado struck Oklahoma City in 1946, damaging many of the aircraft stored at Tinker Air Force Base. Courtesy, Tinker Air Force Base.

intersection of S.W. 59th and Meridian, Municipal Airport opened in 1932. In 1941 the Army Air Corps assumed total control of the airport, renamed it Will Rogers Field, and stationed a light bombardment group there. By the end of the war the base included more than 1,200 acres, 35 buildings, and five hangars.

After the war Will Rogers Airport became an important stop on commercial aviation flight patterns. Eventually, most of the major carriers, including Trans World Airlines, Braniff, American, Continental, and United, would establish operations in Oklahoma City. The potential of Will Rogers Airport was enhanced in 1946 when city and chamber officials convinced the federal government to move the Civil Aeronautics Administration's (CAA) Standardization Center to the field. As an inducement, the city provided $150,000 for moving expenses, two hangars, and a headquarters building. Later in the year the CAA also moved its administration and training centers to the airport.

Like the CAA (later renamed the Mike Monroney Federal Aeronautics Administration) Center, the airport expanded. In April 1965 construction began on an $11.2 million terminal and runway expansion project. On December 2, 1966, the new 200,000-square-foot terminal and the east north-to-south parallel runway were dedicated and opened to use. By 1980 the airport had expanded to 7,400 acres, making it the third largest airport in area in the United States.

The growth of Will Rogers World Airport represented a dramatic transition in American life—from the era of railroading to the age of aviation. As the airport attracted more passengers each day, the Union and Santa Fe depots downtown lost customers. By 1960 the Union Depot was vacant and the Santa Fe Depot was only a shadow of its former self. Another facet of the transportation revolution was the

Workers on this Tinker Air Force Base production line assembled GAM-77 Hound Dog Missiles during the early 1960s. Courtesy, Oklahoma Publishing Company.

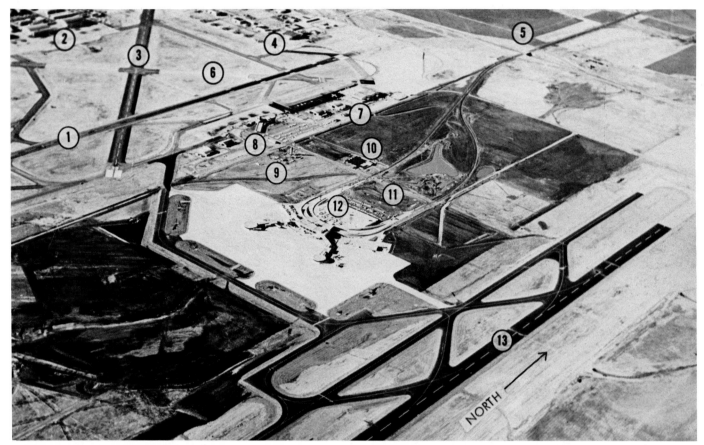

Will Rogers World Airport, renovated and expanded in 1966, is a complex of various agencies and facilities. Shown are: 1) the old instrumented north-south runway; 2) FAA Aeronautical Center; 3) north-west-southeast runway; 4) Oklahoma Air National Guard; 5) Southwest 54th and Meridian exchange; 6) northeast-southwest runway; 7) general aviation facilites; 8) old terminal; 9) new tower under construction; 10) rental car service; 11) Coleman plaza; 12) new terminal and parking; 13) new north-south runway. Courtesy, Oklahoma Publishing Company.

demise of streetcars and interurbans and the increased use of automobiles and trucks. This transition was reflected in the phenomenal surge of postwar highway construction in Oklahoma County.

The first major addition to the highways of the county began in 1947, when businessmen of Oklahoma City and Tulsa proposed a new superhighway between the two urban outposts. They approached Governor Roy Turner with the idea of a turnpike, financed with self-liquidating bonds and retired by revenues from tolls. Turner seized the opportunity and led the fight in the legislature. Finally, with businessmen providing $48,000 for initial expenses, the state created the Oklahoma Turnpike Authority. After spending $48 million raised from bond sales, officials would dedicate the 88-mile Turner Turnpike on May 17, 1953.

In 1948, with plans for the turnpike still in preliminary stages, civic leaders in Oklahoma City developed the idea for a super highway from the turnpike to the downtown business district. The plan included a divided four-lane highway from the toll booth to N.W. 50th Street (N.E. Highway), a traffic circle at the head of Classen Boulevard (where the old streetcars made a turn-around), a four-lane highway northwest from the Classen Circle to May Avenue (N.W. Highway), and a four-lane highway along Route 66 to May Avenue (39th Expressway). The bypass was completed in 1953.

From 1950 to 1956 the county and city governments pushed for four-lane highways in other sections of the metropolitan area. Located on the rights-of-way of former trolley lines, the most important roads

HEART OF THE PROMISED LAND: AN ILLUSTRATED HISTORY OF OKLAHOMA COUNTY

completed were Shields Boulevard south of S.E. 25th, Classen Boulevard from the Classen Circle to downtown, and N.W. 39th Expressway from May Avenue to MacArthur Avenue.

In 1956 highway construction in the state received a major boost when Congress passed the Federal Aid Highway Act, a program under which the federal government would pay for 90 percent of the costs on four-lane, limited access highways. The master plan for this national system of interstate highways included three major routes through Oklahoma—I-35, I-40, and I-44—all of which passed through Oklahoma County.

The first stage of the interstate highway system in the county consisted of the two primary arteries, I-35 and I-40. Much of the right-of-way already was owned, for the city still held title to the right-of-way for Grand Boulevard, which circled the city, and the Chamber of Commerce had been purchasing options on land since 1948. With minimal trouble in securing right-of-way, construction soon was underway. In 1958 the first section of I-35 was opened to traffic, stretching from the N.E. Highway south to N.E. 23rd Street. One year later the highway was extended to Byers Avenue.

Meanwhile, work began on a part of I-40 known originally as the Tinker Diagonal. Costing $4.7 million, this stretch of interstate highway ran from Tinker Air Force Base and S.E. 29th Street west and north until it tied in with I-35. By 1965, I-35 was completed south to Norman and I-40 was completed from Midwest City west across the elevated Draper Expressway and on toward El Reno.

The I-240 and I-35 interchange south of Oklahoma City is shown here under construction. These freeways, planned in the late 1950s, were completed during the mid-1970s. Courtesy, Oklahoma Department of Highways.

With I-35 and I-40 near completion in the county, highway officials turned their attention to an intra-city system of four-lane superhighways that would encircle the city. The first leg completed was Southwest (74th Street) Expressway. Extending from I-35 west to the recently completed H.E. Bailey Turnpike, the highway was opened to traffic in the mid-1960s. Then the rest of I-240 followed after 1969, when contracts were let for pavement along the west side of town and east of I-35. These highways were completed during the mid-1970s.

Many of the postwar advances in Oklahoma County—Tinker Air Force Base, the FAA Center, Will Rogers World Airport, and the interstate highway system—shared a common element: they required the combined resources of city, county, state, and federal governments. The levels of massive spending needed for those developments, however, would have been impossible without an expanding and prosperous business community.

After 1956 the combined influences of industrial expansion and public spending in the Oklahoma City metropolitan area were reflected in an important economic indicator—capital investment. In 1956 business and government committed $131 million to growth in the Oklahoma City metropolitan area. That increased to $216 million in 1960, $280 million in 1962, and $333 million in 1967. Moreover, from 1960 to 1967 the number of industrial jobs in the city increased more than 85 percent. This provided a significant boost to the economy, for every 100 jobs in industry supported 74 additional jobs in service-related fields. With this expansion, the population of the metropolitan area increased from 325,352 in 1950 to 534,902 in 1960.

From 1968 to 1970 the economy of Oklahoma City progressed at an even quicker pace, fueled by urban renewal activity, wartime production, and the rising level of industrial investment. An overt sign of this boom was the burst of major construction in the downtown business district. In 1968 Kerr-McGee announced that it would construct a 30-story tower between Robinson and Broadway just north of Robert S. Kerr Avenue (2nd Street). That same year Liberty National Bank announced plans for a 35-story skyscraper east of Broadway. Then Fidelity Bank N.A. released plans for an 18-story building and park. Together, these additions brought a new spirit of prosperity and hope to a depressed downtown.

During this boom commercial construction also spread along the interstate highways, where land was inexpensive and plants could efficiently utilize the expanding trucking industry. Industrial development just along I-40 during 1969 indicates the scope of this construction boom. During that year, General Electric Company broke ground for a major plant on 1,006 acres of land at I-40 and Morgan Road; Dayton Tire and Rubber Company opened a plant on Meridian Avenue just south of I-40; CMI Corporation constructed a massive plant for the manufacture of paving and earth-moving equipment at I-40 and Morgan Road; and Xerox opened a plant even farther west at I-40 and Mustang Road.

Wholesale and distribution firms added to the construction boom, as many firms abandoned the traditional warehouse district downtown for sites along suburban highways. In April 1969, for example, the

Facing page
This map illustrates the post-World War II distribution of industrial development in Oklahoma County. The dark area in the center is the downtown business district of Oklahoma City, and the dots indicate industrial districts or sites. Courtesy, Bob Blackburn.

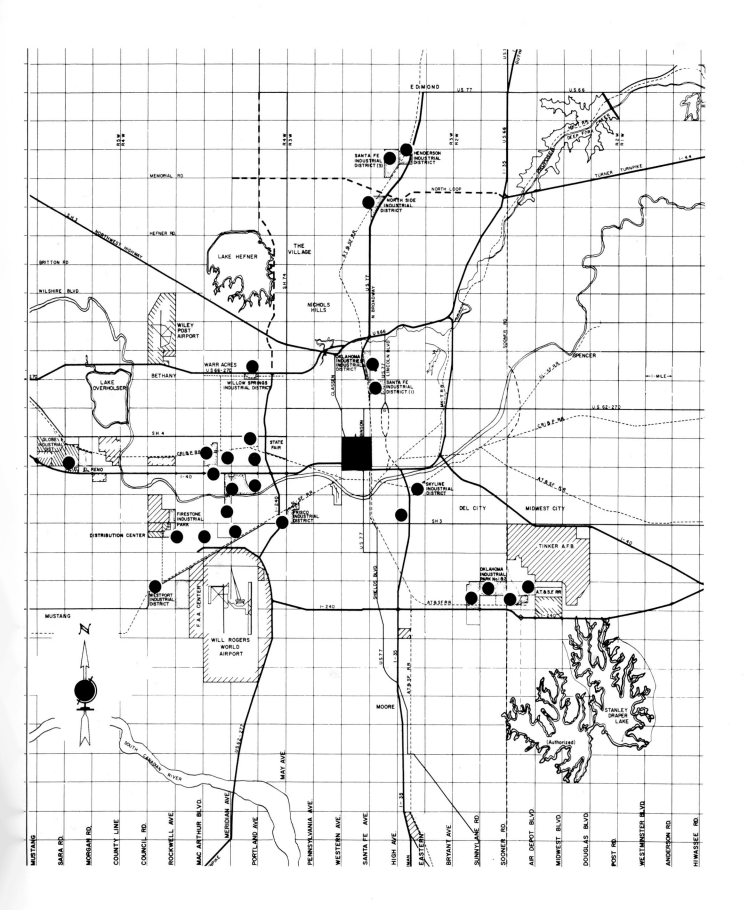

Trammel-Crow Company of Dallas opened a 236-acre industrial park off I-40 at Meridian Avenue. Within a few years the park was filling with companies attracted to the uncongested highways and the unlimited room for expansion, two elements lacking in the old warehouse district.

The economic boom in Oklahoma City came to an abrupt halt in 1974. Two of the most important reasons for this setback were the Arab oil boycott and the decline in wartime production. Urban renewal projects, which had looked so promising in 1970, were abandoned temporarily; inflation soared to record levels; General Motors cancelled plans to construct a large assembly plant; and the construction industry suffered from widespread unemployment, an accurate sign of economic decline.

Located east of the Santa Fe tracks and north of the KATY tracks, this old warehouse district has been largely abandoned by wholesale and distribution firms. The companies moved to industrial districts located on the expanding system of highways. The area is now being renovated as an office park. Courtesy, Bob Blackburn.

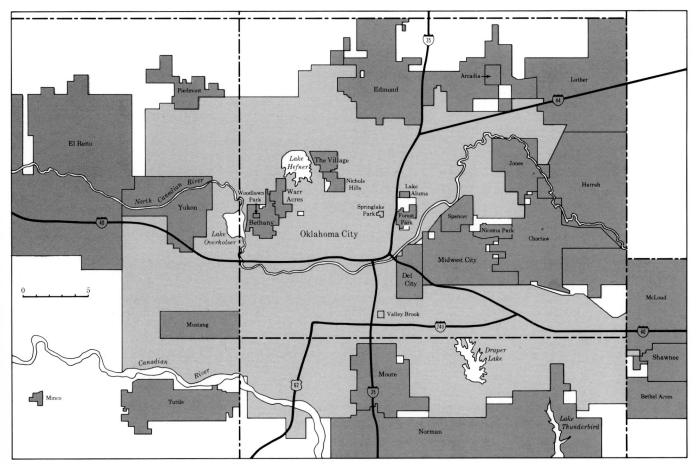

Gradually, the business community fought back. In 1977 a new developer was found for the multi-million dollar retail galleria project downtown; residential construction picked up; and then, General Motors announced that it would proceed with construction of the assembly plant. Located along I-240 east of I-35, the new plant was designed to assemble front-wheel drive, fuel-efficient automobiles. In April 1979 the first automobile rolled off the assembly line. By the end of 1979 more than 5,400 workers were employed at the plant, and more than $120 million in wages were distributed annually.

Although important, the General Motors plant was only one strand in the economic fabric of Oklahoma County in 1980. Officials of the company would not have even considered Oklahoma City if it had not been for the active promotion of the Chamber of Commerce, the availability of investment capital in local banks, and the excellent transportation system. All of this was the legacy of the postwar era of prosperity in Oklahoma County.

As victories were won in business, civil rights, health care, and education, similar advances were made in the cultural environment of Oklahoma County. One of the oldest and most important centers for regional study and education was the Oklahoma Historical Society, located on Lincoln Boulevard southeast of the Capitol. The Historical Society maintains extensive exhibits on Indians, pioneers, and modern Oklahomans, and its library and archives have become nationally famous, while its publications program has made rapid progress.

Oklahoma County consists of a patchwork of incorporated towns and cities. Oklahoma City is represented by the lighter shade of gray. From Historical Atlas of Oklahoma, *University of Oklahoma Press, 1976.*

The Oklahoma Historical Society, housed in this building southeast of the Oklahoma State Capitol, serves as a cornerstone of cultural study and preservation. This photograph, taken shortly after World War II, shows the oil well located to the south of the building. (OHS)

Since World War II Oklahoma County has earned a reputation as a center for museums. In 1965 western history enthusiasts opened the Cowboy Hall of Fame and Western Heritage Center. Located on Persimmon Hill northeast of the business district, the center includes a National Rodeo Hall of Fame, a Hall of Great Western Performers, and extensive art galleries. Acquisitions and new programs are continually developed at this world-famous cultural center.

In 1969 the Oklahoma Historical Society and the Cowboy Hall of Fame were joined in "Lincoln Park Country" by the Firefighters' Museum, founded and operated by the Oklahoma Firefighters' Association. In 1973 yet another museum opened its doors near the Lincoln Park Zoo. The Softball Hall of Fame, moved to Oklahoma City from New Jersey in 1966, maintains a new building dedicated to the national history of softball.

The next addition to Lincoln Park Country was the Kirkpatrick Center. Opened in February 1978, the 800,000-square-foot building houses the Omniplex, the Kirkpatrick Planetarium, the Air-Space Museum, the Center of the American Indian, the African Gallery, the Japanese Gallery, and the U.S. Navy Gallery. Attracting more than 100,000 men, women, and children each year, the Kirkpatrick Center has added greatly to the cultural and educational offerings of Oklahoma County.

Other cultural sites in the county that contribute to the quality of life are: the Oklahoma Heritage Association, formerly the Oklahoma Hall of Fame, which owns and operates the Heritage House at N.W. 14th and Robinson Avenue; the Harn House, an authentic pioneer home complete with furnishings and a reconstructed barn; and the Overholser Mansion, a Victorian-style home located at 15th and Hudson in Oklahoma City. All of this cultural variety is enhanced by numerous art galleries and museums, making Oklahoma County a true center of learning.

The old Union Station in Oklahoma City, abandoned during the 1950s when railroad passenger traffic declined, is one of the historic structures in Oklahoma County that are being renovated for modern use. Courtesy, Bob Blackburn.

To encourage and stimulate the study of local heritage, concerned individuals organized the Oklahoma County Historical Society in 1978. This dedicated group of men and women in just a few years has funded a major survey of historic properties in the county, published and released a book on significant commercial buildings in the county, and carried the fight for preservation and education into the public arena.

Through the efforts of such organizations, and with the support of all men and women who appreciate the value of the past, the history and heritage of Oklahoma County will be preserved. The result will surely be a greater appreciation and understanding of the county's fascinating and inspiring history.

Constructed in 1909-1910, the Oklahoman Building has been renovated with the original design and ornament intact. Such preservation projects enrich the physical environment of the city and county for future generations. Courtesy, Bob Blackburn.

A "Vast and Glorious" Land

n 1826 Thomas James, the first American explorer to enter future Oklahoma County, described the uninhabited land as "a very fertile and beautiful country." Washington Irving, another intrepid traveler who passed through the county six years later marveled at the frontier's flora and fauna, writing in his journal about the "vast and glorious prairie."

The oceans of grass and "impenetrable" forests still exist in Oklahoma County. The 20th century with its revolutionary progress has altered that landscape, but in many ways a new dimension has been added. Where once only shoulder-high grass blanketed the prairies, skyscrapers pierce the clouds. Where once sturdy oaks dotted the red earth, oil derricks probe for black crude.

David Fitzgerald, noted photographer and interpreter of the physical environment of Oklahoma, has captured the spirit and character of our county in photographs. Through his lens we envision the bounty and isolation of rural farmland, the scope and splendor of statuary and architecture, and the vitality and color of native flowers and trees. Using an artist's eye for beauty and a scholar's sense of history, Fitzgerald has preserved an image which reflects the varied life-style possible in Oklahoma County. Indeed, this collection of color photographs reveals the beauty of this "vast and glorious" land.

Facing page
At one time each quarter-section of farmland in Oklahoma County had at least one farmhouse. Today, with mechanized large-scale agriculture, many of those houses stand vacant, monuments to early pioneers who struggled against wind, drought, and low crop prices. Photo by David Fitzgerald.

Large-scale murals by renowned artist Charles Banks Wilson bring the history of Oklahoma to life in the rotunda of the Oklahoma State Capitol Building. Photo by David Fitzgerald.

HEART OF THE PROMISED LAND: AN ILLUSTRATED HISTORY OF OKLAHOMA COUNTY

Above
The Overholser Mansion, a museum of the Oklahoma Historical Society, is a landmark historic house in an elegant inner-city neighborhood of Oklahoma City. Photo by David Fitzgerald.

Left
Union Station Depot, constructed in 1930 by the Frisco and Rock Island railroads, has been renovated by a local business firm. After sitting vacant for 20 years, the Spanish-style structure once again fills an important place in the life of Oklahoma City. Photo by David Fitzgerald.

A VAST AND GLORIOUS LAND

187

Facing page
Looking from north to south, this view of downtown Oklahoma City reveals the flat terrain surrounding the Capitol City. Photo by David Fitzgerald.

Elaborate detail decorates the Southwestern Bell Telehone Building, an ornate structure designed by the architectural firm of Layton, Hicks, and Forsythe (above and right), and the Pioneer Telephone Building in downtown Oklahoma City, a creative masterpiece of architect William A. Wells (top). Photos by David Fitzgerald.

A VAST AND GLORIOUS LAND

Although in the Sun Belt, Oklahoma County receives varying amounts of snowfall each year, ranging from light flurries to blinding blizzards. Photo by David Fitzgerald.

Anyone who has seen a sunset on the western horizon of Oklahoma County understands the lure of "the Promised Land." Photo by David Fitzgerald.

HEART OF THE PROMISED LAND: AN ILLUSTRATED HISTORY OF OKLAHOMA COUNTY

Below
Section line roads divide the rich farmland of the county into 640-acre squares and provide farm-to-market access for stockmen and grain producers. Photo by David Fitzgerald.

Above
Winter wheat, the major cash crop of central Oklahoma farmers, pushes through the sod every fall. Photo by David Fitzgerald.

Facing page
Grain elevators in the western section of the county store rich harvests of wheat each spring. Photo by David Fitzgerald.

A VAST AND GLORIOUS LAND

Downtown Luther is gradually recovering from a decades-long decline, as are many small towns in Oklahoma County. Photo by David Fitzgerald

A view of Northwest Oklahoma City shows St. Anthony's Hospital in the foreground to Lake Hefner on the horizon. Photo by David Fitzgerald.

Located next to the old Route 66, the Round Barn of Arcadia is one of the most recognized landmarks of central Oklahoma. Photo by David Fitzgerald.

Luther's old bus station remains standing as a remnant of the time when Americans traveled west on Route 66. Photo by David Fitzgerald.

A VAST AND GLORIOUS LAND

Above
The Land Run, *an original painting in the collections of the Oklahoma Historical Society, captures the excitement of April 22, 1889. (OHS)*

Held each spring on the grounds of the Civic Center Music Hall, the Oklahoma City Arts Festival attracts thousands of artists, craftspeople, and visitors to the city. Photo by David Fitzgerald.

This mountain gorilla is only one of the many attractions at Oklahoma City's Lincoln Park Zoo. Photo by David Fitzgerald.

Facing page
This wagon, on display at the State Museum of the Oklahoma Historical Society, was used in two of Oklahoma's five land runs. The original owner finally claimed 160 acres of prime farmland. (OHS).

*Oklahoma City's skyline shines at night
as a landmark of prosperity and vigor.
Photo by David Fitzgerald.*

Facing pag
A gas flare from a deep well's rig burn
as a sign of economic strength and cor
tinued prosperity for both county an
state. Photo by David Fitzgeral

A VAST AND GLORIOUS LAND

199

Partners in Progress

Few sights compare with the quiet beauty of the orange sunset in what is now Oklahoma County. The sameness of the spectacle through the years brings a time for reflection and a pleasant awareness of the past as few other scenes do.

The constantly changing and growing skyline of the city and the increasing numbers of people who thrive within it are in sharp contrast to the calm of the sunset. To its citizens, Oklahoma County is still the frontier in both potential and spirit. Two generations ago cattle and the coming of the railroad provided the magnet that attracted new residents. Now it is oil and aircraft that draw people to the area. Here there is a fresh start, and new opportunities that can challenge all who care to accept them.

In recent years the wide-open frontier, cattletown, boomtown appearance has been tempered by the "vestiges of culture"—museums, theater, ballet, symphony, and a recognition that the county has a history and heritage that should be preserved. The residents seem torn between enjoyment of these and a lingering reluctance to admit that their "overgrown cow town" might be losing some of its raw newness.

The small businesses, the wildcat operations, are becoming meshed with national and international companies. The city is being drawn into closer ties with the cultures of other parts of the world, but since the constancy of growth and change are so pervasive its inhabitants take this in their stride.

The citizens of Oklahoma County are, then, a people who have no choice but to go forward with technology into a challenging world. They are a people who must and will come to identify their interests with those of others far away, outside the traditional circle of their loyalties and political responsibilities. Oklahoma companies and institutions are aware of the need for innovation and progress. Its corporate leaders are proud of their efforts to build and modernize. Its citizens exhibit the frontier willingness to work hard and long for their betterment. Their labor and products are part of the increasingly complex global markets.

There is a common thread that links the scenes and memories of Oklahoma—the spectacle of life in all its varied manifestations as it has appeared, evolved, and sometimes died out. The quiet, glorious Oklahoma sunset offers but a fleeting moment for reflection, amidst the dynamic flood of people, ideas, and industry that carries us into the future of this wonderful land.

Facing page
Commercial construction has long been an accurate barometer for the economic climate in Oklahoma. In 1982 suburban commercial construction reached all-time records, reflecting the continued expansion of Oklahoma City. Photo by David Fitzgerald.

Amarex Inc.

In January 1970, a six-month-old Oklahoma City drilling company took a gamble that is now paying big returns. The oil business is accustomed to risks, but when it was announced that the fledgling Amarex intended to spend six million dollars to purchase seismic data on 12,000 miles of land plus 311,000 acres of leases in the Anadarko Basin, older hands wondered. In March 1970 John Mason was made exploration manager. Mason had been a geologist for Standard Oil of Indiana for 20 years and had studied the basin thoroughly. He brought to Amarex a unique, uncanny ability to target the right move at the right time.

Also in 1970 LeRoy Belcher, a certified public accountant who is now executive vice-president, joined the company. His expertise was needed because the ARCO purchase left Amarex with a sizable debt that had to be serviced and with almost no operating capital.

Over the next four years Amarex sold select packages to service the debt and build cash flow. The company sold its first sizable drilling fund in 1971. Through low-risk drilling, it built a strong base of long-lived reserves. All drilling programs were public until 1974, when the advent of the Securities and Exchange Commission's Rule 146 allowed the company to deal exclusively with private drilling funds.

When Congress passed the Natural Gas Policy Act in 1978, the resultant price increase for natural gas discovered below 5,000 feet caused onshore deep gas reserves to become the center of oil and gas exploration in the United States. Amarex decided to focus on the Anadarko Basin and the Tuscaloosa Trend in southern Louisiana. The firm created a favorable position in both areas by aggressive drilling

View of the Antelope Hills in western Oklahoma's Anadarko Basin, whose rich, deep gas deposits have contributed enormously to Amarex's success.

and acreage leasing programs. When it had achieved a sound financial base, Amarex expanded its activities into other areas. It acquired leases in the Rocky Mountain Overthrust Belts and in Alaska. It also moved into related fields by organizing Global Fluids, Inc., to market drilling fluids and assist well operators in the initial design of drilling fluid programs. At the same time the company acquired partial ownership of the historic Colcord Building in Oklahoma City, where

In 1970 John Mason gambled with his unique ability to target the right move at the right time. Today he serves as president and chief executive officer of the highly successful Amarex Inc.

its corporate headquarters is now located.

The outlook for Amarex is bright and its financial posture today is sound by even the most conservative measures—because over a decade ago John Mason was willing to take an extraordinary gamble and LeRoy Belcher was able to devise a highly successful means of financing that gamble. Since then they have both worked to develop a strong team to ensure that the success will continue.

Leroy Belcher brought his accounting expertise to Amarex. He now serves as Amarex's executive vice-president and oversees the company's prosperity.

Baptist Medical Center of Oklahoma

Oklahoma City's first major full-service hospital located outside the downtown area of the city opened its doors on April 15, 1959, just seven days before the 70th anniversary of the Run of 1889. Situated on the city's highest point, Baptist Memorial Hospital represented a dream come true for Oklahoma Baptists.

Dr. Andrew Potter, executive secretary of the Oklahoma Baptist General Convention, in 1946 conceived the idea that became Baptist Memorial Hospital, and later, Baptist Medical Center. He died before the dream became reality, but his successor, Dr. T.B. Lackey, coordi-

James L. Henry, administrator of Baptist Memorial Hospital (left foreground), watches as Edward L. Gaylord, chairman of the Phase Two fund-raising committee (with shovel), begins the groundbreaking ceremony for the expansion project.

nated the project to completion with the help of a planning committee including Dr. H.H. Hobbs, Dr. Auguie Henry, the Reverend Anson Justice, U.S. Senator Robert Kerr, Dr. M.E. Ramay, Bryce Twitty, Judge W.R. Wallace, and R.A. Young.

Former Governor Raymond Gary served as honorary chairman of a fund-raising campaign in which Oklahoma City and County residents contributed one million dollars toward the $4.6-million hospital. The remainder came from Baptist churches as well as a large number of individuals.

The hospital opened under the administration of John Hendricks with 200 beds, a maternity ward, laboratory, pediatrics unit, physical therapy area, diagnostic and therapeutic radiology, 24-hour emergency room, operating rooms, and 206 employees, including nurses. James L. Henry became administrator in 1960; he continues to serve today as president. Henry G. Bennett, M.D., has served as the chief of the medical and dental staff since the hospital's beginning.

Demand for services began to exceed facilities in just three years, with the hospital reaching an occupancy rate of 93 percent. In response, Senator Kerr held a breakfast at his ranch home in 1962,

securing pledges of $800,000 from his distinguished guests and setting a goal of two million dollars for the expansion campaign. The Phase Two addition was completed in 1965, adding the hospital's first intensive and coronary care units and another 200 patient care beds.

More than 27 percent of the total patient load came from outside the metropolitan area. By 1969 occupancy was again past the 90-percent point. Phase Three planning began in 1972, to bring the medical center to a total of 563 beds. That same year the name was changed to Baptist Medical Center to reflect more accurately its comprehensive functions and services. The first adult burn center in Oklahoma City opened on its third floor in 1975.

The institution incorporated as a nonsectarian not-for-profit entity, separated from the Baptist General Convention in 1978. Baptist Medical Center has always led the way in Oklahoma open-heart procedures. Three new 12-bed critical-care units were completed in 1981. In all, Baptist Medical Center combines high technology and concern for quality health care for the region.

Aerial view of Baptist Medical Center of Oklahoma.

Beard Oil Company

Beard Oil Company is a 58-year-old, family controlled independent oil company with exploration, development, and production activities in most of the leading petroleum-producing states in the United States.

The history of the firm began when Joseph Beard, the father of the organization's current chairman, William M. Beard, moved to Duncan, Oklahoma, in 1922 to sell lumber for Dierks Lumber Company. He quickly realized that most of the lumber he was selling was being used to construct drilling rigs, so, appreciating the potential of the oil and gas industry, he built a drilling rig for himself and became a drilling contractor.

A short time later he also became a producer, acquiring a lease in the Empire field in Stephens County, Oklahoma. Operating as a producer-contractor he was moderately successful in the Duncan area. In 1930 he moved his rigs to the newly discovered East Texas field, purchasing several leases, one of which is still producing today. Although the price of oil dropped as low as 10 cents per barrel he survived this period and became a very successful producer in the East Texas field.

Encouraged by this success he sold part of the East Texas production and embarked on a string of consecutive wildcat dry holes in Texas and Oklahoma. Becoming more conservative, he returned to the Duncan area to explore for shallow production, achieving moderate success. He continued to operate as a contractor until his death in 1950.

Following Beard's death the company operated as an estate until 1958, at which time Beard Oil, a partnership, was formed. The present Beard Oil Company was incorporated in June 1969 when John Beard, the older of the two sons managing the partnership, decided to take his proportionate share of the partnership and become an independent oil operator. Today John Beard is a successful independent operator in Oklahoma City.

Immediately following the incorporation of the company, William Beard analyzed the operating environment of the oil and gas industry, and recognized that the industry was in a recession. Crude oil prices ranged between $2.75 and $3 per barrel and natural gas prices ranged from 10 to 15 cents per MCF. Beard made the decision to reinvest most of the firm's available cash flow in additional leasehold acreage. Today one of Beard Oil's most significant assets is its large inventory of undeveloped oil and gas leases, totaling approximately 1.8 million net acres located in 20 states.

In 1973 Herb Mee, Jr., a lifelong friend of Beard, joined the firm as president and director. Mee had previously been president and chief executive of Woods Corporation. One of the first functions Mee coordinated was to take the company public in February 1974. Beard Oil has grown dramatically since then, achieving record revenues of $22 million and profits of $4.4 million in 1980.

Beard Oil Company currently employs 145 people, including those in its Denver exploration office and United States Pollution Control, Inc., a wholly owned subsidiary that provides industrial waste disposal services primarily in Oklahoma. The firm also owns an interest in 12 drilling rigs that operate in Oklahoma and Wyoming and an interest in North American Brine Resources, a newly formed joint venture for the production and sale of iodine recovered from waste brine in North America.

William M. Beard, chairman of Beard Oil Company.

The Bolen Companies

The Bolen Companies are one of the largest complete automotive establishments in the United States, including one of the national sales-leading Oldsmobile dealerships; four imported car dealerships representing Mercedes-Benz, Toyota, Peugeot, Ferrari, Alfa-Romeo, Isuzu, and Fiat; three leasing companies; an automobile insurance agency; three Ajax car rental franchises; and two tire and accessory centers. These firms are all controlled by the family-owned Bolen Investment Company. Ralph L. Bolen, chief executive officer, is an engineering graduate of the University of Oklahoma.

Bolen began his career in the automobile business in 1938. Today he is a nationally known speaker on the successful operation of automobile dealerships with primary emphasis on competent, intelligent management and financial planning. By becoming the dominant industry in the nation, the automobile transformed life in the United States. Because of the distances and lack of public transportation in Oklahoma, the vehicle was an absolute necessity to function in society. In this trend, since 1958 the Bolen automotive enterprises have expanded dramatically and continuously.

The Bolen Companies adhere to the philosophy that each customer must find it rewarding to seek fulfillment of all automotive needs by "Rollin' into Bolen's" year after year. This commitment to service excellence is well-known assurance that here the customer will find 250 highly qualified, loyal employees dedicated to providing first class sales and service at reasonable prices. Continued stability and growth is proof of the success of these policies.

Ralph Bolen, Mrs. Bolen, and two sons, Frank and Don (all active in the operation of the business), are steadily involved in civic, social, charitable, and other worthwhile affairs. Community service and membership on dozens of important boards are all a way of life with the Bolen family.

Ralph Bolen is a leader in the design and creation of the new downtown Oklahoma City and the nationally acclaimed medical center. For years, in the pioneering stages, as chairman of the Oklahoma City Urban Renewal Authority, it was his responsibility to create a mutual understanding between the citizens of Oklahoma City and the various developing organizations involved. Fulfillment of this early dream, sometimes frustrating, is a source of unsurpassed enjoyment.

The Bolen Companies have become a notable part of the history of Oklahoma County, through their leadership and popularity. The Bolen family has helped to ensure the social fabric of the county with their personal efforts in a variety of areas.

Ralph L. Bolen has built his early Oldsmobile dealership into many related companies while giving of his time and resources for civic and charitable causes.

John A. Brown Company

Like so many others, John Albert Brown came to Guthrie, Oklahoma, in 1907 searching for greater opportunity. He had worked in his cousin's dry goods store in Emporia, Kansas, and soon sent for his cousin, Anson Rorabaugh, to join him in the mercantile business in Guthrie. In 1909 he formed another partnership when he married Della Dunkin, a music teacher.

Brown and Rorabaugh purchased the Brock Dry Goods Company in Oklahoma City in 1915. At its opening, this store had the distinction of being the smallest in the city. That didn't last long. The company grew steadily as Rorabaugh-Brown. It continued its growth after Brown bought out his cousin in 1932 and renamed it the John A. Brown Company. By 1934 Brown's had become the largest store in the entire state. Located at 213 West Main, the facility expanded into nine buildings on 11 acres in the heart of downtown Oklahoma City. Countless Oklahomans navigated the conglomerated space that ranged from a full basement and three floors on Main Street to five floors fronting on Parking Avenue. Brown's justifiably proclaimed that it was "Oklahoma Born, Oklahoma Owned, and Oklahoma Managed."

In 1935 an affiliated store, Brown-Dunkin, was opened in Tulsa. Mrs. Brown was the president and treasurer of this venture and her brother ran the store. The experience she gained in Tulsa helped her when, in 1940, John A. Brown died and she became president of the John A. Brown Company. The year 1940 marked Brown's Silver Jubilee, and was also the beginning of an even greater growth period. Under Della Brown's leadership, the College Corner store opened in Norman in 1941 and a Capitol Hill store opened in 1948. During 1960, the Brown-Duncan store in Tulsa was sold so that Duncan could go into the cattle business and the 127,000-square-foot Penn Square branch store was opened.

In 1967, two years after the company celebrated its 50th anniversary, Mrs. Brown died and Laura Ambrose Long guided the business until 1971, when it was acquired by the Dayton Hudson Corporation. Dayton Hudson's offer was accepted because of that firm's proven commitment to customers, employees, and community.

Today, this multimillion-dollar operation is represented by five major department stores, the Norman specialty store, a large distribution center on North Lincoln Boulevard in Oklahoma City, and the headquarters building in the Capitol Hill area. It employs approximately 1,600 Oklahomans.

The firm maintains the traditional Brown quality and supports the worthwhile cultural and civic activities of the community. Its operation and growth continue the Brown tradition in a manner that John A. and Della Brown would commend, as do Brown's longtime and new customers and employees.

The Main Street entrance to the rambling John A. Brown store as it appeared in the 1950s. This building was destroyed by urban renewal in 1974.

CMI Corporation

The extraordinary growth of the young CMI Corporation under the leadership of Bill Swisher is evidence of Oklahoma County's vitality. CMI was formed in 1964 to bring automation to the nation's road-building program. No one had developed a machine to produce grade within the close tolerance needed for the modern interstate expressway work. CMI filled that void with its autograde trimmer, which revolutionized the road-building industry. The autograde could produce and match grade to within one-eighth inch at speeds of up to 60 feet per minute, while trimming up to 30 feet in width.

Not long after the introduction of the autograde trimmer, CMI brought out the autograde placer-spreader and slipform paver. Texturing and finishing machines were added later and CMI soon became the largest manufacturer of automated road construction equipment in the world. CMI currently builds asphalt production plants; asphalt pavers and pick-up machines; asphalt storage equipment; light concrete pavers for sidewalks, curbs, and gutters; median barrier work, concrete finishing machines, motorgraders, and automation systems for Caterpillar Motorgraders; computer-control systems for asphalt and concrete production plants; and a complete line of heavy haul and bottom dump trailers.

CMI produced its second revolution in the highway industry in 1976. The introduction of the roto-mill pavement profilers provided the technology needed to remove worn pavement in a fast, clean, convenient operation. These machines have changed the thinking of pavement maintenance engineers throughout the world. The ROTO-MILL® and roto-cycler have placed CMI in a leadership position within the highway construction business.

More recently CMI has entered the energy field, manufacturing the TORQMASTER™ oil well pumping unit. This highly efficient pumping unit has made CMI an important part of the oil industry as rapidly as the firm's other machines placed it in the forefront of the road construction machinery field.

Other recent CMI activities include a new heavy-duty blasthole drill for the mining industry; a new oil and gas well work-over rig with an advanced design draw works; and a new mobile hydraulic drilling rig—an automatically controlled unit that is highly productive, safe to operate, and easy to move.

Below
The ROTO-MILL PR-750, manufactured by CMI Corporation, facilitates the removal of worn pavement.

Bottom
The TORQMASTER Pumping Unit has made CMI an important part of the oil industry.

Cities Service Gas Company

The discovery well of the Oklahoma City field blew in on December 4, 1928, and was drilled by the Indian Territory Illuminating Oil Company (ITIO). ITIO was subsequently merged into Cities Service Company, a large, integrated energy organization now headquartered in Tulsa. A subsidiary, Cities Service Gas Company, has been headquartered in Oklahoma City since 1944. ITIO also drilled what is probably the most famous well of the field, the Sudik No. 1, which raged out of control for 10 days during 1930. Flowing at the rate of 20,000 barrels of crude and 200,000,000 cubic feet of gas per day, the "Wild Mary Sudik" threw petroleum so high in the air that the wind carried a film of oil as far south as Norman, 11 miles away.

Henry L. Doherty, the founder of Cities Service, was an early proponent of conservation within the energy industry. He instituted scientific research at the firm's Bartlesville facilities, proving that natural gas increased the oil's flowing qualities when dissolved in a reservoir of crude oil. As a result, he fought vigorously for the conservation of natural gas, which was being burned off as waste in the oil fields. When he presented his views in a paper read before the Federal Oil Conservation Board in 1926, his ideas met with little approval from producers. Nonetheless, later developments dramatically proved the accuracy of his arguments.

Doherty's enlightened planning led to the development of the large-volume pipelines for oil and gas that altered the industry not only in Oklahoma, but throughout the nation. Cities Service was joint owner of the first long-distance gas pipeline in the United States.

Extension of this pipeline forms the basis for Cities Service Gas Company's interstate system, which today spans nearly 10,000 miles of main and gathering lines and serves customers in Oklahoma, Kansas, Missouri, Texas, and Nebraska. Included are natural gas storage fields formed from depleted wells, another technique pioneered by Cities Service.

Initially the system drew from the Texas West Panhandle field and the Hugoton field of Oklahoma and Kansas, which still produce after more than 50 years of development. During 1979 the system was extended to Wyoming and the prolific Rocky Mountain Overthrust Belt, where reserves of natural gas will ensure Cities' customers service into the 21st century.

Below
The "Wild Mary Sudik" blowing out of control in the Oklahoma City field between March 26 and April 4, 1930.

Bottom
The newest addition to the Cities Service Gas Company system is the 612-mile pipeline laid between Rawlins, Wyoming, and Hesston, Kansas, dedicated on October 24, 1979.

Crescent Market

When the first shot rang out opening the Oklahoma Territory to new settlers, thousands rushed across an invisible line to stake a claim to a piece of the new land. While others scurried to find the best pieces of property, J.H. Rucks calmly crossed the line with his family in a covered wagon drawn by a team of mules.

Inside that wagon were the beginnings of one of Oklahoma City's oldest stores—Crescent Market. Rucks staked his claim on April 22, 1889, by driving posts into the ground at the four corners of his lot. The area would later be included in the townsite of Guthrie, Oklahoma, but Rucks had no way of knowing this. All he could think of was setting up shop, and he wasted little time in doing just that.

After pitching a tent and moving his merchandise from the wagon to the tent, Rucks opened for business on the same day he made his claim. People clamored to the tent all day long, buying supplies and preparing for the long, hard months ahead. By the end of the day, Rucks, like so many other fledgling Oklahoma businessmen, was exhausted. During the next few months, business steadily increased, but Rucks decided to move the market south to Oklahoma City with a new partner, John D. Thomas.

The market boomed under the new partnership, and Rucks and Thomas constructed a 25-foot by 40-foot frame building on Main Street and did business there until they decided to enlarge and move into the old streetcar terminal on Grand Avenue. In 1923 Thomas purchased Rucks' interest in the market after another move to an even larger building back on Main Street. Foreseeing the expanding growth of Oklahoma City, Thomas then undertook to build the first shopping center in Oklahoma at 10th and North Walker—Plaza Court. The market opened in its fourth location in the fall of 1928.

In 1942 Thomas sold a half-interest in the market to Art L. Pemberton, whose father had opened a grocery and meat market in Muskogee, Oklahoma, in 1905. Pemberton bought out Thomas six years later. Desiring a location near the center of their trade, Pemberton and his son, Art E. Pemberton, who had joined his father in the business in 1951, moved to Nichols Hills Plaza in 1963. The market is still located at this address.

Crescent Market is recognized as the oldest food store in the state, one of only a handful of businesses that opened on the day of "The Run," and is still operating almost a century later.

This view shows the exterior of Oklahoma City's Crescent Market nearly 100 years after its doors were opened for business.

Demco, Inc.

Paul Snetcher and B.C. Christensen organized Drilling Equipment Manufacturing Company in 1946. They rented a small office and a truck garage, which was converted to a shop. With six employees, they began producing equipment for the oil field drilling industry, including 17 different products from drill collars to drag bits. They began, and continued, by emphasizing fine workmanship, appearance, and doing a good job of merchandising. Since there was not room to put the entire company name on the sign, the partners settled on the shortened Demco Mfg. Co. Naturally, the company was called Demco by almost everybody. Not until 1965, when the firm had expanded to a building large enough to accommodate the longer name several times over, was the name officially changed—a change that was made to reflect that the company was no longer just a manufacturer of drilling equipment.

The working conditions for the early employees were a bit primitive in the small space Demco shared with a barber shop and cafe; the first major expansion in 1948-49 was greeted with great enthusiasm. More expansion followed through the years in both plant size and product line. Early additions included mud guns, float valves, safety relief valves, and desanders. One of the giant steps forward came in 1958 when, after four years of testing and development, a line of gate valves was introduced. This was followed by the production of butterfly valves, which gave the company broad sales potential outside the oil field.

Paul R. Snetcher bought out the other stockholders' interest, including that of his partner, B.C. Christensen, in 1950. He served as president until his death in 1965. Snetcher encouraged the aggressive marketing and development programs of the organization. He also believed that stockholders should be content with modest dividends so that money could be available for growth.

After Snetcher's death, C.L. Knight became president. He continued the tradition of conservation of resources and strong development and marketing. Under his leadership four new product lines were introduced—ball valves, sewage treatment plants, through-conduit gate valves, and centrifugal pumps.

In March 1975 Demco, Inc., was acquired by Gardner-Denver and in April 1979 Gardner-Denver became a part of Cooper Industries, Inc., of Houston. Upon the retirement of C.L. Knight in the fall of 1980, William H. Hopf was appointed vice-president and general manager. Demco, now a separate operating division of Cooper, "enjoys the benefits of both independent operation here in Oklahoma City and the support from the fine organization of Cooper," according to Hopf, who is well-suited to continuing the aggressive, conservative Demco approach. Demco now numbers more than 1,000 employees with three plants located in southeast Oklahoma City. The third, most recent plant was completed in 1981 and greatly expands the firm's fabrication capabilities.

Demco has made significant contributions to the history and civic well-being of Oklahoma City over the past 35 years and looks forward to playing a growing role in the future.

The original Demco office building, which was leased by Anderson-Kerr Drilling Company (now Kerr-McGee). Demco eventually bought the property and its offices are still on the same site, although the building has been razed.

The sign in front of the Demco plant and offices. The facility has been expanded frequently since the company's founding in 1946.

Fidelity Bank

Geographically, central Oklahoma is Fidelity Bank's primary marketplace. Today it is an area of vigorous economic growth, and growth that is expected to continue.

When the First State Bank, forerunner to Fidelity National Bank of Oklahoma City, opened its doors to customers in 1908, the state of Oklahoma was five and a half months old. From that beginning through the present, the stockholders and management have seen Fidelity Bank as closely connected with the growth and development of Oklahoma City and the state of Oklahoma.

It was 1921, when the shareholders voted to change from a state bank to a national bank, that the new name of Fidelity National Bank was adopted. The original board of directors included a pioneer educator and a leading physician in Oklahoma City. The leadership of the bank has closely followed its slogan, "As Oklahoma City Grows, So Grows the Bank."

In 1923 the bank was located at the corner of Robinson and Sheridan in what was formerly known as the Baum Building. During the Oklahoma City oil field boom of the late '20s and early '30s, Fidelity Bank was involved. The bank prospered through the Depression years and World War II, continuing to serve the rapidly developing community, providing new trust services.

In 1954 the bank moved into larger quarters at Park Avenue and Harvey. A drive-in facility was first introduced when this move was made. In the early '70s, the bank moved into its current home, Fidelity Plaza, which has become an important showplace for art and history. Realizing that change is a part of substantial development, Fidelity has supported the publica-

The bank's current home, Fidelity Plaza, is an important showplace for art and history.

tions of *Born Grown: An Oklahoma City History* (1974); *The Life of A Successful Bank* (1978); and *One Man In His Time* (1979). In 1983, as Fidelity Bank approaches its 75th anniversary, it will have grown to over one billion dollars in total resources. In every sense of the word, Fidelity Bank has been an integral part of the development of Oklahoma and its capital city through growth, service, and action.

FORMER CHIEF EXECUTIVE OFFICERS AND PRESIDENTS

NAME	YEARS SERVED
C.F. Elerick	1908-1913
S.P. Berry	1913-1915
Irving H. Wheatcroft	1915-1919
Fred P. Finerty	1919-1924
John A. Campbell	1924-1943
Royal C. Stuart	1943-1948
Charles P. Stuart	1948-1964
Jack T. Conn	1964-Present
Wilfred A. Clarke	1978-Present
Forrest D. Jones	1978-Present

The First National Bank and Trust Company of Oklahoma City

On the night of April 22, 1889, Oklahoma City was a sea of wind-swept tents, wagons, and makeshift lean-tos buckling against the plain's wind. In front of a tent on the third lot east of Broadway and Main streets, firmly planted in the Oklahoma soil, was a sign reading "The Oklahoma Bank."

T.M. Richardson, George T. Reynolds (a wealthy Texas banker and rancher who provided the capital), and J.P. Boyle had planned the bank months before the Oklahoma Territory was opened for settlement. Richardson made the tiring journey to Oklahoma on a train only after he had stopped in Dallas to purchase checks, a safe, and some heavy oak desks. He piled all of the equipment and some new lumber in a boxcar and shipped it to the territory only days before the onrush of settlers. When Richardson arrived, he was ready to start business immediately. This he did on the very day of "The Run," when E.E. Elterman brought several large bank drafts to him for safekeeping.

On April 23 a small temporary building was erected for the bank; shortly thereafter Richardson purchased two lots from John R. Tanner, who would later become governor of Illinois. Richardson wasted no time in putting the new land to good use. Using more of the lumber he had purchased in Dallas, he constructed a more permanent 2,500-square-foot building. After a delay the federal government approved the bank's charter on August 20, 1890, and The Oklahoma Bank officially became The First National Bank.

Two years later a three-story stone building was hastily designed and built to offer The First National its first solid home in Oklahoma City. In the years that followed the bank officials erected new stone buildings, and survived customer panics, bank runs, and the Great Depression of the 1930s. In fact, the bank's present home, The First National Building, was started in 1930 and completed in 1931. The board, led by Hugh and Frank Johnson and R.A. Vose, believed in their bank's growth and decided their building dollars would go further during a depression.

Over the years The First has merged with or acquired 21 other banks in Oklahoma City. Today The First National Bank and Trust Company of Oklahoma City has over $2.5 billion in assets and is part of The First Oklahoma Bancorporation, the largest bank holding company in the entire state.

T.M. Richardson, Sr., one of The First National Bank and Trust Company's original founders.

Winter scene of the bank building lighted up.

Glen's Hik-ry Inn

Glen Eaves founded his restaurant years ago on the premise that Oklahomans enjoy and appreciate excellent beef.

Today his wife Alleene and current general manager Kay Eaves Harrison, their daughter, pay close attention to changes in the restaurant business, but have found this original philosophy continues to serve them well. Most of their customers are repeaters. Many come to celebrate anniversaries or special occasions, like the family with 12 children who celebrates each child's 16th birthday at Glen's. The restaurant's staff of 110 takes the motto "delicious food for an evening, beautiful memories for a lifetime" very seriously.

Glen's Hik-ry Inn first opened its door on April 26, 1953. Oklahoma City's first restaurant to feature charcoal-broiled steaks, it grew so quickly that regular additions had to be made. The seating capacity in 1953 was approximately 135; today the restaurant can accommodate 800 guests, making it one of the largest independently owned restaurants in the state. On June 1, 1957, Oklahoma's Semicentennial, Glen's first opened for lunch—featuring Oklahoma City's first "all-you-can-eat" smorgasbord. This, too, was an Oklahoma City original. Today Glen's smorgasbord is enjoyed by thousands on special holidays.

Glen Eaves (1915-1980), founder of Glen's Hik-ry Inn.

Another original was introduced at Glen's in 1960. Until the O-See-O Club was opened, the only private clubs in existence were affiliated with country clubs. The O-See-O Club, a Cherokee word meaning "welcome," was originally located upstairs and was moved to its present location in 1963. The move was made primarily to enable the guests to enjoy dinner as they listen to live entertainment at the piano bar.

Over the years Glen's has become an Oklahoma County institution, basing its menu on ever-popular traditional western foods. Located across from the Oklahoma State Fairgrounds, it remains a place for good food and pleasant memories.

The Horton Company

Neal Horton, a young man who owns a young company, has a keen interest in history—preserving and redeveloping some of Oklahoma City's fine, historic buildings. His enthusiasm is boundless as he explains his activities from an office in the Colcord Building with windows that overlook the Oil and Gas Building of Oklahoma City and the warehouse area.

An Oklahoma City native who attended the University of Oklahoma, Horton began his business career with Fidelity Bank. He reached the position of vice-president in charge of real estate at Fidelity, before leaving in 1969 to found his own company. He began developing housing additions and then small office buildings. By forming subsidiary partnerships Horton was able to invest his profits in large-scale undertakings and retain a portion of the ownership and management of such properties as the Oil and Gas Building at Main and Robinson and the Colcord Building.

Horton first achieved widespread notice when he headed a partnership that purchased the historic Colcord Building, which was constructed on the site of a mule barn and was the first reinforced concrete structure in Oklahoma City. The restoration was a labor of love, a challenge filled with discovery and innovation. Since its completion, the Colcord provides offices that invite firms to "return to the elegance that is the Colcord." With their high ceilings, shining brass, and marble, the office suites are indeed elegant.

Capitalizing on the tremendous response to this project, the Horton Company (again through a limited partnership, Warehouse Development Company), is undertaking its most ambitious project to date—"Bricktown." This project involves the redevelopment of the area known as the Old Warehouse District. When completed Bricktown will encompass a six-block area bounded by Main on the north, Reno on the south, the Santa Fe tracks on the west, and Walnut on the east.

Phase I of the project will transform the aging and neglected warehouses into over 300,000 square feet of office space with parking facilities. Two of the streets are being returned to their original brick pavers. The exterior of the buildings will project a strong, clean visual consistency. Well-lighted pedestrian walkways with greenbelts, and garden plazas with mature shrubs and trees will further beautify the area, making it a most attractive addition to its western neighbor, the central business district.

Neal Horton has discovered the future potential of the charming architectural heritage of Oklahoma City. The enthusiasm generated by his restoration and renovation efforts has reshaped the thinking of many "city fathers." He is literally making history by preserving it.

The architect's rendering of Bricktown, Horton's most ambitious and exciting project to date.

The Oil and Gas Building as it appeared in the early 1900s. Since its restoration and the removal of its 1953 metal skin, it again presents a warm look with a new brick facade.

Liberty National Bank and Trust Company

The year 1918 was an economically uncertain period in Oklahoma and the entire country. Nevertheless, a small group of business and civic leaders decided the time was right to organize a new bank. On September 3, 1918, Liberty National Bank and Trust Company opened in a converted barbershop at the rear of the Lee Building (now the Oil and Gas Building) at Main and Robinson. The bank, whose assets have reached $2 billion, began with a capital stock of $300,000 and a surplus of $30,000.

The bank grew slowly but steadily. Two years after its opening, it was moved temporarily to the Scott-Halliburton Building near Main and Harvey, then returned to occupy the entire first floor and basement of the Lee Building. Eventually it occupied the entire facility. By 1950 Liberty had outgrown even this space and moved to the 33-story Apco Tower at Park and Robinson. Construction immediately began on a 16-story annex to house a drive-in facility and additional floor space.

In 1968 the bank celebrated its 50th birthday with a groundbreaking for the impressive Liberty Tower, the first major structure to be completed in Oklahoma City's sweeping downtown redevelopment program. When even this space proved inadequate, Liberty began building the Mid-America Tower. Construction has just been completed on the 19-story, 350,000-square-foot structure. Eventually a hotel will be constructed as a companion building to the Mid-America Tower; the two towers will then be called the Mid-America Plaza.

Liberty's growth over the years has resulted in large part from sound leadership, the acquisitions of three other Oklahoma City banks, and its expansion into an aggressive group of companies.

The acquisitions began almost immediately after Liberty's formation. In 1921 Guarantee State Bank was merged with Liberty. C.H. Everest, president of Guarantee, then became a vice-president of Liberty. His son, Harvey P. Everest, later served as president for 12 years and his grandson presently serves on the board of directors. Four years later Liberty purchased Oklahoma National Bank, a move that brought an additional $3 million in deposits. The final merger, with the Bank of Mid-America, came in 1960.

In its more than 60-year history, Liberty has had 10 chief executive officers. The first was president L.T. Sammons; the current chief executive officer is J.W. McLean, chairman, who joined the bank as president and chief executive officer on December 18, 1967. His 14-year tenure is the longest of the 10 and, under his management, deposits have grown by more than six times and earnings by almost seven times.

Oklahoma native J.W. "Bill" McLean returned from San Francisco to become president and chief executive officer of Liberty Bank in 1967. He is now chairman and chief executive officer of Liberty National Corporation and Liberty National Bank and Trust Company, one of Mid-America's largest and most diversified financial institutions. (Photo courtesy of Elson-Alexandre—Los Angeles, California.)

Fred Jones Industries

For many years the name Fred Jones has been synonymous with Ford around Oklahoma City. The downtown area is dotted with various buildings that attest to the dominance of Fred Jones in the sale of Ford cars and trucks, Lincolns, and Mercurys. This relationship of names began inauspiciously enough in 1916, when the 24-year-old Jones arrived in Oklahoma City. He had become convinced that the young state of Oklahoma and the young automobile business held the key to his success. On April 10 Jones began realizing his dream when he started work at the new Ford assembly plant in Oklahoma City. The Ford car fascinated him and he learned all he could about every part of the car and its assembly. The young man was hired after he remarked that in spite of being only five foot seven inches tall and weighing only 130 pounds, he could do any job assigned him better than anyone else. He did it!

Jones' career took a new direction when he began visiting the dealerships; he soon determined to become a dealer himself. Always quick to recognize new areas and to dream of new opportunities, Jones usually turned these dreams into reality. Soon after his dream developed of being a dealer, he offered to take over the operations of an ailing dealership in Blackwell as a partner. Since Jones studied the sale of cars as thoroughly as he had studied their manufacture before, the Rice-Jones Ford Agency quickly became one of the most successful dealerships. This success led to his purchase of the agency in Tonkawa in 1921. Many men would have been pleased with this achievement and content to continue as they were. Not Jones.

In 1922 he sold both agencies for a handsome profit in order to return to Oklahoma City. The city already had two dealerships, and friends advised him that he couldn't make a go of another agency. Those friends turned out to be wrong; long after the other two agencies ceased to exist, Fred Jones Ford continues to be a strong dealership. By 1926 it had become the largest Ford agency in the Southwest, and by 1929 the fourth largest dealership in America. By 1940 Jones was awarded Ford and Lincoln/Mercury dealerships in Oklahoma City, Tulsa, and Norman. During the period of May 1920 through March 1966, his simple philosophy of "an enthusiasm for the product you sell and a sincere desire to serve" produced sales of 304,756 automobiles.

Again this might have been more than enough for most men. Not Jones. In 1938 he followed his concern about vehicle service and established a small section in the Oklahoma City service department to produce better reconditioned engines and component parts. This 400-square-foot and four-employee project was the start of the Fred Jones Manufacturing Company. In the beginning the firm sold engines and parts to a dozen dealers in Oklahoma; by 1966 it had become the largest Ford-authorized remanufacturer in the country, supplying over 14 states and 1,000 dealers from Silver City, New Mexico, to Key West, Florida. Warehouses are maintained in Oklahoma City, Orlando, Memphis, New Orleans, Atlanta, Birmingham, and Jacksonville. The company's volume is consistently in excess of one-third of the total dollar sales by all Ford remanufacturers nationally.

Fred Jones celebrated 50 years in the Ford business in 1966. Over 1,000 friends and associates gathered from all over the world to celebrate. Henry Ford II, chairman of the board of Ford Motor Company, proclaimed him "Ford Citizen of the Year." Ford said, "He is a rare blend of an inventive, hard-driving, free enterpriser and a sensitive, considerate humanitarian."

When the celebration was over Jones went back to work on the company's future growth. The manufacturing plant, spread over nine buildings, was at the exploding point. They needed more space but were unable to find a suitable location in downtown Oklahoma City until Ford announced the closing of its parts depot—the same building in which Jones had begun his automotive career a half century before. He was able to buy the building and move his offices and remanufacturing operation into it. His career had, in a sense, come full circle.

From this office Fred Jones planned for the continued growth of his company until his death in June 1971 at the age of 79. His family and longtime associates have continued to follow his forward-looking vision. All new company-owned sales offices were part of Jones' planning. The leadership now rests with Chris V. Speligene, who had previously served as the general manager of the Fred Jones Manufacturing Company.

Under his leadership Nationwide Automotive, Inc., in Winnsboro, Texas, was purchased to provide the Jones concepts of service and quality to all makes of cars. In 1972 the Installment Finance Corporation was added to the Fred Jones family to provide retail financing of automobiles, and to promote owner retention and loyalty. Speligene, with the support of Jones' wife, daughter, and three grandsons, plans to continue the company's expansion.

Fred Jones' unstoppable enthusiasm still permeates the automotive empire he started—and will continue to do so as his family, and his family of companies, look toward an expansive future.

Opposite Top
Fred Jones recognized his dream through the automobile business in Oklahoma.

Opposite Bottom
The original Fred Jones Ford dealership, Oklahoma City, Oklahoma.

Right
Chris V. Speligene and Mrs. Fred Jones christen the 500,000th engine, January 1975.

Below
This Fred Jones Ford dealership opened August 1979.

KTVY Television Channel 4

For almost three quarters of a century, Edward K. Gaylord dominated informational delivery in Oklahoma City and the surrounding area. He began by publishing newspapers, *The Daily Oklahoman* and *Oklahoma City Times*.

When an enterprising Oklahoma Citian, Earl C. Hull, set up a 20-watt radio transmitter in his home in 1920, WKY Radio was born. To E.K. Gaylord it represented a natural expansion area and he quickly acquired it. Under his control the radio station became the first west of the Mississippi with regular daily programming and the first to bring network radio to the Southwest.

Many radio stations moved naturally into television. Gaylord followed this pattern enthusiastically. WKY became the first TV station in Oklahoma, then the first to bring network TV to the state. The first carload of TV equipment arrived on October 9, 1948. Under the direction of P.A. "Buddy" Sugg, the first station manager, it was placed in a studio in the Little Theatre of the Municipal Auditorium (now the Civic Center Music Hall). The plans called for WKY-TV to use the radio station's tower—a 968-foot giant labeled "the world's tallest antenna." Live camera demonstrations soon started. But fire damaged the equipment in November, delaying transmission until it could be replaced. Soon, however, the station was broadcasting test patterns. On June 6, 1949, WKY-TV made its formal debut. The initial operation was from 7 p.m. Sunday through Friday for the 3,300 sets in the market area.

The mobile TV studio allowed the station to "roam the far corners of the state and relay its signal to the main studio." The mobile station permitted the telecast on October 1, 1949, of an OU football game. This event was particularly significant to Oklahomans, for whom football is an essential part of life.

The station continued to add to its list of firsts and to expand programming. On February 11, 1950, Saturday programming put the station on the air seven days a week. The following June the schedule expanded to approximately 40 hours, then to 63 hours in October 1950. Now, of course, the station broadcasts 24 hours a day, five days a week.

By 1951 the television station had outgrown its downtown studio, and in July of that year it moved to the new, ultra-modern studios on Britton Road where the station is still located. The next year, cable facilities linking Oklahoma City to the East were completed, bringing "live" network programming to Oklahoma from the NBC studios in New York.

The innovations in television broadcasting and programming continued rapidly. P.A. Sugg, the station's general manager, was usually prepared to adapt to and progress with the industry. He also had the sagacity to order color camera equipment in September 1949 when that was still in the developmental stage. Because of this foresight, WKY-TV was able to air its first live

Left
Edward K. Gaylord, president of OPUBCO, appears on the first broadcast in Oklahoma on June 6, 1949.

Below
E.K. Gaylord (left), president of OPUBCO, and P.A. Sugg, manager of WKY, explain the procedure minutes before WKY-TV became part of the national NBC network on July 1, 1952.

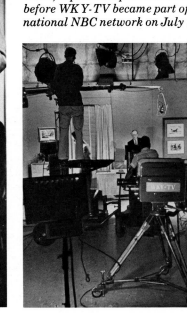

color program from its own studios on April 8, 1954. This made WKY-TV the first independent station anywhere with regular live color program origination. The show was the "Sooner Shindig." On April 26 the station began a more ambitious color stint when it began the daily airing of "Cook's Book" in color. Four months later the color cameras moved outdoors to feed a colorcast of the Anadarko Indian Exposition to the NBC network's "Today" and "Home." This was the first time a local station's facilities fed a colorcast to any network.

Other technological advances followed. Oklahoma's unpredictable weather was monitored and in January 1958 the station inaugurated TV radar coverage for weather reports. In 1959 WKY-TV originated a telecast for NBC, CBS, and ABC of President Eisenhower's address at the Municipal Auditorium. The year 1958 brought the first videotape machine. In 1961 a Collins weather radar was installed on top of the studios, and in February 1964 a contract for a new transmitter tower of 1,602 feet was signed. An order was placed with Jamison Company for the first color film processor installation in Oklahoma City in 1966. For six years the station produced and videotaped the annual "Stars and Stripes Show" for NBC; this was the only network program produced by a local station.

Because of its background, Channel 4 has consistently dominated statewide competition for its outstanding news operation. It is also the only station in Oklahoma to win a prestigious Emmy Award for the program "Through the Looking Glass Darkly" in 1974. Two of its photographers have been named "News Photographer of the Year," the most recent winner being Darrell Barton in 1974. In addition, in 1975 the station was chosen National Newsfilm Station of the Year for the second time—and in 1977 for the third time!

After Edward K. Gaylord's death, the FCC moved to break up media monopolies. Edward L. Gaylord, E.K.'s son and chairman of Gaylord Broadcasting Company, decided that it would be a good idea to sell the television station. The station

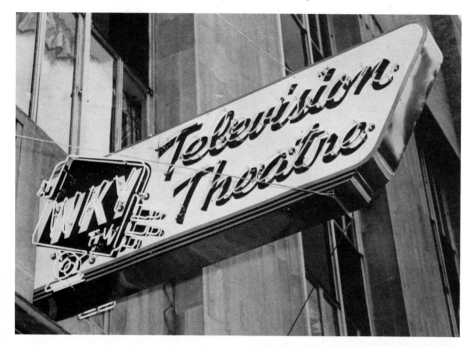

Top Left
The first tangible evidence of television's coming to Oklahoma was this sign, which hung from the Municipal Auditorium.

Left
Danny Williams, who now hosts "Dannysday," as he appeared in the 1950s. He is one of the most popular and longest-standing Oklahoma TV personalities.

was purchased by the Detroit-based Evening News Association for $22.5 million. Because of federal regulations, the new owners had to apply for new call letters. After numerous suggestions, the letters KTVY were selected. The new owners assured their audience that they would change neither the quality nor the personnel at the station. Norman P. Bagwell was retained as vice-president and general manager under the ownership until his death in 1978.

The consistency of leadership continued when Lee Allan Smith, an Oklahoma City native and former assistant general manager of WKY-TV, took over as vice-president and general manager of KTVY on November 1, 1978. He took the reins just in time to preside over the station's 30th anniversary in 1979. Chief among the numerous events scheduled for the celebration was a locally originated ''Mike Douglas Show.'' Douglas had started at WKY Radio in the '40s and it was during this time that he met his wife. The climax of the celebration was a birthday party extravaganza hosted by Bob Hope and Tanya Tucker at the Myriad Convention Center. Will Rogers, Jr., and Governor George Nigh also made appearances on the show. From the rich 30-year tradition that KTVY has built in Oklahoma City has emerged an even greater dedication to the people of Oklahoma. Never satisfied to be ''one among many,'' Channel 4 continues to lead the market with Action 4, their nationally recognized news organization. Recently, when it was determined that the market needed even more information, the station initiated a dramatic change in programming. In November 1980 Channel 4 renamed its news, weather, and sports operation ''Action 4'' and moved the early evening report from the number one position in news in Oklahoma City to an hour earlier—5 p.m. At the same time, this report was expanded from 30 minutes to a full hour of local coverage. This was then followed by national news at 6 p.m. and the new program ''PM Magazine.'' This pro-

vided Oklahomans with two full hours of informational programming daily.

As part of this news, KTVY, which pioneered weather reporting in Oklahoma, continues to offer technologically advanced reporting of the weather. It was first in the installation of the Enterprise Weather Radar System in 1971 and in 1974 the most sophisticated computerized weather system was put on-line. A color radar scan converter was installed in 1977, and today KTVY is pioneering in using a computer

Below
One of the most popular WKY-TV shows during the '50s and early '60s was the ''Bud Wilkinson Show,'' which aired after Oklahoma University football games and featured the winning coach (right) and moderator, Howard Neumann (left).

Bottom
Edward L. Gaylord, chairman of Gaylord Broadcasting Company, signs WKY-TV over to the Evening News Association as Peter B. Clark (seated), president of the association, and Donald T. DeGroot look on.

visual display direct on the air.

Of use to the news department and to other producers and networks are two of the finest mobile units staffed by a crew with a reputation of quality, creativity, and capability. The massive 55-foot tractor-trailer is a production studio on wheels, and the mini-mobile cruiser offers shot-by-shot production on location.

Presenting the programs that Oklahomans prefer is only one goal of Channel 4. The station has always taken an active role in projects of civic betterment. Station management has accepted the leadership role in projects including the United Way, YMCA, OKC Chamber of Commerce, Boy Scouts, Girl Scouts, OKC Zoo, and Allied Arts, to mention only a few. When a worthy cause presents itself, or is conceived by the station, KTVY is always at the forefront in promoting and participating in its success.

Right
Lee Allan Smith, vice-president and general manager, heads the KTVY team of professionals.

Below
The WKY-TV station was ultramodern when it was constructed and has been changing to accommodate new technology ever since. This is how it looked sporting the new KTVY call letters.

Part of the dedication to its community is reflected by the daily presentation of "Dannysday," a talk-variety show, which has kept Oklahomans up to date on current events and personalities for 15 years. This is the only daily talk and variety show produced in Oklahoma City.

Other public service programming includes the long-running "Medicine and You" produced in association with the Oklahoma Medical Association and "Creative Crafts," another 30-minute show that features well-known artists and their works. This is produced in association with the Oklahoma City Metropolitan Library System. "Money and You" is a cooperative

effort of Channel 4 and the Better Business Bureau.

Several times a year, local programs are featured as specials, with the station handling the total production. A recent example is "You're Doin' Fine, Oklahoma!" This outstanding full-hour program followed the reopening of Rodgers and Hammerstein's famous show "Oklahoma!" Crews from the station traveled to Hollywood, Washington, D.C., New York City, and, of course, covered the grand reopening in Oklahoma City. The hour-long special was created from the material they filmed and taped. The program was accepted as a finalist in the Iris Awards national competition held in 1981 by NATPE.

This recognition joins hundreds of other commendations that have been presented to the station. Crowding the trophy cases are Oklahoma's only Emmy Award, News Photography Station of the Year Award, Wrangler awards, Addy awards, and hundreds of other AP, UPI, and Society of Professional Journalists (Sigma Delta Chi) trophies. During its long history, the station's news and public service departments have continually been acknowledged as the best. And the station's current general manager, Lee Allan Smith, and all the dedicated professionals at KTVY plan to keep it that way.

Lippert Bros., Inc., General Contractors

Walter H. and Erick W. Lippert founded their company in 1920 in Boone, Iowa, after returning from the armed forces in World War I. They started with a great deal of desire and drive. Their first jobs consisted of building fireplaces and residential work, as well as pouring sidewalks and driveways. Construction jobs began to increase in scope, with the remodeling of storefronts and buildings. As the business grew, three more of the Lippert brothers joined the enterprise. All were brick masons except for one carpenter.

In 1928 the company received its first large project: the addition to the Boone High School. Increasingly, the firm did more and more large-scale construction, diversifying into sewage- and water-treatment plants in 1930. At the beginning of World War II Lippert built the Camp McCoy, Wisconsin, sewage-treatment plant in record time. Receiving a commendation from the commanding officer of the base for its excellent work, the company was asked to bid on the new Tinker Air Force Base water- and sewage-treatment system and was the successful bidder. During World War II years Lippert completed many projects in the Southwest to help the war effort.

In 1946 Robert L. and Donald E. Lippert, sons of Erick Lippert, returned to Oklahoma City, having served in the U.S. Navy. The Erick Lippert family then decided to remain in Oklahoma, and a permanent office was established in Oklahoma City. Walter Lippert remained in Iowa and in Oklahoma the company

A 1923 photograph of (left to right) Louis T., Reuben C., Erick W., Leo J., and Walter H. Lippert.

grew under the leadership of Erick W. Lippert. In 1947 Lippert Bros., Inc., was formed; the Iowa-based organization had been a partnership.

Many notable structures have been erected by the firm, including the National Cowboy Hall of Fame and Western Heritage Center, the Oklahoma State Department of Health Building, the University of Oklahoma Bio-Medical Science Building, the Citizens Bank Tower, and the beautiful First Presbyterian Church. All of these buildings are in Oklahoma City.

In time, Lippert Bros., Inc. parented other firms, including the Utilities Engineering and Construction Company (in 1955), which specializes in water and wastewater treatment plants and power plants; and the Globe Construction Company (in 1956), which specializes in underground conduits, water, and sewer lines.

Over the years the firm has built hospitals, churches, schools, commercial buildings, and industrial facilities. It has completed projects in a nine-state area: New Mexico, Texas, Colorado, Nebraska, Iowa, Missouri, Kansas, Arkansas, and Oklahoma.

Throughout the years the organization has kept its important sense of family. Today, third-generation boys begin working in the field as laborers at age 14. The girls also have indicated that they want to be "Lippert Bros." as well, by working in the office.

The spirit and concern for excellence has led to growth and many awards. "The Award for Excellence" was given for Dale Hall, the Social Science Building on the University of Oklahoma campus, by the American Concrete Institute.

Right
The Citizens Tower Building.

Below Left
The State of Oklahoma Department of Health Building.

Below Right
The University of Oklahoma Bio-Medical Science Building.

Mercy Health Center

Nightfall on July 2, 1884, found five valiant women, members of the Catholic religious order of the Sisters of Mercy, disembarking from a train at the end of the railroad line in Atoka, Oklahoma. Prairie schooners, carrying the Sisters and their humble belongings, journeyed three days to St. Mary's Academy in Sacred Heart, Oklahoma. There were forged the beginnings of a century of religious education and dedicated nursing service to Oklahomans and Oklahoma Citians in particular. Much credit is due for the progress of the Sisters of Mercy in Oklahoma to those valiant women "who built better than they knew."

The Sisters saw the community mature through days of bitter struggle and difficulty, and days of building, growth, and formation. Their trials imparted inspiration and character, force and fervor, and a love for the primitive spirit still seen in an Oklahoman's fidelity to rules and tradition. The Sisters of Mercy were privileged to be spectators at the unprecedented Run in 1889, and participants in its present prosperous condition. Their influence, hidden and unobtrusive, was felt in the dwellings of the Indian, the sod dugout of the early settler, the shacks of the coal miners and, years later, in the homes of the prosperous and in the hospitals.

From friend and foe alike came opposition at times, yet slowly this gave way to confidence and esteem. Countless Oklahoma youths have been trained in Mercy schools—Indian, parochial, and private. For years the Sisters ministered to the needs of the homeless and destitute, leading lives exemplified by Mother Catherine McAuley, who founded the order in 1831 in Dublin, Ireland.

In gradually expanding their ministry of service to the poor and the sick, the Sisters of Mercy purchased The Oklahoma City General Hospital on July 1, 1947, from a small group of physicians who had owned and operated this original 25-bed hospital since 1917. Located at 12th Street and North Walker on the outskirts of downtown Oklahoma City, it was renamed Mercy Hospital by the Sisters. They purchased additional land and made extensive improvements to bring the patient bed capacity ultimately to 225.

The Mercy School of Nursing, organized in 1927, was continued by the Sisters until 1969, when the last class of 18 nurses graduated. In January 1959 the first open-heart surgery to be performed in a private hospital in the state of Oklahoma occurred at Mercy, which was in the forefront of the burgeoning health care field in Oklahoma City.

Mercy's continuing growth necessitated plans for relocation; in June 1970, after numerous other sites were studied and discarded, land was purchased on the corner of North Meridian and West Memorial roads in northwest Oklahoma City.

In the early 1900s, the Sisters of Mercy traveled over the state to provide care to the sick and needy.

Formal groundbreaking ceremonies, with the Sisters of Mercy hosting a multitude of their friends, were held on December 8, 1971. Later the hospital was renamed Mercy Health Center, to reflect the state's growing trend toward maintenance of health and prevention of disease. On August 17, 1974, the Sisters of Mercy proudly opened the entrances of the new Mercy Health Center, which dominated the northern skyline of Oklahoma City. Two of the five patient floors were utilized.

Immediately adjacent, the 10-story Mercy Doctors Tower opened on October 7, 1974. Mercy Health Center stood alone in its new surroundings; and local authors whimsically referred to Mercy as "the little hospital on the prairie, waiting for its future to catch up." It did, and the Sisters of Mercy were again lauded for their vision and foresight. They had invested in a dream: a hospital to provide the highest caliber of medical care available to the people of their community.

With the help of prayer, energy, and professionalism, the Sisters' dream has grown to become a singular tower of healing—Mercy Health Center. Today the center is a general acute-care health facility with a 400-bed capacity. It includes the only newborn-intensive-care center of any private hospital in the city. Mercy has provided many millions of dollars in charity care to Oklahoma Citians while continuing the finest medical care at the lowest cost available at any comparable hospital in Oklahoma City. In fact, it has cared for so many Oklahoma Citians over the years that virtually every local family has been touched by the work of the Sisters of Mercy.

The Sisters' modest initial dream has provided incredible dividends to their community. Their hospital holds to its pure Friesen concept, while including primary nursing, use of pneumatic-tube systems, nurservers in each patient room, and automatic monorail systems throughout the health facility for easy processing and distribution of needed supplies. This innovation has always paced Mercy's tradition of growth and progress. Not only does the center offer a full range of outpatient services, it also recognizes its responsibility to care for the whole person and the patient's need for spiritual care. Since Mercy's beginning in Oklahoma City in 1947, clergymen from all denominations have been encouraged to minister to their hospitalized parishioners.

The fulfillment of these spiritual needs led to the establishment of a large and active pastoral care department at Mercy, designed to serve all patients, their families, and hospital personnel, whatever their religion. The one thing that has not changed is the hard-to-define "spirit of Mercy" that manifests itself in the special caring concern that everyone at Mercy Health Center has, a special commitment to excellence that makes serving not a slogan, but a way of life.

The new Mercy Health Center rose on the prairie of far northwest Oklahoma City. Since its construction the surrounding fields have become residential neighborhoods and shopping centers.

Musket Corporation

In 1971 Tom Love drove by a cleaning company near his home and noted that the cleaners had added self-service gasoline pumps. This observation sparked an idea that changed the direction of his own gasoline distributing business.

Love had started his business six years before, with the acquisition of an abandoned filling station in Watonga. By 1971 he and his wife Judy were operating a string of about 40 self-service gasoline stations, primarily in smaller Oklahoma communities. The sight of the gasoline pumps in front of the cleaning establishment meshed with an idea that had been forming in Love's mind during his travels throughout the state.

"It was a simple matter of being able to fill a need by adding to our business without adding overhead," Love says. "There was a real need in smaller Oklahoma communities for the same sort of convenience stores that had existed in Oklahoma City for many years. We could meet that need and at the same time begin to diversify, which we needed to do to grow and survive."

The result was a "mini-stop"—a combination of self-service gas station and convenience store in Guymon. When this proved successful, Love opened another store in Buffalo and a third in Boise City.

Today Love is president of Musket Corporation, which owns and operates more than 100 Love's Country Stores in six states. Sales in 1982 are expected to exceed $125 million. Although the company's headquarters offices are in Oklahoma City, Love's Country Stores are better known in the smaller communities (3,000 to 75,000 people) of Oklahoma, Kansas, Texas, New Mexico, Missouri, and Colorado.

Love's Country Stores are no longer merely small convenience stores with gasoline pumps outside. Each 4,000-square-foot facility has three profit centers: the convenience store, gasoline, and a delicatessen operation that serves a variety of prepared sandwiches.

The evolution has been gradual. An important first step was expanding the management of the operation. Larry Dillard, a supermarket chain executive, joined Musket in 1972 as manager of operations. Lindell Pearson joined in 1974 to supervise the acquisition and construction of new stores. That same year Jim Rager joined as vice-president of finance. These three men, plus Tom and Judy Love, form the management team that has made Musket Corporation and Love's Country Stores the 25th largest chain of convenience stores in the country.

Their growth plan for Musket is stated simply by Love: "We intend to occupy the leadership position in the industry. We believe we can roughly double per-unit industry sales standards within the next five to seven years. Our growth pattern has remained consistent over the past five years and we believe we can maintain that pattern throughout the 1980s."

A key strategy in the company's formal growth plan is Love's newest innovation: the Love's Truck Stop. Musket broke ground on its first truck stop facility in Amarillo recently and plans several new locations in 1982.

Unlike the country stores, which are located to draw local customers in small communities, the new truck stops will be situated near interstate highway exits, providing convenient exit and reentry, and along other major highways carrying heavy truck traffic. "Our market is the independent trucker and we hope to serve him by providing inexpensive one-stop service for fuel, food, and other needs," Love comments.

As the stores and truck stops spread across the country, Love and his team keep busy devising new ways to serve their customers better and planning new areas of expansion to ensure that Musket Corporation will continue to be a major force in Oklahoma City's business community in the years to come. "The challenge," says Love, "is in growth and innovation. Finding new areas of diversification is the part of the business I like best."

Above
Tom E. Love founded Musket Oil Company in 1965. Today he is president and chief executive officer of the rapidly expanding Musket Corporation.

Below
One of the many Love's Country Stores, which are located in the smaller communities of six states.

Oklahoma City University

Oklahoma City University (OCU) is an institution proud of its church-related, personalized, value-centered education. Unlike many independent colleges and universities, OCU is prospering—with increasing enrollments, refurbished facilities, new and innovative programs, and an impressive rise in gift and endowment income. The present situation can be credited to the "Great Plan for Academic Excellence" initiated in 1960, and to the enthusiasm, dedication, and leadership of the current president, Jerald C. Walker.

Although OCU experienced several difficult years in the past, it began with an advantage many universities do not have. It was chartered as Epworth University in 1904 under the sponsorship of both the Methodist Church and the Oklahoma City Trade Club (the predecessor of the Oklahoma City Chamber of Commerce). Today partnership between the church and city continues to give OCU a unique potential for service in this region.

The university attracts students from across the state and around the world. More than 75 percent of the students are from the state of Oklahoma with significant numbers from Kansas, Texas, and Arkansas. In fact, more than 20 states and 38 foreign countries are represented among the student body.

Students study in five colleges and schools at OCU, including the Petree College of Arts and Sciences, the School of Law, the School of Religion and Church Vocations, the School of Management and Business Sciences, and the School of Music and Performing Arts. The excellence and professionalism of the performing arts, represented by groups such as The Surrey Singers and the popular musical theater, has gained national acclaim for numerous graduates. Two of these students, Jayne Ann Jayroe and Susan Powell, reigned as Miss America while 11 of the past 15 Miss Oklahomas have been OCU students.

The athletic program at OCU has also gained national recognition through the years. As the home of Oklahoma's great basketball tradition, the OCU Chiefs have received 11 bids to the NCAA post-season tournament and can claim 11 All-American basketball players.

Under the "Great Plan for Academic Excellence" begun in 1960, the university was transformed from a small commuter school into a true university with strong liberal arts teaching and research capabilities. Although the liberal arts continue to be the strength of the university and the performing arts have gained the university national recognition, more than 30 percent of the students at OCU are enrolled in the School of Management and Business Sciences.

Dr. Jerald C. Walker was chosen president in 1979, the first OCU graduate to assume the position. Under Walker, OCU has more than tripled its permanent endowment while increasing the student enrollment by more than 17 percent in two years and launching new degree programs at both the graduate and undergraduate levels.

Today OCU is continuing the tradition of excellence known throughout its 78-year history and is answering the needs of students, churches, and the business community for the future.

The Oklahoma City University campus is a familiar landmark for the many Oklahoma Citians who pass by each day.

Students enjoy the relaxed atmosphere of OCU's 55-acre campus, which provides plenty of outside space to study, sun, and play.

Norick Brothers, Inc.

In 1910 the country was recovering from a financial panic and the rumblings of World War I were far away from the streets of Oklahoma City, where horse-drawn vehicles far outnumbered the cars traveling the predominately unpaved roads. George A. "Lon" Norick had mortgaged his small house to purchase two small hand-fed presses, a hand cutter, and a few cases of type. He was determined to own his own print shop. He painted such a rosy picture of the future of this business that he persuaded his brother, Henry, to give up a $15-a-week job and become his printer's devil at a salary of $3 a week.

As Henry recalled, "Our young business was housed in a tiny frame building next door to a blacksmith and horseshoeing shop. Often the flimsy wall separating us would be kicked by an unruly mule that objected to being shod, and our printing shop would be showered with plaster and dust by the impact." The dust wasn't the only problem the two brothers faced. They made three tries at the printing business before they were able to make a go of it. In between times they "hocked" their equipment and went to work for the paper until they'd saved enough to open up again.

The brothers knew that they needed to specialize rather than being just another job printer if they were ever to succeed. Henry had purchased a one-third share of the company and the brothers had set and exceeded a goal of $10-a-day gross sales when Lon purchased his first automobile in 1917. This purchase became more significant and profitable to the company than any other they ever made because it led them to their specialty—a system of uniform accounting for retail automobile dealers. After working on design and printing forms for several months, the brothers mailed samples of the first system of correlated bookkeeping forms for retail automobile dealers to the 252 Ford dealers in Oklahoma as a test.

Since many of these dealers kept few or no business records at all, the brothers and their two employees anxiously waited for the postman to find out if their gamble would pay off. They had their first reply in

Above
The Norick brothers pose for a picture during the very early days of their printing business.

Below
Some early-day forms are loaded for shipping by an employee in front of the plant at 325 N. W. Second.

three days and more orders came in the following day. Soon their production facilities were taxed to their limit. More printing presses and work space were found so the brothers could cover the entire country with promotions and advertising and subsequent orders. Norick Brothers had found their specialty.

Soon Ford Motor Company officials became interested in the system and cooperated in marketing it to their dealers. Since there were few accountants and dealers in the country who understood automotive accounting, Norick hired six automotive accountants to travel throughout the nation installing the system and training bookkeepers for the dealers. As a further service they began publishing a small periodical in 1922 called *Service News.*

The Norick System was so successful for Ford that in a matter of time, forms were devised and marketed to almost all makes of cars, eventually including foreign dealers of American cars and foreign cars sold in America.

The business weathered the Depression, but in 1936 Lon Norick was forced to retire because of ill health. He decided to sell his portion of the business to his brother Henry. The two had formed the partnership on a handshake and they dissolved it the same way. After 22 years what had been called "the perfect partnership" ended.

The business continued to expand under Henry's sole leadership. The forms were constantly updated and revised and new ones added as more sophisticated information was required. The name of the magazine was changed to the *Motor Dealer* and was eventually circulated to 0,000 dealers before its discontinuance in 1955. The system of regional branch offices which had begun earlier in San Francisco was expanded to the central and eastern parts of the country in order to fill the growing orders more rapidly.

The firm progressed as a family business until 1953, when it was incorporated. Henry Norick became

president. Other members of the family also served as officers. These included James H. Norick, vice-president; Marjorie Norick, vice-president; Frances Norick Lilly, secretary-treasurer; and Dorothy Norick Patton, vice-president.

In 1959 James Norick was elected president of the company and oversaw its continued growth. He took time from the business from 1959 to 1963, and again from 1967 to 1971, to serve as mayor of Oklahoma City. In addition to becoming mayor in 1959, he supervised the last in several company moves to a new plant at 3909 N.W. 36th. By 1977 a new manufacturing facility had been built in Kings Mountain, North Carolina, and branches were located in Los Angeles and Pleasanton, California, and Chicago, Illinois.

The firm recognized the coming of the computer by establishing Norick Data Systems in 1975, which produces software and hardware computer systems in a plant just north of the main building. The year after Data Systems came into being, a million-dollar fire destroyed much of the building. The remains of a million pounds of paper smoldered in the parking lot for two weeks, but employees and management pitched in to become fully operational again

in three months and entirely rebuilt in eight months. Through it all the company maintained its reputation of "never making a customer mad."

With the 1980s came new leadership when Ronald Norick, James' son, became president of the organization which today does business all over the United States and in several foreign countries. The employees now number 360, 300 of whom work in Oklahoma. Over 100 of them have been with the company for more than 10 years. Some of Norick's retired employees served for 50 years, but one, Roy Evans, who was then in his forties, began as editor of *Service News* in 1932 and continues to oversee public relations for the firm.

Norick Brothers continues to improve its product and to expand into the data-processing field and to grow with the worldwide automotive industry. It is the oldest and second largest printing company of its kind, and is devoted to ensuring that it is also the finest.

In session for its final monthly meeting of the 1978-1979 fiscal year is the board of directors of Norick Brothers, Inc.

Oklahoma County Historical Society

The Oklahoma County Historical Society was founded in the spring of 1978 with the purposes of fostering historical research, publication, and the preservation of historical artifacts, manuscripts, and structures in the county. Mike Frew, then director of the Oklahoma City University Business Research Center, was named the first president of the new organization.

Because of the rapid changes that were occurring in the county's metropolitan areas, one of the organization's first projects was an inventory of the historic buildings that were left standing in each of the urban centers, charted in the territorial period—Oklahoma City, Edmond, Luther, and Arcadia. This resulted in the recommendation of a number of these being nominated and placed on the National Register of Historic Places.

This countywide survey led to the first publication of the Oklahoma County Historical Society, *The Physical Legacy: Buildings of Oklahoma County, 1889 to 1931*, written by Bob L. Blackburn, Arn Henderson, and Melvina Thurman. The photographs and text offer an interesting overview of the architectural heritage of the rapid Anglo-American development of the area since 1889.

As the Society enters Oklahoma's Diamond Jubilee year, it is involved in two major projects, in addition to the publication of its Diamond Jubilee history.

One is the organization of an Oklahoma County Museum, designed to bring together into an informative and attractive display the artifacts, photographs, and principal papers of Oklahoma County. Among principal workers in the development of the museum have been Mike and Diane Everman, a husband-wife team dedicated to historical preservation, and Bill Welge.

A major individual in making the museum possible is Howard Melton, owner of the Melton Building at 20 West Main downtown, who has made available to the Society the entire second floor of the building to become the Oklahoma County Museum and the home office of the Oklahoma County Historical Society. He has also conveyed to the Society the facade easement of the building.

The Society is also arranging through James Leake of Muskogee for display cases from the recently closed World Museum of Tulsa. With building space and attractive, secure exhibit cases, the Society will be in a position to seriously seek out the most valuable and historically significant artifacts of Oklahoma County history available.

Another Diamond Jubilee project of the Oklahoma County Historical Society is the collection and restoration of external artifacts of destroyed historical buildings of downtown Oklahoma City and the placement of these artifacts, properly and permanently identified and interpreted, in the Clarence Ford Museum adjacent to the Oklahoma City Chamber of Commerce at One Santa Fe Plaza. Society treasurer Bill Peavler and director Bill Silk, both architects, are directing this project. Others playing significant roles are Walter Nashert, builder and construction historian, Richard Ford, who has made the park possible, and the Chamber of Commerce.

Second president of the Society, following Mike Frew, was Jeannette Gilbert. Current officers are Pendleton Woods, president; Melvina Thurman, secretary; and Bill E. Peavler, treasurer.

Left
Officers of the Oklahoma County Historical Society look over plans for the coming year. From left are Pendleton Woods, president; Melvina Thurman, secretary; and Bill E. Peavler, treasurer.

Below
Museum committee members and directors Bill Welge (left) and Mike Everman look over acquisition papers of the Oklahoma County Historical Society Museum, now being developed.

Oklahoma Health Center

In the mid-1960s the Oklahoma Health Center was only a dream of Dr. James L. Dennis, then dean of the University of Oklahoma College of Medicine and vice-president for Health Sciences. With the support of such leaders as Governor Henry Bellmon, Chancellor E.T. Dunlap, Dean McGee, and the Oklahoma City Chamber of Commerce, the Oklahoma Health Science Foundation was established in 1965 to coordinate the development of that dream. A plan was developed and implemented in 1968. The years since have seen the Oklahoma Health Center develop into a multi-institutional entity of national importance. It has expanded into the 200-acre Oklahoma Health Center and added 22 buildings.

The Oklahoma Health Center is literally an all-inclusive coordinated facility. As such it is a network of autonomous health institutions—both public and private—located in close proximity to each other and capable of producing the full range of services necessary for the preven-

tion and treatment of disease. Included in the area are the Dean A. McGee Eye Institute, the Oklahoma Memorial Hospital, the Oklahoma State Department of Health, the Presbyterian Hospital, the Oklahoma Medical Research Foundation, the Veterans Administration Hospital, the Oklahoma Children's Memorial Hospital, the Oklahoma Allergy Clinic, the Oklahoma City Clinic, the Oklahoma State Medical Examiner's Office, and the University of Oklahoma's colleges of dentistry, allied health, public health, medicine, nursing, pharmacy, and the graduate school.

When the first surge of construction began in 1968 with the University's Family Medicine Clinic, there were only three institutions on campus: the University of Oklahoma, with two hospitals; the Oklahoma Medical Research Foundation; and the Veterans Administration Hospital. These entities occupied eight buildings and there were 920 students. As Robert C. Hardy, executive for the Oklahoma Health Science Foundation, noted: "The basic reason for the initial surge of construction was to increase the supply of health manpower in Oklahoma. Education of health professionals is still the central mission of the Oklahoma Health Center."

Today, 14 years and 30 new buildings later, the Oklahoma Health Center consists of 12 major institutions. The student body of the University of Oklahoma Health Sciences Center has more than tripled to 3,000. The growth during the first 50 years from the 1919 beginnings of the campus were slow, with only the three institutions housed in eight buildings. Even now the projects are continuing. In 1980-1981, the following projects were completed: a dermatology clinic, the central steam and chilled water plant, and the emergency medicine and trauma center. Ground has been broken for new facilities for the College of Pharmacy. The investment in the Dennis dream will reach $382 million when all of these projects are in place. The dream became reality when people recognized that the health of the state depended upon the health of its individual citizens.

Left
Presbyterian Hospital is a part of the all-inclusive coordinated Oklahoma Health Center.

Right
The Dean A. McGee Eye Institute serves the community by providing the services necessary for the prevention and treatment of disease.

Oklahoma Mortgage Company

The Oklahoma Mortgage Company wasn't even a dream when Everett H. Cox left the small town of Anadarko, Oklahoma, in 1940. An experienced country banker, Cox had suddenly found himself without employment but with a strong desire to continue in his chosen field.

He left his family temporarily in Anadarko, and came to Oklahoma City. Because of his experience in making FHA loans, he soon became a contract loan producer doing business as The Oklahoma Mortgage Company for The Liberty National Bank. In those early days his budget was so tight that he lived in a board-

The Hales Building at the corner of Main Street and Robinson Avenue was the first home of the Oklahoma Mortgage Company.

ing house and walked to work to save money. Business picked up quickly, and after the war broke out he handled financing for a number of housing projects. By 1947 Cox had accumulated a working capital of $100,000 and the firm became an FHA approved mortgagee. So, Oklahoma Mortgage Company was founded.

Cox's staff consisted of Louise Jewell and Dale C. Chewgin. All three started working as state loan correspondents for the Mutual Life Insurance Company of New York, in a tiny office in the Hales Building. As the firm expanded it moved to larger quarters in the Perrine Building, and then took over and renamed the old Braniff Building at Third and Robinson, the Oklahoma Mortgage Building.

As the company continued to grow, it opened a branch office in Tulsa and showed sufficient capital to become a FHA-approved mortgagee. Other life insurance companies and savings institutions were added as investors. In 1951 Aet-

na Life Insurance Company appointed Oklahoma Mortgage as its loan correspondent. The relationship with Aetna proved so successful that in 1957 Aetna transferred its servicing of farm loans and mineral interests in seven states to the firm.

The organization continues to grow and has, under the current leadership of president Everett E. Cox, diversified into the fields of oil and gas, real estate sales, private placements, and property management. Cox joined the company in 1960 and has been assisted by John N. Booth, who had joined in 1952.

In 1979 Louise Jewell, who had been with the firm since its beginnings, became president of Closing Service Corporation, a wholly owned subsidiary. Her offices are located across the street from the parent company's current home in Oklahoma Mortgage Tower at 5100 North Brookline.

The servicing volume of the business has grown steadily to over $320 million. Oklahoma Mortgage is justifiably proud of its growth and of its reputation as the most solid mortgage company in the Southwest.

The current headquarters of Oklahoma Mortgage is at 5100 North Brookline in Oklahoma City.

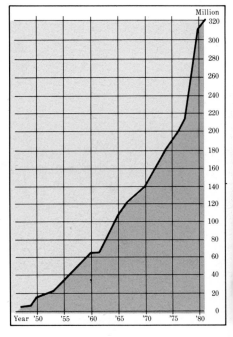

The dollar growth of the company from 1947 through 1981.

Skirvin Plaza Hotel

In 1911 W.B. "Big Bill" Skirvin told Oklahoma City's leading architect, Solomon Layton, to build him "the showplace of the Southwest." How well he succeeded is still evident today, over 70 years later, as the Skirvin Plaza reflects the elegance and warmth of the Gilded Age amid the steel and glass of modern Oklahoma City.

Skirvin, who had made an enormous fortune in oil, spared no expense or effort in creating the city's finest hotel. His generous, outgoing personality made him an ideal host; he insisted that his staff consider the hotel's guests as his personal guests. (He passed this gift of hospitality along to his daughter, Perle Skirvin Mesta, whose Washington, D.C., parties were legendary.)

Skirvin's grand hotel and equally grand manner attracted the cream of local and national society, as well as celebrities from all over the world. The hotel became so popular that Skirvin added a new section in 1918, two more floors in 1923, and an entire new building, the Skirvin Tower, in 1929.

Until his death in 1944, Skirvin continued to adapt and improve his hotel. The next owner, Dan James, followed in the same tradition of excellence, showcasing the best entertainment, big-name bands, and Hollywood stars. Unfortunately, the growth of motels and the decline of the downtown area forced James to sell out in 1960 to a group of Chicago and New York businessmen.

Over the next 15 years, the Skirvin changed hands several times and finally went into bankruptcy. Then, as the downtown renewal project gathered momentum in the 1970s, a group of local businessmen decided that it was time to restore the Skirvin to its original glory.

They bought the hotel and embarked on a massive renovation program. The lobby was restored to its original two-story height and highlighted with crystal chandeliers imported from Czechoslovakia; a sweeping staircase was installed near the drive-in lobby; all 210 guest rooms were redecorated with the finest furniture and fabrics; a new club, Pinstripes, was created on the mezzanine; and the basement was transformed into Skirvin Place—a marvelous array of specialty shops and restaurants.

Today, as businessmen again meet in the elegant lobby, and the city's major social events are again held in the hotel, the Skirvin Plaza is once again what Big Bill Skirvin originally dreamed it would be: "The showplace of the Southwest."

Oklahoma Teaching Hospitals

Created through an act of the Oklahoma Legislature, OTH came into being on July 1, 1980. However, the history of those hospitals which make up the OTH is much more extensive than that date indicates.

OTH is made up of four parts. They are Oklahoma Memorial Hospital, a comprehensive 430-bed teaching hospital for adult patients; Oklahoma Children's Memorial Hospital, a 402-bed tertiary care teaching hospital serving young people from birth to 21 years; the Don H. O'Donoghue Rehabilitation Institute, a 120-bed teaching facility that provides evaluation and rehabilitative services to all ages; and the Child Study Center, an outpatient facility for children with behavior and developmental problems.

Administratively, these facilities function under the Oklahoma Department of Human Services. Operationally, they function as teaching facilities for the University of Oklahoma Health Sciences Center (OUHSC). They are staffed by OUHSC personnel and others.

OTH also operates an emergency air transport helicopter service—Medi Flight Oklahoma—staffed by highly trained emergency medical professionals who provide stabilization to patients en route to required comprehensive medical care and treatment. Medi Flight is a statewide service, providing assistance to other hospitals on request.

Oklahoma Memorial Hospital first came into being when it was established as a part of the University of Oklahoma Medical School on October 12, 1911. At that time it was christened the State University Hospital. Housed in a converted private hospital owned by Dr. Joseph B. Rolater, it had a total of 60 inpatient beds, a dispensary for ambulatory patients in the basement, and used a kitchen for its clinical laboratories.

The university obtained its own hospital building in 1919, thanks primarily to the efforts of Dr. Francis B. Fite of Muskogee, a member of the State Board of Education, Dr. Leroy Long, Dean of OU Medical School, and Governor Robert Lee Williams. The hospital had 176 inpatient beds and included 25 private rooms. In 1921 administrative offices and nurses quarters were added to the hospital.

By 1970 a new building program was under way at University Hospital. In that year a structure was erected on campus. It was Everett Tower, named after former Dean of the OU Medical School, Dr. Mark R. Everett.

Through the next 12 years the reconstruction program continued. Today Oklahoma Memorial Hospital, as the hospital was renamed in 1980, is recognized as one of the most modern, up-to-date medical facilities in the country. In addition to its 430 inpatient beds, which serve the general medical and surgical needs of adults, it has established more than 40 specialized outpatient clinics. OMH is a regional center for patient care, teaching, and clinical research.

Oklahoma Children's Memorial Hospital was first established in 1928 as part of the old University Hospital. It was, and is today, a teaching hospital. At that time it

Above
Oklahoma Memorial Hospital, one of the most modern medical facilities in the country, is a comprehensive 430-bed teaching hospital for adult patients.

Below
Oklahoma Children's Memorial Hospital is equipped to handle numerous pediatric specialties and is designed to cater to their needs.

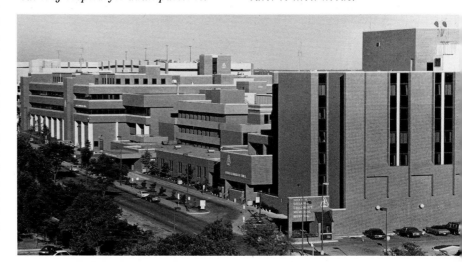

was known as Oklahoma Crippled Children's Hospital, and provided an additional 160 beds to the University Hospital total. Children's Hospital was transferred to the Oklahoma Department of Human Services, known then as the Oklahoma Department of Institutions, Social and Rehabilitative Services (DISRS), in 1973.

When that transfer occurred, OCMH began a similar program of reconstruction and expansion as that experienced by OMH. By 1981 OCMH had been modernized, expanded, and enlarged to accommodate such pediatric specialties as neonatology, cardiology, cardiac surgery, hematology and oncology, pediatric surgery, burn therapy, nephrology, urology, neurology, genetic diseases, dental and oral surgery, orthopedic surgery, and growth problems.

The Don H. O'Donoghue Rehabilitation Institute is a 120-bed multipurpose inpatient and outpatient facility designed to provide short-range, intermediate medical and rehabilitation services to physically disabled children and adults. Opened in 1981, the institute is named after Dr. Don H. O'Donoghue of Oklahoma City, a pioneer orthopedic surgeon whose work on behalf of crippled children, leadership in medical education, and professional abilities have brought him well-deserved national recognition.

With its opening, the institute established a new tradition in patient care, education, and research. Clinics meet at various times throughout the month and include (but are not limited to) spinal cord, hemophilia, cerebral palsy, urology, myelomeningocele, hand, amputee, orthotics, screening, and neuromuscular care and treatment programs.

The Child Study Center of OTH was established in 1958. It is a multidisciplinary unit designed to provide outpatient evaluation and treatment for children with neurological, developmental, social/emotional, and school learning problems. Patients range in age from newborn to 21 years.

Primary services of the CSC include comprehensive assessment by a multidisciplinary team; medical

Above
Medi Flight, a statewide service, provides stabilization to patients en route to medical care and treatment.

Below
The Don H. O'Donoghue Rehabilitation Institute provides short-term, intermediate medical, and rehabilitative services to physically disabled children and adults.

follow-up of problems; psychological and social work services for children and their families, including family therapy, play therapy, individual psychotherapy, supportive parent groups, consultation for management of behavior problems, and a respite aide program for deaf-blind/sensory impaired, Down's syndrome, and multi-handicapped children; and psychoeducational programming of autistic, emotionally disturbed, abused, and language-disordered children. Consultation from health professionals throughout the OTH and the OUHSC are available to all CSC patients.

The State of Oklahoma Teaching Hospitals were established to serve the medical care and treatment needs of the people of the state. No patient is ever turned away from any of its institutions because of an inability to pay for the care and treatment available through its programs. OTH is affiliated with the University of Oklahoma Health Sciences Center. It is a major teaching base for the OUHSC's six colleges—the College of Medicine, the College of Nursing, the College of Pharmacy, the College of Dentistry, the College of Health, and the Graduate College. Working hand in hand, OTH and the OUHSC are home to faculty and residents of these health-related institutions of learning.

While justifiably proud of its past, the staff of OTH concentrates on the present and the future. Historically, OTH has had three major goals. The first was to provide the most comprehensive medical care and treatment available to its patients. That tradition goes on.

Second, the hospitals were designed to provide educational programs for the training of health care professionals. They have evolved into a major teaching center which enjoys a national reputation for excellence. That tradition goes on.

Finally, the hospitals have dedicated themselves through the years to the support of clinical research on the part of the faculty and staff. That tradition goes on.

Presbyterian Hospital

Oklahoma City's history of medicine is as varied and intriguing as the chronicle of its political, social, and economic heritage. Presbyterian Hospital and its predecessor institutions, the Oklahoma City Clinic and Wesley Hospital, have been at the center of this history during the 20th century. The Wesley Hospital was established in Oklahoma City in 1910 by Dr. Foster Camp and operated under his administration until 1919. Just after the completion of their military service in World War I, Drs. A.L. Blesh, Marvin E. Stout, W.W. Rucks, D.D. Paulus, J.Z. Mraz, and W.H. Bailey established the Oklahoma City Clinic and acquired the Wesley Hospital. Dr. J.C. McDonald joined the organization within the first year of operation, adding his specialty.

The Wesley School of Nursing was established in 1920. It prepared students for professional status until 1952, when the baccalaureate pro-

gram in nursing was established in a cooperative form between Oklahoma Baptist University and Wesley Hospital. This new program was granted full accreditation. Currently the Oklahoma Baptist University nursing program, in conjunction with several other nursing programs, forms an important component of Presbyterian's role as a teaching hospital.

Presbyterian Hospital has maintained a continuous intern and residency program in surgery, general medicine, gynecology, and obstetrics. In 1937 the hospital established a teaching affiliation with the University of Oklahoma Medical School. It consisted of clerkships in the departments of medicine, gynecology and obstetrics, pediatrics, and radiology. Through this connection, in 1965 Dr. James L. Dennis, director of the University of Oklahoma Medical School Center, requested that Presbyterian Hospital consider moving to the Oklahoma Health Center in northeast Oklahoma City. Medical education and a broader and more diverse base became major factors in the decision to move.

Expanded health care has remained as a major factor in the continuing growth of the hospital throughout its existence. The main building, located on Northwest 12th Street, was constructed in 1927. The west wing of the complex was built three years later, and the east wing

came into being in 1947. Further expansion at that location took place in 1951, 1960, and 1964.

In 1964 the Washita Presbytery of the United Presbyterian Church affiliated with the Wesley Foundation Hospital, which had been designed to promote charitable, scientific, and educational goals. The foundation had assumed operation and control of Wesley Hospital in 1961. Physician members of the Oklahoma City Clinic continued to utilize the hosptial and new physicians with needed specialties were invited to practice at the hospital. With the new arrangement in 1964 came the new name—the Presbyterian Medical Center of Oklahoma, Inc. In 1973 the name was changed to Presbyterian Hospital, Inc.

Intensive planning went into the move and expansion of the hospital. The planning committee included Drs. Robert C. Lawson, R.B. Carl, Ted Clemens, William L. Hughes, James P. Luton, Edward R. Munnell, as well as Mr. Stanton L. Young. Their efforts led to the decision to construct a $36-million private acute-care hospital. On December 1

The leadership and foresight of doctors A.L. Blesh, Marvin E. Stout, W.W. Rucks, D.D. Paulus, J.Z. Mraz, and W.H. Bailey led to the formation of the Oklahoma City Clinic and the acquisition and development of the Wesley Hospital (later to be Presbyterian Hospital).

On October 1, 1919, the Oklahoma City Clinic purchased the 50-bed Wesley Hospital, owned by Dr. Foster W. Camp. When Camp bought St. Luke's Hospital in 1910, he renamed it for his wife's alma mater, Wesley Hospital Training School in Chicago.

1974, the staff of approximately 500 took up their duties at the new building on Northeast 13th Street and Lincoln Boulevard. That first year the hospital nearly doubled its staff size, opened a pulmonary functions laboratory, instituted an electroencephalography laboratory, expanded its patient service capabilities, expanded its educational programs, and initiated innovative management techniques. A new working relationship with the Oklahoma Medical Research Foundation brought about the housing of their inpatients in Presbyterian Hospital.

The hospital currently consists of two separate buildings, containing 407 beds, 384 private patient rooms, 23 beds in intensive care and coronary care units, and 31 nursery bassinets. Continued growth has brought about a $6-million expansion project, which will be completed in 1982. The hospital chapel, open 24 hours a day, is located on the first floor. The ecumenical chaplaincy program is a vital part of the care for the patients' spiritual needs. In this, too, the hospital is a teaching institution, for ministers and priests are trained in the program for work across the state.

Presbyterian Hospital maintains services including endocrinology, urology, general medicine, general surgery, cardiovascular and thoracic surgery, microsurgery, neurosurgery, neurology, nuclear medicine, obstetrics-gynecology, oncology, orthopedics, pediatrics, plastic surgery, ophthalmology, otorhinolaryngology, special procedures, and X-ray. Also available are 13 operating suites, an intensive care unit, coronary care units, hemodialysis, a progressive coronary care unit, complete laboratory services, gastroenterology, and pulmonary medicine.

A variety of other services are available, including Presbyterian's remote cardiac monitoring network, which is the largest in the nation. The sleep disorders center began operation in 1976, and is one of only 25 accredited centers in the United States. The genetics diagnostic center, opened in 1979, provides genetic diagnosis, counseling, and education. The oncology program fosters a family-centered cancer care effort. Additional services include the chemical dependency treatment unit and the counseling center. The hospital operates its own schools of radiologic technology and medical technology, as well as maintaining other teaching relationships. Presbyterian is the only private, not-for-profit hospital in the Oklahoma Health Center. Through its wholly owned subsidiary, Innovative Health Programs (IHP) Corp., it provides management and contract services to more than 40 hospitals and clinics throughout Oklahoma.

Presbyterian Hospital employs approximately 1,700 trained persons on full-time and part-time basis. The volunteer auxiliary consists of more than 300 people who contribute thousands of hours. In every facet of the hospital's work the patients and their families are treated in an intelligent and sensitive manner. Presbyterian Hospital, the "Patient People Place," is a historical example of "sharing life by caring for it."

The modern and attractive Presbyterian Hospital continues to grow at its current location on the corner of Lincoln and Northeast 13th—an important part of the Health Science Center complex.

The maternity ward—and especially the nursery—is one of the happiest parts of the hospital whose total commitment is preserving and restoring good health.

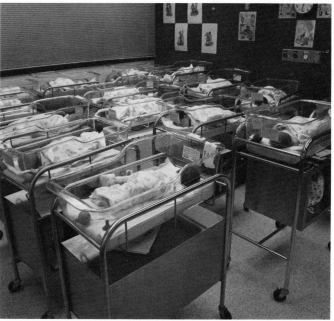

Scrivner, Inc.

Enoch Scrivner bought a 160-acre farm near Meshak (where Tinker Field now stands) in 1901. It was here that he first went into the grocery business. Mrs. Scrivner helped operate the store and Enoch hauled produce the 17 miles to Oklahoma City. Most of the time these loads consisted of rabbits and quail, piled as high as the sideboards of the wagon would hold.

Scrivner moved to Oklahoma City in 1905 to open a retail grocery store. He formed a partnership with his brother-in-law, J.H. Stevens, and by 1917, when it was sold, their firm operated three retail grocery stores and was one of the largest in the Southwest.

The partners took the money from the sale of the retail outlets and for-mally organized as the Scrivner Stevens Company, Wholesale Grocers. They leased space until their "modern" warehouse at 122-136 East Washington Avenue was completed in 1927.

As the organization grew in Oklahoma City, it branched out. In 1929 the partners formally opened a warehouse in Shawnee, and by 1939, had added another in Tulsa to service the northeastern part of Oklahoma and the southern part of Kansas.

The company continued to expand and develop the quantity and quality of its operation during the next years. In 1955, when its founder, Enoch Scrivner, died, plans were under way for a new warehouse in Tulsa. Henry W. Dean, who took over as president, presided at the opening of the warehouse. At the time of Scrivner's death, the firm's payroll exceeded $700,000 paid to 298 employees. The company's annual sales amounted to over $15 million. Dean followed Scrivner's example of improving and streamlining the wholesale operation, which served numerous independent and company-owned Red Bud stores. Scrivner Stevens acquired Bouldin Fruit Company in July 1958. Scrivner Stevens became a publicly owned company in 1960 and two years later the Oklahoma City food distribution center was relocated to its present site at Southeast 59th Street and Interstate 35.

A. Dean Cutsinger became Scrivner Stevens' president in 1962. In an effort to increase the scope of operations, Cutsinger arranged a merger with Boogaart Supply Company of Concordia, Kansas, in November 1965. This merger brought 19 retail supermarkets and 60 independent

Enoch Scrivner, founder of Scrivner Stevens Company.

James V. Kunstel, chief executive officer, president, and chairman of the board of Scrivner, Inc.

stores into the fold along with ice cream and bakery plants. Soon after, the newly named firm of Scrivner-Boogaart acquired the Golden Krust Bakery in Alva.

J.V. Smith was elected president and chief executive officer of the company in 1968. During his 10-year leadership term, he spearheaded a diversification move into the general merchandise business and negotiated the acquisition of Pay Cash Grocery Company, a wholesale food organization in Knoxville, Tennessee. Scrivner-Boogaart became a listed company on the American Stock Exchange in 1971. The firm's name was shortened to its present Scrivner, Inc., in 1974.

Today Scrivner, Inc., an Oklahoma corporation and wholly owned subsidiary of Hanamerica, Inc., is led by chairman, president, and chief executive officer James V. Kunstel. Like his predecessors, his goals are the effective and efficient operation of the existing six divisions and growth through new acquisitions. In 1980 the company purchased Groce-Wearden, a wholesale grocery company operating in southern Texas. That same year the corporation moved its principal offices to a new corporate headquarters facility. The year 1981 saw the completion of a large new perishable products warehouse in Oklahoma City.

Annual sales are hovering at the billion-dollar level from distribution centers in Oklahoma City; Concordia, Kansas; Knoxville, Tennessee; and Victoria and Donna, Texas; food service for restaurants and cafeterias is handled in Oklahoma City and Bay City, Texas. The company owns over 70 retail stores, including Bestyet, Food World, and Sharp stores in Oklahoma, Tennessee, Georgia, Louisiana, Kansas, and Texas; as well as Boogaarts and Buy for Less Stores in Kansas and Nebraska.

Scrivner, Inc., continues to receive recognition as one of the most efficient and best managed wholesale-retail operations in the country and all plans call for it to continue to pioneer ways to expand its service and increase its scope of operation in the coming years.

James V. Kunstel and city officials break ground for the firm's corporate headquarters.

T.G.&Y. Stores

T.G. & Y. Stores began as the warehouse operation of a new company, Central Merchandise, in 1936 in Oklahoma City. The venture was formed by R.E. Tomlinson, E.L. Gosselin, and R.A. Young. They put their wholesale operations under unified management in order to increase their buying power. Tomlinson operated variety stores in Frederick and Grandfield; Gosselin had stores in Cordell, Hobart, and Elk City; and Young owned stores in Kingfisher, Weatherford, Hennessey, Crescent, Guthrie, Geary, Watonga, and Medford.

In 1936 they opened the first combined retail store, a T.G. & Y., in Norman and the second was opened the following year in Oklahoma City. The chain continued to grow until in 1944 all of the individually owned stores were combined into one company. The organization was incorporated under the laws of Delaware as T.G. & Y. Stores Company in 1946. By that time the chain operated more than 30 outlets. Central Merchandise, a wholly owned subsidiary, was retained for the wholesale operation.

When asked about the tremendous growth of T.G. & Y., which now has an annual volume exceeding two billion dollars in sales, R.A. Young explained: "We just kept taking advantage of every opportunity. I have never been much for budgets or long-range plans. What happens if an opportunity comes along and it's not in your plan? You're liable to miss it. You should use your best intelligence at the time to take advantage of new opportunities that appear."

The first warehouse was located in Oklahoma City on 11th Street; the operation then moved to North Broadway in 1938. In 1950 T.G. & Y. moved into new headquarters on North Santa Fe, the first industry to locate north of 36th Street. As the company continued its rapid expansion into the southern and southwestern states, branch warehouses were opened in Shreveport, Louisiana, in 1961; Lubbock, Texas, in 1965; La Mirada, California, in 1966; Montgomery, Alabama, in 1969; Kansas City, Kansas, in 1970; Edmond, Oklahoma, in 1972; and Houston, Texas, in 1974. In 1977 T.G. & Y. introduced distribution warehouses, which distribute promotional, seasonal, and new-item goods to the respective area. Five of these are in operation in Orlando, Florida; Hattiesburg, Mississippi; Edmond, Oklahoma; Shelbyville, Kentucky; and Macon, Georgia. In 1979 a new import warehouse was constructed in Oklahoma City.

T.G. & Y. operates three classes of stores—the expanded variety store, the family center, and the larger family center. Based upon the size, the goods and services range from convenience merchandise to clothing, sporting goods, fabrics, hardware, and automotive center, pharmacy, and outdoor garden materials.

In 1957 T.G. & Y. merged with Butler Brothers and both became a subsidiary of City Products Corporation, which is now a subsidiary of Household Merchandising, a Household International Company.

The current president and chief executive officer of T.G. & Y. is D.S. "Dan" Kelly, who was born in Drumright, Oklahoma, and worked his way up through the organization to this post, living the "excitement of retailing" that is T.G. & Y.

D.S. "Dan" Kelly, T.G. & Y. president, started working in a Ben Franklin store in 1936. By 1945 he was an assistant T.G. & Y. store manager; he progressed to the presidency in 1980.

An early T.G. & Y. small variety store which through the years has been replaced with the larger, more modern family center.

Thomas Concrete Products Company

Oklahomans who refer to Thomas Concrete these days are talking about Thomas Concrete Products Company, whose 85-acre plant in south Oklahoma City is the largest precast, prestressed concrete manufacturer in the Southwest.

However, in the days of the Dust Bowl and Great Depression, they would have been talking about Thomas Concrete Pipe Company, founded by Tom A. Thomas, Sr., in Ada, Oklahoma, in 1934.

From the outset, Thomas concentrated on research and development and became the first to master a new technique of manufacturing six-foot concrete pipe segments by machine. Soon Thomas machine-made segments 8 feet and 12 feet long. The firm was first to produce a 72-inch inside diameter concrete pipe by machine, and then went on to manufacture concrete pipe 84 inches in inside diameter. When World War II broke out, Thomas Concrete Pipe Company had more pipe-making equipment than anyone in Oklahoma or Texas.

Thomas added concrete blocks to the company's line and became the largest producer of concrete blocks in the Southwest. Growth accelerated. Thomas built plants in Oklahoma and Texas until he had six permanent and nine temporary plants. He made partners of his father, Charles A. Thomas, and his brothers; Lewis, Ray, Wilbur, and Churchill.

Among the lasting achievements of the Thomases is the FAA supply depot built in 1956 to 1957, near Will Rogers World Airport. This seven-acre facility was the largest structure to have been made of precast, prestressed concrete at that time.

In 1959 the firm merged with another company which would become Martin Marietta, but in 1962 Tom A. Thomas, Jr., and his brother, Jimmie C. Thomas, left Martin Marietta and established Thomas Block Company. This enterprise was soon renamed Thomas Concrete Products Company and located at 5500 South High.

Tom A. Thomas, Jr., now chief executive officer of the firm, has long held a leadership position in the Prestressed Concrete Institute (PCI), the industry's premier association, with a national membership and international affiliations linking 256 plants throughout the world. In 1981 he became president-elect of PCI.

Jimmie C. Thomas is secretary-treasurer of the firm. Other Thomases in the business are Tom Jr.'s sons, Tom A. Thomas III and Michael C. Thomas; and Jimmie C.'s sons, Timothy N. and Ted N.

Early in its history, Thomas established the eight-foot-length of pipe as an industry standard. Later Thomas established the eight-foot-wide double-T as an industry-standard building component, and then developed the TOTALCAST®, a multi-story office building system.

Because of its pioneering in the industry, consultants from throughout the United States and foreign nations have come to Oklahoma City to study Thomas techniques, which have received great acceptance.

It has been said that no one single company has contributed more to the advancement of precast, prestressed concrete than has Thomas Concrete Products Company of Oklahoma City.

Tom A. Thomas, Jr., chief executive officer (above), and Jimmie C. Thomas (below), secretary-treasurer, of Thomas Concrete Products Company.

The founder of Thomas Concrete Pipe Company, Tom A. Thomas, Sr., (fourth from left), is shown with his brothers, whom he made partners in the firm during World War II. From left to right are Churchill, Lewis, Ray, Tom, and Wilbur.

Tinker Credit Union

Since World War II Tinker Air Force Base has been a major employer in the Oklahoma City area as well as an integral part of our national defense system. In March 1946 seven civilian employees of Tinker recognized the cooperative advantages of the credit union movement, and they incorporated the Tinker Field Employees Credit Union to serve the base's civilian employees and their dependents.

The credit union began operation in Building 3001 on base, and in that same year, 1946, it printed its first annual report, listing a total of 152 members and assets of $4,190.

From those modest beginnings the organization has grown steadily. In 1949 it hired its first full-time employee, and in 1953 added the Area A branch office in Building 203. Two years later the credit union opened a third office on base. The board of directors opened the field of membership to include the base's military employees and their dependents in 1958.

The membership continued to grow, and in 1967 the organization changed its name to Tinker Credit Union and opened a branch office at Vance Air Force Base in Enid. By 1975 its funds on deposit greatly exceeded loan requests, and in order to find borrowers for those unused funds the credit union began searching for new members.

That same year Tinker Credit Union began allowing corporations to affiliate with it, and these affiliations, in turn, made the corporations' employees eligible to join the credit union. To accommodate the growing membership, two additional branch offices were opened—one in Midwest City in 1975 and another in Bethany in 1977. That year Tinker moved its Area A office into new quarters, and two years later moved the Midwest City branch into a new facility.

Today Tinker Credit Union's membership is located throughout the world, and it is growing at a new rate of approximately 600 members per month. With a total membership of approximately 90,000, the organization has assets of $200 million. It is the largest credit union in Oklahoma and the 16th largest in the nation. It operates seven branch offices, employs 160 people, and has its own computer system.

Tinker Credit Union offers a wide range of services, including share accounts, share draft accounts, share certificates, money market certificates, all savers certificates, individual retirement accounts, trust accounts, safe deposit boxes, money orders, and travelers checks. The credit union also offers an Automated Teller Machine card (ATM), Command 24, which may be used at approximately 150 locations across Oklahoma.

The expanding Tinker Credit Union serves a worldwide membership from this building on base. (Photo courtesy of Sherryl Warrick.)

United Engines, Inc.

United Engines is a company growing rapidly in Oklahoma. The chairman of the board and founder believes that's the way it ought to be. He's 78-year-old James W. Morton who lives in Shreveport, Louisiana. He got his start in the Louisiana oil fields. In 1946 he became the General Motors distributor for diesel engines in Louisiana and Arkansas.

In 1967 the Mortons purchased the Diesel Power Company founded in Oklahoma in 1934. James Morton's son, Jerry, merged Diesel Power Company with United Engines, Inc., and subsequently moved to Oklahoma City as president and general manager of the firm.

The company that started in the oil field is still heavily involved in oil field equipment. United Engines is official distributor for Detroit Diesel Allison, a division of General Motors Corporation. It sells, services, and remanufactures Detroit diesel engines and Allison automatic transmissions for oil field equipment as well as the trucking and busing, agricultural, and construction industries. The firm also manufactures customized diesel driven generators for computer operations and hospitals, as well as emergency support systems.

President and now chief executive officer, Jerry Morton, has appointed his son, Jay, a graduate of the University of Oklahoma, vice-president and general manager of corporate affairs. Like all of United Engines's executives, Jay has grown up with the business. He started at the bottom and has earned his credentials.

From its original location United Engines has expanded into three new facilities in Oklahoma City spanning over 215,555 square feet. The home office is located at 5555 West Reno Avenue. In addition to Oklahoma City, United also has complete sales and service facilities in Tulsa, Oklahoma; Shreveport, Louisiana; and Texarkana, Arkansas. In 1982 United plans to open a complete sales and service facility in Duncan, Oklahoma, and a parts and service depot in Elk City, Oklahoma.

The business climate in Oklahoma City agrees with the company's youthful management group. In 1967 sales totaled $3 million. Now the group, whose average age is 30.2 years, employs over 400 people and accounts for over $83 million in annual sales.

Above
James W. Morton, chairman of the board and founder of United Engines, Inc.

Below
Diesel Power Company at the time of its purchase by United Engines.

Unarco Commercial Products

UNR Industries, Inc., is a diversified manufacturer and marketer of a broad range of industrial, commercial, and consumer products. It is comprised of a number of divisions, each of which is a leader in its respective field. Steel fabricating is the common thread permeating most of its divisions. The headquarters of the corporation is in Chicago, but it has a unique connection with Oklahoma County.

In the 1950s, Unarco purchased the patent for the shopping cart that had been designed, manufactured, and marketed from the county. This was the original "Folding Carrier" shopping cart. Unarco Commercial Products remains the leading manufacturer of this indispensable product line for the supermarket and mass merchandising commercial enterprises. To meet the requirements of all types of stores, large and small shopping carts are manufactured and marketed in the United States, Europe, the Middle East, and Asia. It remains a mainstay of the mass merchandising supermarket industries.

The Vendall and Vendex lines of stack baskets, mobile bins, and gondola baskets are new concepts of handling and displaying products for mass merchandisers. They permit merchandise to be bulk-dumped, thereby eliminating the need for individually handling products. The Unarco Food Handling division manufactures a complete line of equipment for preparing, storing, and displaying foods.

In 1979 Unarco Commercial Products introduced a new line of Lifestyle KD Furniture. Market accept-ance has proven to be outstanding and the line is now sold nationally by the country's leading furniture retailers.

Unarco Home Products manufactures stainless steel sinks, faucets, charcoal-fueled cookers, and other stainless steel and porcelain-enamel coated products. Unarco-Leavitt is among the nation's largest producer of standard and specialty electric-welded steel tubing from three-sixteenth-inch to five-inch diameter. The division's highly automated tube mills produce more than 75,000 miles of finished tubing per year.

Unarco Lighting is a major supplier of lighting and venting systems for recreational vehicles and mobile homes. These include modular and combination rear lamps; clearance, identification, and side marker-reflector lamps; back-up and license lamps; dome lamps; and porch lights. The Unarco Materials Storage division manufactures a wide variety of industrial racks and other storage equipment. An important feature in some of these rigid-rack systems is the patented Float Wedge Connector, which holds components together without pins, screws, or other con-

Marvin Weiss, senior vice-president and general manager of Unarco's Commercial Products division.

Unarco's new generation of Checkmate shopping carts feature a new "swing down and under hideaway gate" that allows for full basket loading and easy unloading.

ventional fasteners.

The Unarco-Midwest Steel division is a major supplier of rail, trackwork, and tools used in industrial railroad installations. The division also provides pre-drilled, cut-to-length rail sections, joint bars, special machine bolts, fasteners, and crane stops. Unarco-Midwest Tele-Communications is involved in the sales, engineering,

Below
The Unarco Commercial Products division is based in Oklahoma City.

installation, and servicing of complete closed circuit television systems. For almost 30 years, Unarco-Rohn has been a major manufacturer of towers for a variety of uses, including towers for supporting residential, television, CB, and ham radio antennas, radar towers, microwave towers for cross-country voice and data transmission, radio broadcasting towers, lighting towers for meteorological equipment, and livestock confinement equipment.

Unarco Rubber Products division, located in Tulsa, is a major producer of molded solid rubber wheels for industry and sport. Simple in appearance, rubber wheels require precise engineering and rigid manufacturing techniques. Unarco Transportation Equipment Division is well known to the transportation industry for its load bearing, protecting, and segregating systems, as well as boxcar side doors and freight car hand brakes. The division also rebuilds, repairs, and reconditions railroad freight cars and freight car equipment. These products and services minimize in-transit damage and permit faster and more efficient loading and unloading of freight cars and trailers.

The Unarco Commercial Products division, based in Oklahoma City, is directed by Marvin Weiss, senior vice-president and general manager, and is one of the innovative arms of the multifaceted corporation that is another example of the creative elements of free enterprise. Since 1937 the shopping cart has evolved with the supermarketing and mass merchandising efforts. The invention was so revolutionary that it has earned an honored place in the Smithsonian Institution in Washington, D.C., where it is displayed. It is one of the principal stories of a timely idea made a reality, spanning four decades, to provide for modern existence

Left
In 1979 Unarco Commercial Products introduced a new line of Lifestyle KD Furniture. The line is now sold nationally by the country's leading furniture retailers.

University of Oklahoma Health Sciences Center

One of the nation's youngest state universities, the institution first began in September 1892, in a rented store building located in what is now the Norman business district. David Ross Boyd served as the first president, and with three other faculty members made up the teaching staff. The curriculum first provided for preparatory courses and two years of college work.

In 1908 several important appointments made the medical school, which ultimately was to be in Oklahoma County, a new reality for the university. These included Dr. C.S. Bobo as dean and Dr. L.A. Turley as professor of pathology, with the additional duty of organizing the bacteriological laboratory for the State Board of Health and also acting as state bacteriologist. John Dice McLaren was appointed head of the department of physiology; Edwin DeBarr, head of the department of chemistry, taught chemistry in the medical school and served as the state chemist.

The University of Oklahoma Medical School absorbed the Epworth College of Medicine of Oklahoma City in 1911. The State University Hospital was established in a converted private hospital owned by Dr. Joseph B. Rolater, housing a total of 60 inpatient beds, a dispensary for outpatients in the basement, and a kitchen for its clinical laboratories. The University Medical School was provided with a new building in 1919. The new University Hospital, constructed on Northeast 13th, just southeast of the state capitol, housed 176 beds and included 25 private rooms. The University of Oklahoma School of Nursing, which had been created in 1911, also was headquartered in the new facility.

The original College of Medicine Building, presently the home of the Colleges of Allied Health and Public Health at the University of Oklahoma Health Sciences Center.

Administrative offices and nurses' quarters were added to the new hospital in 1921. The dean of the medical school at that time was Dr. Leroy Long.

As the University of Oklahoma went through many years of turbulent growth, the medical school grew in somewhat calmer seas in Oklahoma City. The Medical Center, as it became known, grew into the primary medical education center of the state and an impressive monument to medical progress in the Southwest. The complex of buildings that line the street combined the objectives of medical education, community medical service, and medical research. Opened by the post-World War II period were the University of Oklahoma School of Medicine, the University Hospital, the University's School of Nursing, the Crippled Children's Hospital, and a Speech and Hearing Clinic. Also on the grounds, completed in 1953, were the Veterans Administration Hospital and the unique Oklahoma Medical Research Institute, which is privately owned and operated, with its adjacent research hospital.

In the mid-1960s Dr. James L. Dennis, then dean of the University of Oklahoma College of Medicine and vice-president for Health Sciences, proposed the creation of a coordinated health science center to be a multi-institutional teaching facility. It has expanded into a 200-acre Oklahoma Health Center with a complex of 22 buildings which rival the main campus in Norman in size and structure. In 1980 the University Hospital was renamed Oklahoma Memorial Hospital as a part of Oklahoma Teaching Hospitals. Memorial is one of four hospitals that are part of the educational enterprise. The other three are Oklahoma Childrens' Memorial Hospital, the Don H. O'Donoghue Rehabilitation Institute, and the Child Study Center.

The University of Oklahoma colleges of medicine, nursing, pharmacy, dentistry, public health, allied health, and graduate college now comprise what is known as the University of Oklahoma Health Sciences Center. In a cooperative effort, the coordination of the many institutions in the Health Sciences Center and particularly the Oklahoma Teaching Hospitals allows dramatic growth potential for the future.

Oklahoma University Health Sciences Center's Bio-Medical Sciences Building.

W & W Steel Company

The most important elements of the firm are "our employees and our customers," according to Allen E. Coles, chairman of the board and chief executive officer of the steel fabrication company.

W&W Steel Company was founded on October 1, 1945, by W.G. "Jerry" Wilson and John H. Winneberger. They worked together for another steel company as general sales manager and chief engineer, respectively, and soon recognized the need for a more progressive steel company.

With their vast knowledge and experience in the steel industry and dedication to providing service to their customers, their teamwork stimulated instant success. W&W Steel had grown to over 60 permanent employees by 1949. Winneberger's valuable services and long years of experience in the steel business were lost to the organization through his untimely death in an auto accident May 14, 1949.

As demand and sales increased in the fabrication of reinforcing steel, structural steel, and ornamental iron for commercial and industrial construction, the growth resulted in three fabricating plants. These plants currently provide 496,000 square feet of shop fabrication and over 46,500 square feet of office on 63 acres. The Oklahoma City plant has remained the headquarters. The firm has experienced constant growth in serving customers proficiently. In addition to the enlargement of the original plant, the company acquired a manufacturing plant in Norman, Oklahoma, in 1966. This plant manufactures over 30,000 electrical transformer tanks annually. Additional steel fabricating facilities have been acquired in Albuquerque, New Mexico (1967), and Lubbock, Texas (1976). Total operations employ over 660 people, with sales over $60 million serving 20 southwest and western states.

Allen E. Coles, chairman of the board of W&W Steel Company.

The firm's original plant in Oklahoma City began operating in October 1945.

he acquisition in 1981 of the facilities of the Rio Grande Steel Company in Albuquerque, New Mexico, added 280,000 square feet of steel fabricating buildings and 4,000 square feet of office space located on 25 acres of prime industrial land.

W.G. "Jerry" Wilson headed the firm from 1945 to 1967 as it grew to prominence in Oklahoma. The employee stock ownership plan that he introduced in 1951 gave permanent employees the opportunity to invest in their company. Thus are efforts and dedication rewarded, as only active employees can participate.

Most of the firm's growth in Oklahoma followed the master plan of Wilson and Winneberger. W&W Steel introduced a critical preplanning method for scheduling production in 1967. This plan was revised in 1971 to a long-range and short-term internal scheduling of all labor. Referred to as the schedule control system, it was implemented throughout all four plants. Preplanning enables all employees to work as a solid, active efficient unit. W&W Steel Company has joined the computer age with the installation in October 1981 of a new Hewett-Packard 3000 computer.

The leadership of Allen E. Coles has enabled the organization to maintain a high degree of efficiency and productivity. Coles started working for the firm during the summers while still a student at the University of Oklahoma. Upon his graduation in 1951 he became a permanent employee in management training. Coles became executive vice-president seven years later, and president and chief executive officer in 1967. Upon Wilson's retirement in 1979, Coles assumed the duties of chairman of the board. His relaxed and positive outlook and genuine concern for both employees and customers is reflected by all W&W employees. It is this positive can-do attitude that accounts for the fact that the firm hasn't lost a customer in 15 years and draws new clients through the recommendations of its established ones.

Structural steel for Mountain Bell Headquarters Building in Salt Lake City, Utah, was provided by W&W Steel Company.

A 1980 view of the company's main plant location in Oklahoma City.

Western Electric Company, Inc.

The story of Western Electric in Oklahoma City has paralleled the technological advances of America's telecommunications industry.

Western Electric, a subsidiary of AT&T, came to Oklahoma City on August 15, 1957, with the arrival of Joseph T. West, the first plant manager. He directed the start-up of the leased pilot plant at Northwest 39th and Tulsa. Oklahoma City Chamber of Commerce officials Stanley Draper and Paul Strasbaugh worked with West to develop a site for Western Electric's own plant.

On a blustery December 10, 1958, Senator Robert S. Kerr and Western Electric president Arthur B. Goetze ceremoniously set off dynamite charges to break ground for the new plant at West Reno Avenue and Council Road. On May 24, 1960, the factory, encompassing 30 acres under roof, was completed.

The Oklahoma City Works was established with the primary mission of producing "state-of-the-art" technology for telephone central office switching equipment. In the '60s and early '70s the Oklahoma City Works was the "Crossbar Capitol" of Western Electric. The electromechanical Crossbar equipment introduced in 1938 is still in reliable use in the nation's telephone network of the 1980s.

Western Electric introduced its first Electronic Switching System (No. 1 ESS) in 1965, and three years later the Oklahoma City Works was the high-volume producer of No. 1 ESS used in metropolitan areas. The ESS family grew with No. 2 ESS for suburban offices and No. 3 ESS used in rural exchanges. Oklahomans began building these products in 1972 and 1977, respectively.

Two powerful switching system processors known as the 1A Processor and the 2B Processor went into production at Oklahoma City in 1977. The 1A Processor can handle over a quarter of a million calls per hour. It serves throughout the Bell System network and has also been sold to foreign countries from Saudi Arabia to the Republic of Korea. The call-processing workhorse of small communities has been the 2B Processor.

In the 1980s the Oklahoma City Works remains on the leading edge of telecommunications technology with the 1981 and 1982 introductions of the 3B Processor and No. 5 ESS. The 3B Processor is a multi-application mini-computer. No. 5 ESS is a modular digital switching system designed to serve all sizes of central offices from metropolitan to rural.

Production of the electronic systems at the Oklahoma City Works is handled by a work force normally totaling 4,500 to 5,000 employees. The 1981 payroll amounted to $102 million and another $34 million was spent on purchases within the state. Throughout the nation, Western Electric has some 155,000 employees. Corporate sales in 1981 totaled $13 billion.

Western Electric had its beginning as Gray and Barton in Cleveland, Ohio, in 1869, and took its present name in 1876. In 1881 the American Bell Telephone Company (forerunner of AT&T) acquired a major interest in Western Electric.

Above
A powerful circuit pack showing the complex integrated circuit technology utilized in the 3B Processor is displayed by Gilman Burris, a Western Electric Oklahoma City Works employee.

Below
Western Electric Oklahoma City Works employees show off the first "frame" of electromechanical telephone switching equipment shipped from the pilot plant on March 12, 1958.

FIRST CROSSBAR FRAME PRODUCED at OKLAHOMA CITY COMPLETED MARCH 12.1958

Willmann's Furriers

Lew Willmann came to Oklahoma City in 1925 to work in the fur department at Al Rosenthal's, the fine women's clothing store. He worked hard and dreamed of owning his own store some day. After managing fur repairs at Halliburton's for two years, he ventured out on his own in 1935. Because of the enormous expense of operating and maintaining a furriers, Willmann was forced temporarily to abandon his dream after two years. He returned to Halliburton's to manage its storage and repair departments. Recognizing his ability, Kerr's department store hired Willmann in 1940 to manage its fur department.

The dream of owning his own store had not died. Willmann's wife and son shared in that dream. When son Bob finished his tour in the Marine Corps in 1945, the family plans were reactivated. The three of them, Lew, Ona, and Bob, opened a showroom at 519 West Main, but they soon realized that they had too much space and moved to 1114 North Robinson. This time the business caught on. Lew Willmann had the pleasure of watching his dream grow and prosper until his untimely death in 1963.

Under the leadership of his son, Bob, the store was moved in 1965 to its present location at 46th and Classen. The furriers now covers about 6,000 square feet of space devoted to showrooms, work rooms, a storage vault, and cleaning operation. The first store relied heavily on the sale of ladies' stoles. Now Willmann's has a sumptuous array of jackets, coats, and hats for ladies in mink, Persian lamb, sable, lynx, fox, muskrat, coyote, broadtail lamb, beaver, and rabbit. In recent years men's coats and jackets in coyote, muskrat, and beaver have been added.

Another addition to the store is the third generation of the family. Bob's son, Kirk Willmann, is now manager along with his sister, Kit Willmann Daggs; her husband, Steve Daggs, manages the cleaning operation. Because all the Willmanns grew up in the business, they are experts in the designing and redesigning of furs and in caring for them.

Because Lew Willmann refused to abandon his dream, Willmann's is the only family-owned furriers in the state and is also the oldest business devoted only to furs. The sumptuous furs displayed in the showrooms and the 12 busy employees are a far cry from the early store—but without that early determination yesterday, today's Willmann's Furriers wouldn't be possible.

When Lew, Ona, and Bob Willmann first opened their own shop, they relied on canvas models of coats.

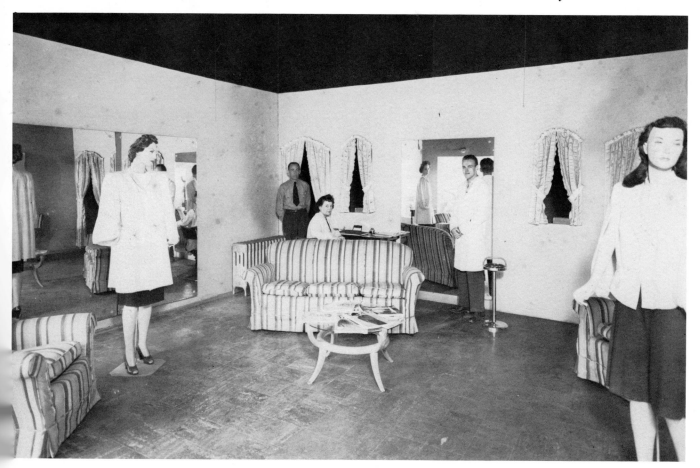

Acknowledgments

In researching and writing *The Heart of the Promised Land*, I incurred many debts to librarians, historians, friends, and co-workers, without whom this book would have been impossible. Their skills, knowledge, and encouragement made this history more accurate and readable.

First, I must thank the Oklahoma County Historical Society, the group that sponsored this history, and particularly Howard Meredith, who supported me as the author.

In compiling this book I called upon the expertise of various librarians in the search for materials. Among the most helpful were Sandra Schuler of the Metropolitan Branch of the Oklahoma County Library System; John Heisch, Sandy Smith, Manon Atkins, and Mary Moran of the Oklahoma Historical Society Library; and Monteray Nelson, chief librarian for the Oklahoma Publishing Company. They opened their minds to my quest and responded with thousands of manuscripts, vertical files, newspaper accounts, and photographs.

In addition to primary documents, I relied on the works of other historians, the men and women who have opened the frontiers of knowledge in Oklahoma history. Foremost among them is Roy Stewart, longtime journalist in Oklahoma City and renowned commentator on his times, who wrote *Born Grown*, an encyclopedic treasure chest of information about Oklahoma City. Other historians and writers who have preserved the history of Oklahoma County include: Angelo Scott, B.B. Chapman, W.F. Kerr, Albert McRill, Gilbert Hill, Mary Jo Nelson, and George and Lucyl Shirk. I hope I have added to the legacy of these pioneers.

During the painstaking process of writing a manuscript, every historian needs editorial assistance. Fortunately, I had access to some of the best professionals in the field. The editorial staff at Windsor Publications was highly cooperative and helpful with their suggestions, and Windsor's sales representative, Bob Moffatt, did a commendable job of eliciting the participation of local organizations whose stories are told in the final chapter of this book.

Many of the rough edges were brushed from the manuscript by Dr. Odie B. Faulk, distinguished Professor of History at Northeastern Oklahoma State University and Oklahoma's most accomplished author and historian. For the seven years I have known him, Odie B. Faulk has represented the values of meeting deadlines, honoring agreements, and working diligently toward goal after goal.

Much credit belongs to Jack T. Conn, Earle Metcalf, and LeRoy Fischer, three men who appreciate and promote the study of local history. Their support at the Oklahoma Historical Society has been invaluable in completing this book.

Finally, I must give thanks to my family, who supported me through the years and served as a mooring during stormy days. My wife, Deborah, sacrificed countless weekends and evenings while I labored on the manuscript, and she endured the highs and lows experienced by all authors. To her I dedicate this book.

Bibliography

Academy of Medicine. *Oklahoma City Academy of Medicine, 1910-1951.* Oklahoma City: Oklahoma Academy of Medicine, 1951.

Allen, Stephen J. "An Analysis of Urban Planning Problems Created by the Evolution of Oil Field Development in Oklahoma City, Oklahoma." Unpublished Master's Thesis, University of Oklahoma, Norman, 1969.

Annual Report of the City Auditor, Oklahoma City, 1915. Oklahoma City: Times-Journal Publishing Company, 1915.

Baker, June Anne. "Patterns of Black Residential Segregation in Oklahoma City, 1890 to 1960." Unpublished Master's Thesis, University of Oklahoma, Norman, 1970.

Ballentine, Thomas McClellan. "The Oklahoma City Annexation Program, 1958-1963, Purposes, Processes, and Planning Implications." Unpublished Master's Thesis, University of Oklahoma, Norman, 1964.

Brandes, Kay. "Theatrical Activities in Oklahoma City from 1889 to 1964." Unpublished Master's Thesis, University of Oklahoma, Norman, 1965.

Bunky. *The First Eight Months of Oklahoma City.* Oklahoma City: The McMaster Printing Company, 1890.

Capitol Hill Beacon. *An Early History of Capitol Hill.* Oklahoma City: Capitol Hill Beacon, 1965.

Casey, Naomi Taylor. "Miss Edith Johnson: Pioneer Newspaper Woman." *The Chronicles of Oklahoma,* vol. LX, no. 1 (Spring 1982).

Chapman, Berlin B. *Oklahoma City, From Public Land to Private Property.* Oklahoma City: n.p., 1960.

Classen, Anton H. "The Future Possibilities of Oklahoma City." *Sturm's Oklahoma Magazine,* vol. VIII, 1909.

Colcord, Charles F. *The Autobiography of Charles F. Colcord, 1859-1934.* Tulsa: C.C. Helmerich, 1970.

Doherty, Henry L., comp. *The Story of Indian Territory Illuminating Oil Company.* New York: Henry L. Doherty Company, 1930.

Eastman, James N. "Founding of Tinker Air Force Base." *The Chronicles of Oklahoma,* vol. L, 1972.

_____. "Location and Growth of Tinker Air Force Base and Oklahoma City Air Material Area." *The Chronicles of Oklahoma,* vol. L, 1972.

Fischer, LeRoy H. "The Fairchild Winery." *The Chronicles of Oklahoma,* vol. LV, no. 2 (Summer 1971).

Fulkerson, Fred Grover. "Community Forces in a Negro District in Oklahoma City, Oklahoma." Unpublished Master's Thesis, University of Oklahoma, Norman, 1946.

Harlow, Rex. *Oklahoma City's Younger Leaders.* Oklahoma City: The Harlow Publishing Company, 1931.

Hill, Gilbert. "City Rolls Up Score in Industrial Game." *Oklahoma City Times,* Oklahoma City, June 23, 1960.

_____. "History of the Oklahoma City Chamber of Commerce," a series of articles published in the *Daily Oklahoman.* A complete set of these articles is located in the vertical files of the Metropolitan Branch of the Oklahoma County Library System.

Kelley, E. H. "When Oklahoma City was Seymour and Verbeck." *The Chronicles of Oklahoma,* vol. XXVII, 1950.

Kerfoot, John. "The Jobbing Center of the Southwest." *Sturm's Oklahoma Magazine,* vol. VIII, 1909.

Kerr, W. F., and Ira Gainer. *The Story of Oklahoma City.* 3 vols. Chicago: S.J. Clarke Publishing Company, 1922.

Knowles, Malachi. "A Study of the Non-White Population Distribution and Housing Characteristics in

Oklahoma City, Oklahoma, 1940-1960."
Unpublished Master's Thesis, University of
Oklahoma, Norman, 1965.

Lockwood Greene Engineers, Inc. *Oklahoma City Business and Its Trade Territories: A Study and Plan for Expansion.* Oklahoma City: Industrial Department of the Oklahoma City Chamber of Commerce, 1931.

Lucke, Ray W. *Who's Who in Oklahoma City.* Oklahoma City: Mid-Continent Publishers, 1931.

McConnell, Leona Bellew. "A History of the Town and College of Bethany, Oklahoma." Unpublished Master's Thesis, University of Oklahoma, Norman, 1935.

McRill, Albert. *And Satan Came Also: An Inside Story of a City's Social and Political History.* Oklahoma City: Semco Color Press, 1955.

Mahar, Janette I. "Social Changes in Oklahoma City From 1889 to 1930." Unpublished Master's Thesis, University of Oklahoma, Norman, 1933.

Maver, George J. "Oklahoma City: In Transition to Maturity and Professionalization," in Leonard E. Goodall, ed., *Urban Politics in the Southwest.* Tempe: Institute of Public Administration, 1967.

Merchants and Manufacturers Record. *Oklahoma City: The Industrial Prodigy of the Great Southwest.* Oklahoma City: Tindall and Nockel, n.d.

Meredith, Howard L., and George Shirk. "Oklahoma City: Growth and Reconstruction, 1889-1939." *The Chronicles of Oklahoma,* vol. LV, 1977.

Mid-Continent Life Insurance Company, comp. *Glimpses of Oklahoma City.* Oklahoma City: Harlow Publishing Company, 1917.

Mid-Continent Publishers, comp. *Who's Who in Oklahoma City.* Oklahoma City: Mid-Continent Publishers, 1931.

National Publishing Company, comp. *Greater Oklahoma City Illustrated.* Oklahoma City: Oklahoma Engraving and Printing Company, 1909.

Nelson, Mary Jo. *History in Mortar.* Oklahoma City: Oklahoma City Times, 1972.

Oklahoma City. *Citizens' Year Book, City of Oklahoma City: First Annual Report of the City Manager, 1927-1928.* Oklahoma City: n.p., 1928.

Oklahoma City Chamber of Commerce. *Bigger Possibilities for Factories in the Great Southwest: Oklahoma City.* Oklahoma City: Oklahoma City Chamber of Commerce, 1912.

Oklahoma City Chamber of Commerce. *Oklahoma City Yearbook for 1911.* Oklahoma City: Oklahoma Printing Company, 1911.

Oklahoma City Chamber of Commerce. *Production Sheet of Oklahoma City Chamber of Commerce and Projects for 1933.* Oklahoma City: Oklahoma City Chamber of Commerce, 1932.

Oklahoma City Junior Chamber of Commerce. *Who's Who in Greater Oklahoma City.* American Yearbook: 1965.

Oklahoma Publishing Company. *Fifty Years of Progress: The Story of the Growth Together of a Great Community and a Great Newspaper.* Oklahoma City: Oklahoma Publishing Company, 1953.

"Oklahoma! the Territory, the County, the City." *McMaster's Magazine,* vol. XI, 1899.

Peery, Dan W. "The First Two Years." *The Chronicles of Oklahoma.* vol. VII, 1929.

Petty, A. E. "New Downtown: Oklahoma City's Goal for its 1989 Centennial." *Journal of Housing,* vol. XXXIV, 1977.

"Prosperous Year For Oklahoma City." *McMaster's Magazine,* vol. XIII, 1900.

Red Corn, James L. *The Forgotten Poor: The Indians of Oklahoma City.* Oklahoma City: Native American Center, 1976.

Robertson, Leo L. "Geographical Changes Resulting from Oil Development in Oklahoma City and Vicinity." Unpublished Master's Thesis, University of Oklahoma, Norman, 1937.

Scott, Angelo C. *The Story of Oklahoma City.* Oklahoma City: Times-Journal Publishing Company, 1939.

Shirk, George. *Report of the Citizens Committee, Oklahoma City.* Oklahoma City: n.p., 1955.

Shirk, Lucyl. *Oklahoma City: Capital of Soonerland.* Oklahoma City: Oklahoma City Board of Education, 1957.

Smallwood, James. *Urban Builder: The Life and Times of Stanley Draper.* Norman: University of Oklahoma Press, 1977.

Smith, Larry. *Survey of Industrial Parks in Oklahoma City.* Oklahoma City: Oklahoma City Urban Renewal Authority, 1972.

Steinmeyer, George. "A History of the Oklahoma Gas and Electric Company to the Year 1912." Unpublished Master's Thesis, University of Oklahoma, 1961.

Stewart, Ronald Laird. "The Influence of the Business Community in Oklahoma City Politics." Unpublished Master's Thesis, University of Oklahoma, Norman, 1967.

Stewart, Roy P., and Pendleton Woods. *Born Grown: An Oklahoma City History.* Oklahoma City: Fidelity Bank, N.A., 1974.

Thoburn, Joseph B. "Product of Pulling Together." *Sturm's Oklahoma Magazine,* vol. IX, 1910.

Woods, Pendleton, and Frank Boggs. *Myriad of Sports . . . A Profile of Oklahoma City.* Oklahoma City: All Sports Association, 1971.

Zalewski, Ronald A. "Economic Development and Urban Renewal in Oklahoma City." Unpublished Master's Thesis, University of Oklahoma, Norman, 1968.

This photograph shows Oklahoma City on May 21, 1889. The grove of cottonwood trees on California Avenue survived only a few years. (OHS)

Index

Page numbers in italics refer to illustrations.

Partners in Progress Index

Titles in the Windsor Local History Series

St. Paul: Saga of an American City, by Virginia Brainard Kunz (1977)

The Heritage of Lancaster, by John Ward Willson Loose (1978)

A Panoramic History of Rochester and Monroe County, New York, by Blake McKelvey (1979)

Syracuse: From Salt to Satellite, by Henry W. Schramm and William F. Roseboom (1979)

Columbia, South Carolina, History of a City, by John A. Montgomery (1979)

Kitchener: Yesterday Revisited, by Bill Moyer (1979)

Erie: Chronicle of a Great Lakes City, by Edward Wellejus (1980)

Montgomery: An Illustrated History, by Wayne Flynt (1980)

Omaha and Douglas County: A Panoramic History, by Dorothy Devereux Dustin (1980)

Charleston: Crossroads of History, by Isabella Leland (1980)

Baltimore: An Illustrated History, by Suzanne Ellery Greene (1980)

The Fort Wayne Story: A Pictorial History, by John Ankenbruck (1980)

City at the Pass: An Illustrated History of El Paso, by Leon Metz (1980)

Tucson: Portrait of a Desert Pueblo, by John Bret Harte (1980)

Salt Lake City: The Gathering Place, by John S. McCormick (1980)

Saginaw: A History of the Land and the City, by Stuart D. Gross (1980)

Cedar Rapids: Tall Corn and High Technology, by Ernie Danek (1980)

Los Angeles: A City Apart, by David L. Clark (1981)

Heart of the Commonwealth: Worcester, by Margaret A. Erskine (1981)

Out of a Wilderness: An Illustrated History of Greater Lansing, by Justin L. Kestenbaum (1981)

The Valley and the Hills: An Illustrated History of Birmingham and Jefferson County, by Leah Rawls Atkins (1981)

River Capital: An Illustrated History of Baton Rouge, by Mark T. Carleton (1981)

Chattanooga: An Illustrated History, by James W. Livingood (1981)

New Haven: An Illustrated History, edited by Floyd Shumway and Richard Hegel (1981)

Albany: Capital City on the Hudson, by John J. McEneny (1981)

Kalamazoo: The Place Behind the Products, by Larry B. Massie and Peter J. Schmitt (1981)

Mobile: The Life and Times of a Great Southern City, by Melton McLaurin and Michael Thomason (1981)

New Orleans: An Illustrated History, by John R. Kemp (1981)

Regina: From Pile O' Bones to Queen City of the Plains, by William A. Riddell (1981)

King County and Its Queen City: Seattle, by James R. Warren (1981)

To the Setting of the Sun: The Story of York, by Georg R. Sheets (1981)

Buffalo: Lake City in Niagara Land, by Richard C. Brown and Bob Watson (1981)

Springfield of the Ozarks, by Harris and Phyllis Dark (1981)

Charleston and the Kanawha Valley, by Otis K. Rice (1981)

Dallas: Portrait in Pride, by Darwin Payne (1982)

Heart of the Promised Land: An Illustrated History of Oklahoma County, by Bob L. Blackburn (1982)

Winnipeg: Where the New West Begins, by Eric Wells (1982)

City of Lakes: An Illustrated History of Minneapolis, by Joseph Stipanovich (1982)

Rhode Island: The Independent State, by George H. Kellner and J. Stanley Lemons (1982)

Calgary: Canada's Frontier Metropolis, by Max Foran and Heather MacEwan Foran (1982)

Greensboro: A Chosen Center, by Gayle Hicks Fripp (1982)

Norfolk's Waters: An Illustrated Maritime History of Hampton Roads, by William L. Tazewell (1982)

Metropolis of the American Nile: An Illustrated History of Memphis and Shelby County, by John E. Harkins (1982)

At the River's Bend: An Illustrated History of Jackson County, by Richard D. McKinzie and Sherry Lamb Schirmer (1982)

Beaumont: A Chronicle of Promise, by Judith W. Linsley and Ellen W. Rienstra (1982)

Boise: An Illustrated History, by Merle Wells (1982)

Broome County Heritage: An Illustrated History, by Ross McGuire and Lawrence Bothwell (1982)

Hartford: An Illustrated History of Connecticut's Capital, by Glenn Weaver (1982)

Raleigh: City of Oaks, by James Vickers (1982)

At the Bend in the River: The Story of Evansville, by Kenneth P. McCutchan (1982)

Duluth: An Illustrated History of the Zenith City, by Glenn N. Sandvik (1982)

The Valley and Its Peoples: An Illustrated History of the Lower Merrimack River, by Paul Hudon (1982)

The Upper Mohawk Country: An Illustrated History of Greater Utica, by David M. Ellis (1982)

Chicago: Commercial Center of the Continent, by Kenan Heise and Michael Edgerton (1982)

Corpus Christi: The History of a Texas Seaport, by Bill Walraven (1982)

Cape Fear Adventure: An Illustrated History of Wilmington, by Diane Cobb Cashman (1982)

The Lehigh Valley: An Illustrated History, by Karyl Lee Hall and Peter Hall (1982)

Windsor Publications, Inc.
History Book Division
Editorial Office
21220 Erwin Street
Woodland Hills, California 91365
(213) 884-4050

THIS BOOK WAS SET IN
CAMBRIDGE EXPANDED TYPE,
PRINTED ON
ACID FREE 70 LB. WARRENFLO
AND BOUND BY
WALSWORTH PUBLISHING COMPANY
HALFTONE REPRODUCTION BY ROBERTSON GRAPHICS
TEXT AND LAYOUT DESIGNED BY
PAMELA MOSHER